D1260638

BLACK *and* WHITE *Power Subreption*

By the author of

Black Religion: The Negro and Christianity in the United States

The Politics of God

BLACK
and
WHITE
Power Subreption

by Joseph R. Washington, Jr.

BEACON PRESS BOSTON

E185
.W33

The author gratefully acknowledges permission to reprint passages from the following copyrighted works: "Shroud of Color" from *On These I Stand* by Countee Cullen, Copyright 1925 by Harper & Brothers, renewed 1953 by Ida M. Cullen, by permission of Harper & Row, Publishers, Incorporated; "From the Dark Tower" from *On These I Stand* by Countee Cullen, Copyright 1927 by Harper & Brothers, renewed 1955 by Ida M. Cullen, by permission of Harper & Row, Publishers, Incorporated; "Africa," "If We Must Die," and "White Houses" by Claude McKay from *Selected Poems of Claude McKay,* by permission of Twayne Publishers, Inc.; "Tempo di Marcia" of "Dark Symphony" from *Rendezvous with America* by Melvin B. Tolson, by permission of Dodd, Mead & Company; "For My People" from *For My People* by Margaret Walker, Copyright © 1942 by Yale University Press, reprinted by permission of Yale University Press.

Copyright © 1969 by Joseph R. Washington, Jr.
Library of Congress catalog card number: 72–84799
Beacon Press books are published under the auspices
of the Unitarian Universalist Association
All rights reserved
Printed in the United States of America

For the triple-power persons in my life who have shaped

My Past: SOPHIA

And Present: BRYAN

Toward Future: DAVID

06146

Contents

Preface

Black Power is for many people a paradox surrounded by an enigma containing a mystery. Black Power raises more questions than answers, but this is more indicative of strength than weakness. There are certain memories in the experience of black people to which Black Power puts an answer beyond any question. One of these experiences comes out of the writings of the beloved mystic William Blake. "The Little Black Boys," his hymn, is taught at Albion College and other institutions by professors of English who cannot understand its renouncement and denouncement by Black Power's children:

> My mother bore me in the southern wild,
> And I am black, but O, my soul is white!
> White as an angel is the English child,
> But I am black, as if bereaved of light.
>
> My mother taught me underneath a tree,
> And, sitting down before the heat of day,
> She took me on her lap and kissèd me,
> And pointing to the East, began to say:
>
> "Look at the rising sun: there God does live,
> And gives His light, and gives His heat away,
> And flowers and trees and beasts and men receive
> Comfort in morning, joy in the noonday.
>
> "And we are put on earth a little space,
> That we may learn to bear the beams of love;
> And these black bodies and this sunburnt face
> Are but a cloud, and like a shady grove.

"For when our souls have learn'd the heat to bear,
The cloud will vanish, we shall hear His voice,
Saying, 'Come out from the grove, my love and care,
And round my golden tent like lambs rejoice.' "

Thus did my mother say, and kissèd me,
And thus I say to little English boy.
When I from black and he from white cloud free,
And round the tent of God like lambs we joy,

I'll shade him from the heat till he can bear
To lean in joy upon our Father's knee;
And then I'll stand and stroke his silver hair,
And be like him, and he will then love me.

This book seeks an understanding of Black Power's means and ends, sources and resources, through an examination of the anatomy of Black Power. The confusion of meanings surrounding Black Power is instructive. Black Power means many things to many people; therefore it is many things. It is not my intention to defend or offend Black Power. What I hope to reveal is that Black Power's roots lie deep in the social, cultural, economic, political, and religious experience of black Americans. The significance of this movement is not in whether it proves right or wrong, idealist or realist, right-spirited or wrongheaded, defused or refused or re-fused—the significance of Black Power is that it is the crucial response to the critical plight of black people. If there centers around this dynamic an impression of reckless abandon, there is also an indomitable expression of black heroism and courage to fight for the right. It begins in ignominy, but its ubiquitous drive against infamy is ineluctable and influences every sphere and penetrates every level of American life in all directions at once: black and white, rich and poor, urban and rural, sophisticates and illiterates, young and old, Negro and Afro-American, religious and nonreligious, liberal and racist, moderate and reactionary, politician and diplomat, powerful and powerless, hopeful and hopeless, revolutionary and counterrevolutionary.

Whatever its destiny, Black Power is destined to recharge old hate and love, resistance and persistence, suffering and joy.

Some see in Black Power the hope of glory; others believe it to say, "If your enemy smites you on one cheek turn the other, but if he smites you on the other cheek knock the hell out of him." This much is certain—the much-discussed revolution in America has not come. At the moment, Black Power is not revolution. The power of Black Power is the question it begs. Will the revolution or the Kingdom come?

Joseph R. Washington, Jr.
Beloit College
Beloit, Wisconsin

Subreption

Secret, underhanded, unlawful, or unfair representation, through suppression or fraudulent concealment of facts; a deduction drawn from such representation. *Canon and Scots law:* the obtaining of or attempting to obtain a dispensation from ecclesiastical authority or a gift from the sovereign by concealing the truth.

from *Webster's Third New International Dictionary*

1.

WHITE POWER Failure

Ethical effectiveness in achieving civil rights is the idea and therefore the test of white power—white people, white systems, white structures.

While I was researching this book, my ten-year-old son remarked, "Dad, you know the white man has everything going for him. Even nature is on his side; he can bask in the sun and become as black as we are. If there is no sun, he turns on the electric lamp he invented and in midwinter becomes as brown as brown can be. He can even pass for a black man if he wishes. Dad, have you ever known a black, black man who became white and then black again?"

Of course, my son has a point. The difference between being black and being white is the difference between being powerless and powerful. There is another difference between blacks and whites which my son has yet to understand. Blacks have used their powerlessness with ethical effectiveness in the struggle for civil rights. But since blacks have been fooled into attempting to achieve what is not in their domain, there is a growing question among some blacks as to whether or not their powerlessness has been put in a trick. The trick bag is that powerlessness in a power struggle can hardly be called ethical since it cannot be effective. Whites have all the power necessary to achieve civil rights for all Americans, but they have not been ethical or effective.

The fact is that whatever improvement has come about in civil rights has been at the initiation of the powerless black minority. It would appear that the problem and its resolution are issues for blacks alone rather than issues for all. American white power has withheld civil rights from black Americans by demeaning the black man and depriving the black child. White America has been playing with black America, toying with black America. The 90 percent withheld civil rights from the 10 percent and now says to the 10 percent you can have as much civil rights as you can gain by pleasing or teasing us. It is the old elephant and mouse game. Black Americans have played the game with limited skill but with great earnestness only to discover the amount of civil rights gained is in proportion to the extent they, the mouse, scare the white elephant. There comes a time when limited skill and powerlessness versus gamesmanship and power becomes a dangerous game. The unskillful may forget it is powerless and act as if it possessed power. The powerful may not then react with skill but with all of its might. Frightened by the irritation in its trunk, the elephant first becomes resentful and then threatens to stomp. We are at the brink of a time when the powerless may go wild and the powerful may go mad. Therefore, the issue of moment is whether the white power majority will effectively, ethically achieve civil rights. Instead of merely reacting to the initiatives of the blacks and insisting that the 10 percent become perfect democrats in a system that guarantees failure, white America must take the initiative. With regard to civil rights, whites determine not only the ends but the means as well. At best, blacks share in some areas where their destiny is involved.

This, then, is the thesis of this chapter: given democratic structures and institutions, there is no guide for the 90 percent from science, philosophy, psychology, sociology, religion, or ethics as they exist today for ethical effectiveness in achieving civil rights. Put another way, we are engaged in a chess game, the rules of which whites made up, and they know all the possible moves that can be made by blacks. They are also in a position to check most moves made by blacks and do so as a defensive measure. But whites are somehow unable to move at their own initiative and easily win the game of democracy. As a result, a growing number of blacks and whites are saying that we not only have failed to achieve any real measure of civil rights, but that it is impossible to do so. For these Americans, the achievement of civil rights is no longer of moment. They are calling for an effective way for blacks and whites to live in peaceful coexistence, and whether it is ethical or not, it is believed that semiseparatism is the way.

The white majority has accepted, and continues to do so, the presupposition that the inferior position of blacks in this society is an objective result of their objective and natural inferiority. This presupposition was reinforced as long as blacks were predominantly located in Southern rural areas. As of 1910, 73 percent of blacks lived in the rural South. The presupposition of black primitive inferiority remains, but a measure of its reinforcement was lost through the in-migration of blacks to the urban North and West. In fifty years blacks changed from being a predominantly Southern and rural people to a predominantly Northern and Western urban people. As of 1960, 73 percent of the blacks lived in urban areas, increasing all the while in poverty and fertility.

In the face of this persistent presupposition, blacks have believed in the equality of humankind and on this assumption never strayed from their objective of full citizenship. Blacks were never in complete agreement as to what full citizenship meant in positive terms, integration or acculturation or assimilation, for example. They were in full agreement that full citizenship and second-class citizenship were incompatible. Organizations for the advancement of blacks existed from the beginning of this century, but they were limited in their possibilities. It was not until industrial America called the blacks up and out of the South to man their industries that the black movement began. With the exodus the dynamics of change were set in motion.

Blacks early protested the role of second-class citizen in every area of life, including the military. They were largely unsuccessful until the post-World War II period. Blacks were off and running with the Supreme Court Decision of 1954. It was widely held that the reason blacks did not receive their full due centered around their acceptance of the situation without solidified and massive action demanding a change. The opportunity, the time, the man, all converged in 1955, precipitated by the dignity of a lady. There followed from this event massive marches, protests, sit-ins, and passive resistance. These direct actions were launched with high hopes. As a result, the solid South was formally changed, and some would say the informal structures as well, although the evidence here is less formidable.

This unbelievable direct action shook the nation and the world. There were enough people who believed substantial changes took place in our society to make it appear that they did. But this great movement of black people joined by white people came at a time when the majority of blacks no longer resided in the South. This fact does not minimize one bit the significance of the movement in the South and the continuing needs there. However, the movement of desegregation in the South directly effected the increase in discrimination in the North. By this time the objective of integration was generally accepted. Some believed that the important gains through the protest movement in bringing about desegregation indicated a pattern, that the protest movement could bring about dramatic changes in discrimination. The evidence is not yet all in, but if Milwaukee is the best example, it appears this method of protest is effective in segregation situations, not in those which are discriminatory. We have yet to see the full use of a correlative tactic in the North, the tactic of economic boycott.

Nevertheless, the movement has shifted with the population to the North. Blacks were told that the major problem was no longer their inaction but discrimination. That is, blacks were told the reason integration was stymied in the North was that blacks moved North too fast and in too great numbers, the implication being that this would be a short-term phenomenon. Further, it is said, discrimination is enhanced by two other factors, besides the presence of too many blacks in too short a time period. For one thing, blacks lack a strong family organization so necessary for psychological self-help as well as for changing the image held by middle-class whites that blacks are different. For another thing, blacks failed to bring with them from the rural South, or develop, solid community institutions which are necessary for mutual assistance to raise the level of both individuals and the group as a whole. Blacks, then, are disadvantaged by the disorganization of the family and community institutions.

Thus, discrimination is seen as basically an economic problem. Consequently, blacks have been at work demanding equal opportunity in employment. The pressures applied in this area are accompanied by efforts to increase the opportunity of the male to earn sufficiently to increase the family bond, and, at the same time, efforts are made to bring cohesion in the black community. In the meantime, there does not appear to be a direct relation between the qualifications of the black person and the amount of employment or income or occupational status when compared with whites in the society. This blacks are told is due to the lack of quality education. So, blacks have been about desegregation of schools. But desegregation of schools is not possible in black ghettos; thus the push for open occupancy. But open occupancy is to no avail because if blacks were allowed to move into neighborhoods, they could not afford to do so in numbers relative to the need.

Whites have then said to blacks, tell us what needs to be done. So, blacks have worked up a freedom budget and set forth a blueprint for equal opportunity. But such methods are filled with too many political problems. As a consequence, blacks are told that they need to become a political power to effect decisions. As blacks move into positions of political power, whites are fleeing ever faster from the major cities, and thus set in motion regional governments. Those who claim there is no difference between the blacks in urban areas and the previous immigrants need to reflect upon the fact that previously no major city approached a take-over by one group in the society, but for blacks, this is a national movement.

The point is that blacks have followed up and initiated action on every excuse that has been made for discrimination and the exclusion of blacks in the society. We are now in a period where great expectations continually meet great disappointments. Some blacks perceive the continual tossing of the ball back into the laps of blacks as a great hoax. The move now is toward building up black institutions for power integration. What is called for is a power base for "group-exploitation deterrence-capability." The combination of group solidarity and political-economic unity for power skillfully used has come to the fore. The initiative still lies with blacks.

Now it is important to move into our thesis more specifically. Why is it that the 90 percent is not guided to ethical effectiveness in achieving civil rights? Of course, the majority, the whites, have the power and the know-how, but there is no guide from them in the matter of achievement. I believe this is partly due to a low priority, limited interest, and lack of the general will. Clearly, the fact of White Power as subreption is not to be ignored. In order to see this, it is necessary to recall the numerous and conflicting positions dominant in the intellectual communities.

In the first place, there is no common agreement as to the problem. In my view, there is a white folk religion, a preconscious color prejudice that is irrational, a white preference for whites and indifference to blacks. On the one hand, social psychologists claim there is a "color stigma" attached to being black in America. This color stigma centers on the presupposition that blacks are an inferior primitive group, a presumption which is reflected in the expectation that blacks play the subservient role and in the response to intermarriage. Though not necessarily a permanent disadvantage, this stigma precludes an entire class of people from participating fully in the society.

On the other hand, we are told that blacks are victims of a caste-deprivation system which operates to prevent blacks from sharing in the "material and nonmaterial" products of the society for which they are in part responsible. This victimization is seen in the limited access of blacks to the dynamics by which a people rises in the society. Blacks are victims in that they are means for other people's ends to which they have not given consent. They are victims in the sense that the system permits manipulation to the disadvantage of blacks by the clever, vicious, cynical, and powerful. Victimization reaffirms the problem as the powerlessness of blacks.

Another view of the problem holds blacks to be the latest in the parade of immigrants which are to be understood as no different from other groups (i.e., Jews, Catholics, Spanish-Americans, and Japanese-Americans). Here blacks have the problem of becoming more acceptable to middle-class standards.

Others hold that the immigrant analogy is misleading because it provokes the response, "What's so different about blacks?

We made it in our merit and they will have to make it this way as well." It is worth looking into just how the previous immigrants made it in this society. What is further objected to is that the immigrant analogy overlooks the slave status of the blacks in this society, which makes the situation different from "Jew baiting" or castigating the "shanty Irish"—Jews as "Christ killers" and Catholics as "papists." Above all else, it is held, the color of the skin cannot be left behind however high one may rise.

One other view holds that the color stigma is only a symbol. When the conditions change, that symbol can be a positive rather than a negative factor, and the problem is the lack of family structure and community organization whereby blacks can rise together.

Still another view holds that the problem is the white middle class which seeks at all costs to protect its life-styles from deterioration by blacks whom they believe to have different life-styles. The pattern of protection is not to act solely in terms of class but to ghettoize the black. An indication of this fact is that most whites oppose integration in housing. It is true that the better-educated white differentiates between the professional and the assembly line working black, but the less-educated white tends to make no distinction. It is also true that when it comes to integrated housing even the educated white believes the black of whatever level has a different life-style. Discrimination at all levels by whites is believed to be the crux of the problem.

Still others hold that the single most important problem is the poverty of blacks and the accompanying high fertility—inadequate education, housing, occupation, and income. Whatever the problem, we are somewhere between desegregation and nondiscrimination.

If there is little agreement among intellectual whites as to the nature of the problem, there is even less as to the objective. We can fairly assume that nearly all intellectuals have in common a belief in desegregation.

Some hold the objective to be integration beyond desegregation. By integration is meant the social process of interaction and effective communication between blacks and whites whereby there is a sharing of societal life. Integration in this sense means developing a style of life compatible with the white middle class in terms of education, occupation, income, housing, and basic values.

One group holds the objective is assimilation beyond integration. By assimilation is generally meant the process of racial homogenization through intermarriage.

Still another group holds the objective to be acculturation, the melting-pot approach. In this view, blacks should not only be compatible with the dominant middle class but also be indistinguishable from them in every area of culture and religion. Acculturation is neither the presence of similar but different interacting groups, nor the loss of group identity through assimilation, but the emergence of the individual who is accepted by rising to the top through ability and will.

For yet another group, the objective is a more limited one: desegregation and the resultant admixture of people in functional relationships but not in social and informal relationships.

Perhaps the dominant objective is that of inclusion or full citizenship via pluralism. It is contended that this objective is the only American way. Pluralism means the preservation and strengthening of the black community to the level where it is viewed by blacks as valuable to be black. It is "full participation combined with preservation of identity," as distinguished from assimilation and separatism. This pattern is seen to be set by Jews and Catholics.

Still another objective is the separation of blacks into a group for either temporary or permanent purposes of identity and equality.

There is some difficulty with each of these objectives and a segment of the black community finds each attractive. Integration is simply not working in the society; whites are rapidly moving away and leaving the city to blacks. Assimilation appeals to a very few whites or blacks, and, at best, it would take five to ten centuries to accomplish. Acculturation may work for a few individuals but it is ineffective as regards the black group. Separatism results more from frustration than real desire, but it may yet be the short-run, if not the long-run, objective.

Equal partnership in a pluralistic society is considered the best single objective, but it has difficulties as well. A dynamic pluralism is dependent upon middle- and upper-class blacks providing mutual aid and support to blacks who have done poorly. Pluralism assumes that color is a sufficient bond to keep a people united, or else it must assume the debatable—that black people have distinctive particularities comparable to Jews and Catholics: religion, culture, and life-styles. Pluralism also assumes that blacks would choose the pluralistic way if they were free to choose. Pluralism resulted from the inclusion of Jews and Catholics into the society once dominated by WASPs. This unique contribution of Jews and Catholics, in the perspective of pluralism, means the pattern is frozen, and the full participation of blacks in the society would not bring about another basic change. That is, pluralism applauds, with some condescension, the accomplishments of blacks in the society and, if brought to a conclusion, will mean "the elimination of any category defined as inferior in itself." Such a successful resolution might mean a society where differences are not protected by defensive measures but through the welcoming of any who wished to participate at any level. In a really open society pluralism might well have a very difficult time maintaining separate identities. Most of all, pluralism is dependent upon the removal of the color stigma and presupposes that its removal will result from blacks' being solidified in family and community structures whereby they will change, and therefore change the way they are viewed by others.

We have highlighted some of the conflicting views intellectual whites hold with respect to the problem and objective in civil rights. We now need to look at some of the conflicting solutions.

One of the difficulties with the solutions proposed is the tendency to lump all blacks together. Blacks are not a homogeneous group. The movement of civil rights has resulted in a small group of blacks who are rising and, in some instances, may be said to get preferential treatment, because they are at a premium. Within the black community differences in life-style tend to be more effected by education and values than by income. Blacks within similar incomes may have middle-class or lower-class life-styles although at the lowest income level, an unorganized lower class exists with still another set of values. Some hold that were all the barriers down, the black upper class would welcome social integration, leaving the black institutions to the middle class, but as long as barriers remain, social integration will continue to be taboo. The black middle class focuses upon better jobs, better living, and has little interest in rising into the black upper class or engagement in integration. If they have a concern, it is for a good education for their children. The agony of middle-class blacks who live on the gilded edges of the ghetto is over separate but equal education. Since separation is seen to be inevitable because of housing discrimination, can there be equal education? If not, security is threatened at all levels. Those blacks who are partially integrated have special identity problems since they are limited, on the one hand, by whites and, on the other, by blacks who deride them as being uppity. It is true that all blacks suffer the primary problem of color stigma, but the value of solutions depends upon their meeting the needs of the great masses and the small minority simultaneously.

Some intellectuals believe the solution lies in resolving the disorganization of the black family. The American social system has been such as to prevent the black male from assuming the expected male role in the society. Whether or not it is too late to bring wholeness into the black family as a unit is not clear. What is clear is that the unemployment rate for blacks is not decreasing but is moving beyond double the unemployment rate for whites, and in the ghettos, one out of three is unemployed. The occupational patterns are creeping into line with those of whites but not rapidly enough. Black income has risen, but the gap is widening instead of closing; where the gap has closed it is in employment of women. The solution, then, is to provide opportunity for work for blacks, especially the men, to dramatically increase their employment rate, occupational patterns, and income.

Another solution concerns itself with the question of blacks' being below the median of the nation. Blacks in 1965 were economically where whites were in 1945, but the black continues to suffer the psychological disadvantage of being behind, which was not the case with whites in 1945. Problems facing blacks are difficult indeed, but they are not insurmountable. According to this solution, blacks have going for them a dynamic economy and their own rise in educational attainments, so that they are not falling further and further behind because the standards are continually rising in education and job employment. There is some dissipation, but not complete. The fact is that in 1963 the median income for a black high school graduate was $4,530; for whites, it was 55 percent higher—$6,991. Whites with eight years of elementary education earned 20 percent more than blacks with high school education—$5,454. With the rise in black education, even though one corrects for differences in quality, the solution assumes education among the young is better and will continue to be so, but education is not the answer since discrimination is inflicted irrespective of education. The solution, then, is to effect nondiscrimination in employment through preferential treatment of blacks to speed progress, to upgrade deficiencies, and to increase the general welfare of all. The solution of nondiscriminatory practices in employment through special efforts for blacks means this is to be done in such a way that whites are not held back as blacks rapidly rise.

Another solution is based on the assumption that national economic progress spells progress for blacks, that they are not as a whole caught in the backwash of poverty. It is necessary to engineer over the next twenty years the uplift of the blacks, through achievement in education and professional spheres, into fields where salaries and wages are already high, as well as in less well-paying jobs calling for skill. The solution is one of reducing the "inequality in earning capacity." At the same time, help must be given to those who do not have the capacity to earn a median standard of living. Here the solution suggested is the negative income tax.

Still another solution argues that nothing is holding blacks from advancing if they will put forth the effort and ability, that the color of skin is no deterrent, nor is the change in the economic system. However, some believe opportunities to be closed by the traditional route since the trade unions are more interested in keeping jobs for present membership than in controlling conditions for work.

Some hold the solution of equal status is light years away and the immediate solution is that of equal opportunity, which itself will take decades. This solution is one that is strictly dependent upon blacks' pulling together over the long haul, exerting strong pressure and leadership for change in the American society whereby blacks will change the society so there is no inferiority category, and in the process will change being black into a symbol of value rather than the symbol of inferiority as is presently the case.

Others believe the solution lies along multiple lines of desegregation, nondiscrimination, and the provision of equal opportunity without equal status. This view of the vicious circle is that blacks are caught in the wheel of poverty and residential segregation that imposes social segregation through isolation from whites, which in turn produces educational segregation and inferior education that restrict occupation and income which reinforce poverty. The solution requires simultaneous provisions for open occupancy, compensatory education and training, preferential treatment in job employment, or special jobs set aside for blacks to enter the job market, and change in life-style of blacks. Only through a massive attack on discrimination whereby there is full equality of opportunity will the problem be solved.

One solution calls for massive action against discrimination, but specifies the need to attack prejudices directly. Gordon Allport states that prejudice is decreased when two groups "possess equal status, seek common goals, are cooperatively dependent upon each other, and interact with positive support of authorities, laws or customs." It is nearly impossible in our society to create such conditions apart from isolated, and therefore special, situations. The solution is to erase the color stigma of blacks, and this can be done only through attacking all the patterns of prejudice directly, for changes on the job do not eliminate prejudice in the neighborhood or in the family. This solution calls for experiment with basic institutional changes.

It is strongly believed by some that the solution lies in massive intervention by the federal government, but to be effective, the conditions must be created whereby federal civil rights processes are both activated as to the law and responsive to the need. Such a solution depends upon the mobilization of civil rights groups and others to bring forth the complaints which set off the enforcement mechanism. This solution is said to be ineffective at present because the preoccupation with urban pathologies deters energy necessary to make federal civil rights work. It is also believed that in such areas as housing, the role of the federal government could be enormous, but this is the lowest of priorities among blacks.

Another solution holds that only the massive forces of federal, state, and local governments working together can bring about a resolution, in cooperation with private business and other organizations. What is called for is the channeling of the cause so as to gain the support of the most influential elements in the society.

The solution for a small segment is for all Americans to become color-blind. For others, the solution is for blacks to form a single political alliance with liberals. The solution for others is for blacks to make multiple alliances with every segment of the society where they have common interests. While such political alliances would be often conflicting, they would not be ineffective. Economic boycotts on a local, state, and national level are still another solution.

A growing number of intellectuals are affirming that the solution lies with revolutionary changes. Some hold that the revolutionary changes can be done within the American system and framework. Those who hold radical and rapid changes can take place within the existing system deem it necessary to modify the relations between man and man, man and his work, and man and his social-political environment. A corollary to this is the radical change among blacks so that they become able to ward off group exploitation. Blacks must be able to exploit their group solidarity for common goals. Group-exploitation and deterrence-capability require power and/or ability to get people to act the way desired, the use of this power for group purposes, and the skillful deployment of this power. Such power takes shape in politics, economics, and group solidarity.

In another view, the solution lies with revolutionary changes that will reorder the basic values through reordering the social, economic, and political system. This group is not opposed to black solidarity and its strategic, skillful deployment in politics and economics. It believes, however, that no matter how concentrated and wisely this deployment is set forth, blacks are in a minority and cannot reasonably hope for changes through their best efforts. Moreover, it is held that the political and economic system is such that only limited gains can be made. The assumption is that these limited gains are inadequate and will not satisfy blacks. It is held that the sentiment will grow for radical gains in American values, economy, and society that will alone wipe out victimization. It is believed that radical demands reflect themselves in summer tragedies which will get worse if the shift is not made toward such a solution as the guaranteed income.

In another view, the solution lies in separatism of white and black groups, the building up of the black community for peaceful coexistence.

It is a singular view that blacks must build up their community structures for mutual support and assistance for the deprived majority as a group and the individuals within the group. At the same time, the blacks in the middle class must continue to rise, and every barrier which prevents the natural growth of this group and the freedom of choice of the individuals within the group must be attacked and knocked down. The organization of the black community to aid in the breaking of the vicious cycle which victimizes it cannot be separated from the pushing up of those of the black middle class. The fact that members of the black middle class live outside the black ghetto does not mean they must lose identity with the less advantaged. It does mean that this generation of middle-class blacks must change its pattern of indifference with regard to the lower class of blacks and aid in pulling it up and out.

One thing is definite—blacks are not opposed to gaining civil rights for everyone as well as for themselves. The problem and the solution do not lie in the objective and "qualifiable" shortcomings of the black people. The problem and solution lie in the past and present "subjective attitudes of whites." Whites generally do not want equal opportunity for everyone. They certainly do not want integration in housing and schools.

The black community has been uneven, but ethical, in its attempts to achieve civil rights. It has been ineffective and will continue to be so, irrespective of how perfect blacks become in all the objective areas, if achievement of civil rights is left to blacks alone. Nevertheless, although the whites do not want it, the blacks must use their powerlessness to enable rather than disable civil rights.

Ethical effectiveness in achieving civil rights is not a strategy or goal to be determined by black people. Of course, there are those who have everything riding on the backs of blacks to break all inferiority statuses for the sake of America and its ideological fight with communism. The strategy, objective, and action depend upon whites, not upon blacks. Irrespective of national policies, whites have not accepted the concept of total integration. If whites are to be ethical and effective, they need to set forth a massive education-action program for whites to change the society and thus their subjective attitudes, wherein lie the problem and solution to achieving civil rights. However much blacks struggle, only whites can determine the means and the ends. To be ethical and effective means to me that whites are required to take the ball and run with it. It is the white community, not the black community, which affirms discrimination, the color stigma, ghetto enforcement. It is the white community that possesses both the knowledge and the power. What is needed now is for whites to bring their knowledge and power together into a program for action among and for whites. Blacks can and will continue to do better in themselves, but they cannot do for whites what whites must do for themselves. Many would like to see a Marshall Plan for Whites in America that was political, social, as well as economic in nature. Many would like to see whites put into action a plan whereby the color stigma would be erased, and put that plan into action within two years.

Until such time as the 90 percent do for themselves as they insist the 10 percent do, there will be no agreement upon the problem, the objective, or the solution. More than this, there will be no convergence of knowledge and power in action, only the continuation of this unconscious or conscious subreption. What really matters is what whites care about passionately. It is sheer wishful thinking, if not condescension, to believe that blacks are superpeople who can do what whites do not wish to be done.

So blacks cannot tell whites what is ethical, or effective, or achieving, or civil rights. Until whites decide, it would be presumptuous to determine the how, the why, the what, the when, and the where of ethical effectiveness in achieving civil rights. To date, the emphasis of whites has been on analyzing "effectiveness" or the "ethical," and precious little emphasis has been placed on "achieving civil rights." In fact, the civil rights confusion and its lack of achievement are the best evidence of white power failure.

The thesis of this chapter: that there is no guide for the 90 percent to take the initiative does not mean there can be no guide. In fact, a guide is possible and expected.

Among white intellectuals there is a welter of relativistic perspectives representing different disciplines and interests. What is needed is not an ideological confrontation at a higher level of understanding where particularities and complexities are transcended in commitment to universal reconciliation. Conflicting empirical knowledge brings forth a variety of views as to the problem, objective, and solution vis-a-vis black-white relations which are helpful to the extent they are reconciled in a unity with imagination or transformation. Beyond an analysis of particularities, there must be a sense of the whole through participation with feeling, which alone provides imagination, with knowledge of the right and desire for the right. This is the path of reconciliation and transformation, of ethical effectiveness. If there is to be a guide for the achievement of civil rights, psychology, sociology, ethics, theology, economics, together with other disciplines, may need more agreement over policies. Such unity in policy does not call for less but more differentiation, not less complexity within the different disciplines but more unity within each discipline and between disciplines for the transformation and reconciliation of this society.

The combination of science, sociology, and technology creates an enormous potential for knowledge of the processes by which social systems may be regulated for an integrated whole. We have the imagination, too, for creative transformation. The question is whether or not we have the desire to bring into being the good life with blacks and whites together in minimal conflict and maximum cooperation. The mobilization of whites for the good life might begin with a view to reconciliation through transformation of the society and therefore the destruction of a number of myths:

1. The myth that acts of discrimination against blacks are caused by objective and qualifiable deficiencies among black people.

2. The myth that formal education will make blacks more acceptable and whites less discriminatory in housing, education, and social interaction.

3. The myth that logic and information will lead to non-discrimination.

4. The myth that achievement of a pluralistic but equal society will bring about absolute equality for all.

5. The myth that equal opportunity can be achieved under a system of color stigma.

6. The myth that it is impossible to bring about rapid and radical voluntary changes in the middle-class discrimination-bound North.

7. The myth that the shape of black-white relations can be changed through legislating beliefs and morals apart from creating private groups that work persistently and consistently for voluntary changes in discriminatory attitudes and behavior.

8. The myth that equal opportunity for all blacks must be achieved before action can be taken to bring about equal status for some blacks.

9. The myth that there is a set order of rational change; that economic or political or social relations must be modified first and others later.

10. The myth that nonviolence is the only method of direct social change effective in this society.

11. The myth that violent eruptions are to be met with rigid enforcement of law and order as a substitute for making the changes which brought forth the violence.

12. The myth that black-white relations are adequately understood and dealt with if they are viewed as not fundamentally different from minority-dominant group relations involving Jews and Catholics.

13. The myth that there can be no real changes without violence.

Researchers have developed an impressive array of knowledge from a number of fields which could be put to use for the effective changing of black-white realities. This prodigious knowledge has yet to be combined with anything like the unity possible for effective and dramatic changes in black-white relations. We know that blacks develop or not within the basic communities of business and industry, religion, the military, the professions, the labor unions, health, welfare, education, politics, and community organizations. We know that blacks are rebellious because the local ties which once bound are loosening through mass migration, mass communication, technology, urbanism, and the permeation of the democratic ideal throughout the world, which has unleashed the demand for freedom and equality now. We know that these demands are irreversible and that our society has the resources, the precedents, the laws, the economic growth, the stability, the intelligence, the managerial capacity, and the technical capability to achieve civil rights ethically and effectively. One thing and one thing only is lacking: the will of the people, the will of the white majority.

Alfred North Whitehead put it this way: "It is the task of the future to live dangerously." Evidence from the past does not give the black masses in America much hope as to the future of civil rights. In fact, the history of White Power so far largely spells subreption. This power failure of whites is evidence of their inability or unwillingness "to live dangerously." The failure of White Power has created the idea of Black Power. Is Black Power reverse subreption of White Power? The future for black people is Black Power. The shape of the future is measured by the extent to which advocates of Black Power and participants in this idea "live dangerously." Black Power is a powerful idea recently exploded upon the American scene. One question remains: Is Black Power an idea whose time has come?

2.

BLACK POWER
Precursors

It is generally held that the ultimate goal of Black Power, violent revolution for a just society in which black and white share equally, has no historical precedence. This understanding has been common because the black slave was interpreted so authoritatively by historians who saw in him what they expected. A clear example of this self-fulfilling prophecy was written in 1913 by Sir Harry Johnston in his *A History of the Colonization of Africa by Alien Races*:

> He is possessed of great physical strength, docility, cheerfulness of disposition, a short memory for sorrows and cruelties, and an easily aroused gratitude for kindness and just dealing. He does not suffer from homesickness to the over-bearing extent that afflicts other peoples torn from their homes, and provided he is well fed, he is easily made happy. Above all, he can toil hard under the hot sun and in the unhealthy climates of the torrid zone. He has little or no race-fellowships—that is to say, he has no sympathy for other negroes; he recognizes, follows and imitates his master independently of any race affinities, and, as he is usually a strong man and a good fighter, he has come into request not only as a labourer but as a soldier.[1]

Reliance upon this description of black men makes the appearance of Black Power in its violent dimension seem out of character. The black man is supposed to be blessed with Christian qualities to the extent that in virtue he is the example for the white masters. Where else in the annals of history has an entire cross section of people had attributed to it such Christian achievement? To be black was to be depicted as one born to be a slave, and instinctively Christian. Whites still believe that blacks are the only group in America with Christian vitality, really alive in the spirit. Perhaps the weight of guilt and the continued enslavement of blacks make it necessary to disavow their capacity for retaliation.

This picture of black men as superhuman, nonviolent, and Christian beyond the level of those reared in Christian environs was distorted by the angle of those who drew the conclusion. Black men were not unlike other men. They were sparked to revolt by cruelty. Less immediate factors than cruelty also conditioned the grounds for revolt. Those environmental factors inducing revolts included economic strains and stresses, the extraordinary happening, wars, industrialization, and urbanization.

The violent black man was not the creation of Black Power in 1966. Black Power is but the rebirth of the will to freedom and equality which black people expressed from the beginning. A funny thing happened on the African coast.

> A Sloop commanded by a Brother of . . . Capt. Ingledieu, slaving up the River Gambia, was attacked by a Number of the Natives, about the 27th of February last, and made a good Defence; but the Captain finding himself desperately wounded, and likely to be overcome, rather than fall into the Hands of such merciless Wretches, when about 80 Negroes had boarded his Vessel, discharged a Pistol into his magazine, and blew her up; himself and every Soul on Board perished.[2]

This happening took place in the summer of 1759. It was not an isolated or exceptional occurrence. The historical record shows ships like the *Creole* and the *Amistad,* one American and the other foreign, overturned by slaves in revolt, who thereby gained liberty. Thus, Black Power has its inception on the African shores and continued on the high seas. The black uprisings in these very early days were not always successful. As *The Boston Post Boy* of June 23, 1750, reports:

> By a Vessel lately arrived here from the West-Indies, we have Advice, that a Ship belonging to Liverpool coming

> from the Coast of Africa, with about 350 Slaves on board, and when in Sight of the Island Guardaloupe, the Slaves, as 'tis supposed, being admitted to come upon Deck to air themselves, took an Opportunity on the 28th of May, N.S. and killed the Master and Mate of the Ship and threw fifteen of the Men overboard, after which they sent the Boat with two white Lads and three or four others to discover what Land it was, meanwhile the Ship drove on to the Leeward, which gave the Lads an Opportunity to discover the Affair to the Commandant of that Quarter of the Island, who immediately raised about 100 Men, and put them on board a Sloop, who went in Pursuit of the Ship, and in a few Hours took her and carried her into Port Louis.[3]

Blacks were aware of the penalty possibilities in an unsuccessful rebellion, but this was not a sufficient deterrent. Elizabeth Donnan documents an example:

> Why, Captain Harding weighing the Stoutness and Worth of the two slaves, did, as in other Countries they do by Rogues of Dignity, whip and scarify them only; while three other, Abettors, but not Actors, nor of strength for it, he sentenced to cruel Deaths; making them first eat the Heart and Liver of one of them killed. The woman he hoisted up by the Thumbs, whipp'd and slashed her with Knives, before the other Slaves till she died.[4]

Thus, it was not innate slavery or Christianity which turned on black slaves, it was Black Power, the longing for liberty or death. The records are frequented with more than two hundred and fifty land revolts. A desire to be free and human took precedence over being bound in slavery or Christian virtues. Were these the inhibiting factors, slaves would have revolted more often and more successfully. They were stymied by militias, restricted movement which limited their communications with each other, small numbers on small farms, and the ubiquitousness of spies, overseers, or owners. It is worth recalling that the two hundred and fifty revolts on record do not take into account those which undoubtedly transpired but were not reported in print. Nevertheless, there is evidence enough of a very human and revolting spirit among blacks from the outset of slavery. It follows, too, that this spirit should find expression in ways less spectacular. Thousands upon thousands escaped to freedom, many of whom were lost in the statistical accounts just as today we are unaware of just how many black males there are in urban centers. The history books are full of indications that the desire for freedom found reality in slaves' purchasing their freedom, gaining it through military duty and engagement in freedom movements. Slave revolts took place throughout the last half of the seventeenth century, when slaves had landed here in some numbers. They continued into the American Revolution, which gave them impetus, especially a spirit like that of Mrs. John Adams in a letter to her husband:

> I wish most sincerely there was not a slave in the province; it always appeared a most iniquitous scheme to me to fight ourselves for what we are daily robbing and plundering from those who have as good a right to freedom as we have.

There were three insurrections which especially give credence to the historical connections of Black Power. They were preceded by many others in Surry County, Virginia; Charleston, South Carolina; Georgia; and New York City. Most of these insurrections are set forth by Herbert Aptheker in his *American Negro Slave Revolts*. The first memorable insurrection was masterminded by a slave known only as Gabriel, of Henrico County, Virginia. The plot was kept secret for a number of months, only to be revealed by two slaves on the eve of execution. Evidence for the extraordinary preparations and time in which the plot was developed is clearest in the numbers appearing that night. Some one thousand slaves were involved, but they retreated when the rain broke forth with such a flood that they were unable to gain a footing against the militia. Interestingly enough, though only a thousand strong, the devastating possibility of this force lay in its organization, secrecy, timing, and commitment to a religious cause. The religious dimension was the impressive way in which Gabriel convinced these blacks they were, on the authority of the Bible, the new Israel called upon to rise up and overthrow their masters. The timing was also a significant lesson which Black Power has not forgotten. The insurrection took place when Jefferson was spearheading a democratic revolt against the Federalists.

It is to be noted that although scores of the thousand actually taking part in placing their bodies on the line were captured and executed, none of them would involve others or leak any information about the plot. They were impelled by liberty and were willing to face death without a whimper. Perhaps this was due to a confidence that the many engaged in the plot would try again with more success. It is reported that a thousand slaves were involved, plus Indians and some French, and the hope of the poor whites as well. This historical event shook the region, a singular reminder to black militants that with intelligence, organization, charisma, and the involvement of the masses themselves, they can be united in the cause. This rebellion was unsuccessful due, at least in part, to the intervention of forces of nature. There followed from its waves many smaller and less ingenious revolts throughout the area.

Prior to and following, but especially during the War of 1812, all kinds of revolts, rebellions, and insurrections were smashed before they could get started. During this period of expectance that the British would come to their aid, a battle song was written by a slave which has few marks of docility:

> Arise! arise! shake off your chains!
> Your cause is just, so Heaven ordains;
> To you shall freedom be proclaimed!
> Raise your arms and bare your breasts,
> Almighty God will do the rest.
> Blow the clarion's warlike blast;
> Call every Negro from his task;
> Wrest the scourge from Buckra's hand,
> And drive each tyrant from the land!
>
> Firm, united let us be,
> Resolved on death or liberty!
> As a band of patriots joined,
> Peace and plenty we shall find.

The second and perhaps most spectacular insurrection was planned by Denmark Vesey in 1822. It took place in Charleston, South Carolina. Denmark Vesey, who had purchased his freedom for $600 in 1800, held in common with most of the conspiracy leaders Christian convictions, if not Christian virtues. For Denmark Vesey and his fellow rebels, Christianity had basically to do with justice, freedom, and equality now. Christianity had to do with gaining these human longings through any means necessary. This was God's word to his people in Israel made plain to them in the scriptures.

Denmark Vesey was influenced by antislavery speeches surrounding the Missouri Compromise. The successful uprisings in Haiti were known to him. These unusual events combined with the Bible were powerful factors Vesey put together to form a cohesive band of true believers. His ability to lead consisted of a sense of dignity and the belief in the equality of blacks with whites. An excerpt from his trial reports:

> Even whilst walking through the streets in company with another, he was not idle; for if his companion bowed to a white person he would rebuke him, and observe that all men were born equal, and that he was surprised that anyone would degrade himself by such conduct; that he would never cringe to the whites, nor ought anyone who had the feelings of a man. When answered, We are slaves, he would sarcastically and indignantly reply, "You deserve to remain slaves"; and if he were further asked, What can we do, he would remark, "Go and buy a spelling book and read the fable of Hercules and the Waggoner"; which he would then repeat, and apply it to their situation.[5]

Those slaves not impressed by the Bible of the white man or by his ancient myths were brought into the movement through their own conventional wisdom. Vesey had as his second in command a practitioner of sorcery, Gullah Jack, who was extremely successful in organizing and gaining the allegiance of those who found the past ways of their ancient homeland most convincing. In Vesey and other early leaders of violent revolts, Black Power has a heritage of intelligent command and heroic models, as well as ingenuity. The commitment of Vesey to freedom included his rejection of the back-to-Africa movements for free black men. He preferred to give his life here in the cause of freeing all his brethren. Escape through personal privilege or the creation of separatism in any form found no response from black rebels with courage.

Denmark Vesey planned the insurrection for a Sunday when slaves were permitted in the city. It is said that the original plans called for the revolt in the month of July when most whites were vacationing. The preparations included the take-over of ammunition centers, and more than two hundred of the slaves were to be armed previously with stolen blades such as bayonets and knives. Contact had been made with Haiti. Wigs were in preparation for disguises. But the plans all went awry due to betrayal by black men. Denmark Vesey and thirty-seven others were hanged; an equal number were deported. Many more were arrested. But the conspiracy included a far larger circle of stalwarts such as members of the black Methodist congregation who were spared. Those who died followed their leaders to the end: "Do not open your lips! Die silent as you see me do." [6]

Terror filled the countryside for miles around following the breakup of this plot. The white response was much the same as the backlash which occurs today in the wake of rebellions in our cities. But the blacks were catching so much hell on the frontlash that they could not be contained by the backlash. Just as whites today draw on these real slave images to get back at blacks, so blacks draw on these heroes for ferment in the present movement. Though foiled, the Denmark Vesey revolt reached the blacks beyond the vicinity, as well as the whites, and there was real cause for alarm at the spreading of this disobedience. Voices of whites were heard everywhere demanding the stamping out of the blacks for safety in the streets. Containment by militia was the response. However, the whites' economic investment took precedence over the will to eliminate the blacks.

The third great black awakening came with the advance of Nat Turner. He was a deeply religious man, a mystic in whose vein John Brown followed. Historically, he has been reputed to be plainly superstitious because of his mixture of Christianity with belief in the signs of the stars. In this he was not alone; the practice of omens from the heavens was widespread among blacks and whites of the region.

Nat Turner believed that the rebellion should begin at home and then spread abroad. Accordingly, in 1831 he led a small band of slaves on a Sunday in August in the massacre of his master and the family. The last shall be first, the first shall be last. This was the spirit of Christ which led Nat Turner on. Thus, there was no well-planned plot. There was but the charisma of this moving spirit leading a band of followers which increased as he moved from place to place. They blindly killed every white in sight, more than fifty in all. They confronted a militia and were easily overcome. Nat Turner, in hiding for six weeks, was finally captured. He pleaded "Not guilty!" This was the perspective he had on the matter. As with his comrades in arms, he was hanged by the neck until he was dead.

The unrest of the slaves and their revolts were in evidence all during this period leading up to the Civil War. Whites were committed to the attainment of freedom for the blacks, even by violence, in circumstances less grand than those of the Civil War. This kind of support a few whites are ready to give Black Power in the present has precedents. Few of them have been reported, for their attunement to black people was out of harmony with the dominant thrust of the age. Whites were indoctrinated with the belief that blacks should never be placed on an equal footing with whites and found their voice in such men as Thomas Jefferson. Virginia was Thomas Jefferson's love. In this area slave revolts were plentiful. Thus, Thomas Jefferson might hesitate

> to degrade a whole race of men from the work in the scale of beings which their Creator may *perhaps* have given them. . . . I advance it therefore, as a suspicion only, that the blacks, whether originally a distinct race, or made distinct by time and circumstance, are inferior to whites in the endowment both of body and mind. It is not against experience to suppose that different species of the same genus, or varieties of the same species, may possess different qualifications. Will not a lover of natural history then, one who views the gradations in all the races of animals with the eye of philosophy, excuse an effort to keep those in the department of man as distinct as nature has formed them.[7]

One such white move to counter the general white antiblack and antiblack violence was that of Harpers Ferry, Virginia, some distance from the Virginia home of Jefferson. Old John Brown was the leader. In this raid of October 16, 1859, John Brown sought guns and ammunition to arm blacks and create of them a real guerrilla fighting force from the mountains of what is now West Virginia. He was trapped with his black brothers while in possession of the armory.

Black revolts, rebellions, insurrections, and conspiracies were means justified by the end of freedom. They were not successful in this objective. They did serve to throw the white South into the throes of fear, which, it is not difficult to argue, only served to bring the hatred to the surface. Thomas Jefferson's standpoint, held in common by whites, makes clear that there was nothing blacks could do which would add to the overwhelming and unshakable bond of hate in which they were held. If the fear did not serve to change the hearts of whites, it did cause them to keep on the alert a very expensive militia. Even more, during the Revolutionary War and the War of 1812, the fear of violent insurrections resulted in a limited involvement by whites of the South, as well as in a general national weakness.

So, the general proneness of the South to produce military men results in part from the necessity of large militias throughout the era prior to the Civil War. If the South was in many quarters an armed country of patrolling militia, it was a price Southerners were willing to pay to keep slavery. Blacks were kept in chains; the freedom of whites was thereby necessarily restricted. It was as if everywhere blacks could be heard to sing

> Jesus make de blind to see
> Jesus make de cripple walk,
> Jesus make de deaf to hear.
>   Walk in, kind Jesus!
>   No man can hinder me.

The year 1816 was one of continuous uprisings. It was also the year of birth for the Colonization Society for the removal of free blacks to Africa. Some support for this movement came as the reaction to fear of conspiracies. Even more, the Abolitionist

Movement was furthered by the knowledge of these revolts and the direct participation of agitating blacks in the movement. These black precursors of Black Power were not simply singing

> Yes, we all shall be free
> Yes, we all shall be free,
> Yes, we all shall be free,
> When the Yankee shall appear,

they were engaged in bringing him directly into the movement and eventually into the Civil War. The insurrections convinced the Abolitionists that this was the inevitable consequence of slavery. So, while whites of the South were proclaiming how obedient, imitating, and docile were their blacks, insurrectionists were the final confirmation to Abolitionists that blacks were men who not only longed for freedom but fought for it. There was something added by these black men which increased the participation of whites in the fight to end slavery. This something was not their self-pity, it was their aggressiveness. To give their lives for freedom led whites to do no less than extend their hand to help with enthusiasm.

No American was more important in the fight for freedom through Abolition than the magnificent ex-slave Frederick Douglass. He spoke out on every hand. Frederick Douglass supported Radical Abolition, welcomed secession, urged emancipation as a war measure, and on occasion attacked Abraham Lincoln for policies he was critical of, although he admired the man as a whole. If one seeks to discover a resource for the inflammatory speeches of Black Power, it would be useful to turn to Frederick Douglass. When Lincoln overruled General David Hunter's order that slaves in Georgia, Florida, and South Carolina under his military command were forever free, Douglass said:

> ABRAHAM LINCOLN is no more fit for the place he holds than was JAMES BUCHANAN, and the latter was no more the miserable tool of traitors and rebels than the former is allowing himself to be.[8]

When the conservative Emancipation Proclamation with its revolutionary promise was issued, this same Douglass wrote, "We shout for joy that we live to record this righteous decree." His opposition to blacks' emigrating to Africa or to Haiti was based on this standpoint: "The hope of the world is in Human Brotherhood; in the union of mankind, not in exclusive nationalities." [9] When the Civil War came and with it the question of duty of blacks or their right to fight, Douglass was in the forefront:

> Colored men were good enough to fight under Washington. They are not good enough to fight under McClellan. They were good enough to fight under Andrew Jackson. They are not good enough to fight under Gen. Halleck. They were good enough to help win American independence, but they are not good enough to help preserve that independence against treason and rebellion.[10]

In this same spirit, James Madison Bell, who served with John Brown, wrote from San Francisco where he worked as a poet:

Shall we arm them? Yes, arm them! Give to each man
A rifle, a musket, a cutlass or sword;
  Then on to the charge! let them war in the van
Where each may confront with his merciless lord,
And purge from their race, in the eyes of the brave,
The stigma and scorn now attending the slave.

I would not have the wrath of the rebels to cease,
  Their hope to grow weak nor their courage to wane,
Till the Contrabands join in securing a peace,
  Whose glory shall vanish the last galling chain,
And win for their race an undying respect
In the land of their prayers, their tears and neglect.

Is war one for Freedom? Then why, tell me, why,
Should the wronged and oppressed be debarred from the fight?
Does not reason suggest, it were noble to die
  In the act of supplanting a wrong for the right?
Then lead to the charge! for the end is not far,
When the contraband host are enrolled in the war.[11]

Despite the two hundred years blacks fought for their freedom with knife or pen, underground or overground, on the land or on the sea, with whites or against them, in war or in slavery, as slaves or as free men—despite this history, the question arose as to whether they should fight in the Civil War. The two basic oppositions were the prejudice of whites in the North who did not want to fight with "Niggers" and their basic belief that blacks were cowardly. Blacks knew themselves to have been engaged in massacres, mutilations, assassinations, propaganda, setting fires, escapes, poisoning, and other guerrilla warfare. So, they sought to put an end to the struggle once and for all by giving their best in the Civil War. This was the opportunity. But they had to protest for the right of free, black, and Northern men to engage in the war. There was official opposition from the War Department in Washington. But through the events of losses and the extension of the war, Northern opposition gave way. This was assisted by the willingness of Generals David Hunter and Andrew Johnson. In April, 1862, President Lincoln wrote General Hunter:

> I am glad to see the accounts of your colored force at Jacksonville, Florida. . . . It is important to the enemy that such a force shall not take shape, and grow, and thrive, in the South; and in precisely the same proportion, it is important to us that it shall.

In late March President Lincoln wrote General Johnson:

> I am told you have at least *thought* of raising a negro military force. In my opinion the country now needs no specific thing so much as some man of your ability and position to go to this work. . . . The colored population is the great *available* and yet *unavailed of* force for restoring the Union. The bare sight of 50,000 armed and drilled black soldiers upon the banks of the Mississippi would end the rebellion at once. And who doubts that we can present that sight if we but take hold in earnest?" [12]

The performance of blacks in the war were consistent examples of desperate courage. Blacks never thought for a moment they were fighting simply to save the Union—the fight for them was the fight for freedom. By the end of the 1863 summer, there were fourteen black regiments in the field, twenty-four more being organized. In August, 1863, President Lincoln set his pen to this public letter: "Some of the commanders of our armies in the field who have given us our most important successes, believe the emancipation policy, and the use of colored troops, constitute the heaviest blow yet dealt to the rebellion." [13]

This statement of Lincoln's found truth as well in the South where blacks formed more than 35 percent of the population. The good fortune of the North with black troops and the defeat of whites in Santo Domingo along with the French troops sent by the masters raised in the minds of some the thought of enlisting blacks on the side of the South. General Lee responded favorably to the idea. The inducement was to be that of freedom with the consent of the masters. Jefferson Davis consented after a long period of indecisiveness. It was toward the end of the Civil War that at Richmond a few black companies were put together. Before they could fight, the war ended.

Meanwhile, the South had tightened its security with patrols, refusing assemblage of slaves without the presence of persons who took the responsibility for their gathering, mounted guards, and well-armed volunteer riders. The shortage of manpower was acute. Yet, a white man was deferred for every fifteen slaves. Heavy guards were necessary to cover slaves forced into labor on behalf of the Confederacy. This worked very well as long as the experienced overseers were wise enough to keep these blacks a substantial distance in the rear from any frontline troops. These precautions cut into the troop numbers the South was able to put on the line.

The great majority of slaves were watched so closely that they were unable to escape, fight, or in other ways directly challenge their masters. But freedom was on their minds. They wished to find ways to encourage the North and upset the South. During the Civil War blacks engaged in disruptive tactics with increasing vigor. They took the risk of refusing to work because a certain overseer was disliked, food was distasteful, or the hours were too long more often than they had in the past. Sometimes they won more than the reward of simply being disruptive. Cases are known where wages were paid or punishment was eliminated. Beyond their own acts of refusing to lay their bodies on the work line, they often engaged in the destruction of tools, the mistreatment of animals, and the ruination of property, including crops and fences. The death penalty was not unusual in these matters. Best of all, these blacks were in the service of Union troops as spies who supplied them, and Confederate deserters, with food, shelter, clothes, and directions. In fact, it was not unusual for Confederate espionage to take the form of spies for the South dressing as Union soldiers and thereby gaining information. Thus, intensive hatred of slavery led to conspiracies, assassinations, and arson, which slaves offered as their contribution to freedom.

Guerrilla warfare has come to prominence as a possibility in America only in the 1960's. This was a form of reaction to slavery blacks took during the Civil War. The brave slaves who slipped away would reside in swamps, woods, and mountains which then became escape centers for runaway slaves. These hideouts were also beehives for raids upon masters. They became as well refuges for white Unionists of all kinds and Confederate deserters, who did some harm to the Confederacy in their robbing and stealing and killing.

These small, but menacing activities in defiance of the Southern way of life were possible in part because of the information blacks received from that tiny band of whites who were Southerners but hated the system of slavery. These Southern blacks also gained information from their black brothers in freedom who were their hearts. As any concentration camp or prison system has the most active and dependable grapevine imaginable, so blacks in slavery had their unbelievable system of communication, which was accurate and fast.

There may be a generation gap among blacks today. The young everywhere cry out for black history which many of us were brought up on. It is certain, though, that as we received black history from social groups, family teachings, and church schools, where it was not taught in public schools, a letdown in this area grew with the coming of civil rights and the expectation that we have made it. The past could be put aside because the whole society was to be ours. This did not occur. Moreover, the demand everywhere by black youth for black history is different. It is as much for whites as for blacks. Whatever the result, black militants are in earnest search of black heroes who were men of brains and brawn. They search history not just for the acceptable and respectable black heroes like Booker T. Washington and George Washington Carver. They seek those blacks whom many have rejected for their disdain of the American way of death. There is every reason to look with pride at the black warrior heroes sketched here. In them there is courage and confidence enough to continue the struggle for freedom and equality toward the long awaited era of revolutionary reconstruction. The singular fact that black militants should grasp is that this heroic movement for freedom was the work of a heroic people. The individuals who stand out may not be overwhelming in numbers. What is overwhelming is the unity of a people for freedom and their determination, even while in the throes of slavery, or handcuffed by fellow blacks who were chained forever to the system. There is one other reminder here. In the just and right cause there are those whites who have in the past and will in the future extend their hand of fellowship and risk their lives for the common freedom and equality they know to be the need of all. Black Power knows this and finds support in the past for the present, when in the question of political equality, there are still the Senator Vardamans who speak for many:

> . . . it matters not what his [the Negro's] advertised mental and moral qualifications may be. I am just as much opposed to Booker Washington as a voter, with all his Anglo-Saxon re-enforcements, as I am to the cocoanut-headed, chocolate-covered, typical little coon, Andy Dotson, who blacks my shoes every morning. Neither is fit to perform the supreme function of citizenship.[14]

The language of today is different; the spirit is the same.

The Civil War differed from previous wars and other dimensions of the American experience very little with respect to the mutual involvement of blacks and whites. The significance of the Civil War was that it united for the first time the black people in America. Blacks expected that its conclusion would launch them on the way to being full men and women in the events ahead. Recalcitrant disdain and hatred of blacks were endemic in the American mainstream as Reconstruction in the South and migration to the North were to prove. Blacks deserved their freedom and the hopes of equality because this was their right as men and women created by God for responsible manhood. They went further and proved their manhood for all time through the most courageous acts under the persistent gun. But the simple desire of being accepted as brothers of the one God was denied by the white society which continued to use its freedom to check the freedom of blacks, as well as its own.

Black Power is the living embodiment of this memorable past and ignoble present. Its task is to complete the revolution and bring into being those forces which will, once and for all, make concrete in the context of America the illusive reality of black manhood. As blacks were once united in the fight for freedom and the union of a nation torn asunder, there is no question but that they can be united again in the fight for freedom through a civil conflict in the name of the unity of all, rather than in the name of special privileges for the white majority. The Civil War united black people with forces initiated beyond their control. Yet, freedom remained an illusive expectation. Black Power sees this experience and seeks to build a unified black people out of their own internal dynamic. This may be the only real counter to systematic exclusion. There is more light and truth yet to break forth from the historic anvil of Black Power amidst the burning that is to shape the new America.

3.

BLACK POWER
Surrogates

The Civil War not only ended the violence of blacks for a cause that was not entirely of their making and certainly not in their control, it also brought to an abrupt halt their unity. Pride in being black people, which once formed them into fearless fighters for freedom, became in the wake of the post-Civil War period an oppressive colored millstone cast around their necks. The hope of freedom did not die in the masses, but the consciousness that black people, precisely because they were black, were everywhere a despised lot gave pause. Black leaders were unable to draw a demoralized people into unity with their enthusiasm broken by the post–Civil-War Black Codes like the one in Mississippi. It read that

> all the penal and criminal laws now in force in this State, defining offenses, and prescribing the mode of punishment for crimes and misdemeanors committed by slaves, free Negroes or mulattoes, be and the same are hereby reenacted, and declared to be in full force and effect, against freedmen, free Negroes, and mulattoes, except so far as the mode and manner of trial and punishment have been changed or altered by law.[1]

Both North and South blacks were unacceptable. There was no intention of granting them decency with respect in opportunity anywhere. As one reporter observed:

> Wherever I go—the street, the shop, the house, the hotel, or the steamboat—I hear the people talk in such a way as

> to indicate they are yet unable to conceive of the Negro as possessing any rights at all. Men who are honorable in their dealings with their white neighbors, will cheat a Negro without feeling a single twinge of their honor. To kill a Negro, they do not deem murder; to debauch a Negro woman, they do not think of fornication; to take the property away from a Negro, they do not consider robbery. The people boast that when they get freedmen's affairs in their own hands, to use their own expression, "the Niggers will catch hell."
>
> The reason of all this is simple and manifest. The whites esteem the blacks their property by natural right, and however much they admit that the individual relations of masters and slaves have been destroyed by the war and by the President's emancipation proclamation, they still have an ingrained feeling that the blacks at large belong to the whites at large.[2]

In response there arose the Reconstruction Acts, the demand of blacks for "forty acres and a mule," black participation in Reconstruction governments, and the quest for education. These efforts failed not by the good efforts of blacks, but because of the stubborn will of whites that blacks would remain on the bottom. Blacks caught hell in this period on the frontlash of racial embroilment epitomized by the Ku Klux Klan, which threw white supremacy back into power and undermined the will of blacks and whites to the good. Lynchings increased rapidly "to keep the Negro in his place."

At the turn of the century, nine tenths of the blacks were locked in the Southern system of disenfranchisement, paternalism, violence, poverty, and fear, which flared up in the 1906 Atlanta race riot. In this riot, as in all other conditions of the South, blacks received a beating. In the North, though their numbers were small, the life lived by blacks was so marginal as to make the migration of blacks from South to North seem not worth the effort. If blacks kept quiet and accepted the life of inferiority, they were economically better off in the South. It was this facet of the dilemma Booker T. Washington fastened to with tenacity. Black people, distracted, their dream denied, their hopes deferred, their power delayed, issued forth in their recoil from Black Power. Fighting Frederick Douglass spoke for black men throughout the nation. All that he fought for nearly slipped away by the time he died. In the year of his death, with the civil rights of blacks in the South revoked, there arose a spokesman for blacks in the South proclaiming in his inaugural speech of 1895 in Atlanta: "In all things that are purely social we can be as separate as the fingers, yet one as the hand in all things essential to mutual progress." Washington spoke for the masses of blacks and there was hope in this, but in keeping with the time in which he lived, reaction set in against him.

> The radical and conservative tendencies of the Negro race cannot be better described than by comparing, or rather contrasting, the two superlative colored men in whom we find their highest embodiment—Frederick Douglass and Booker Washington. . . . Douglass was like a lion, bold and fearless; Washington is lamblike, meek and submissive. Douglass escaped from personal bondage, which his soul abhorred; but for Lincoln's proclamation, Washington would probably have arisen to esteem and favor in the eyes of his master as a good and faithful servant. Douglass insisted upon rights; Washington insists upon duty. Douglass held up to public scorn the sins of the white man; Washington portrays the faults of his race. Douglass spoke what he thought the world should hear; Washington speaks only what he feels it is disposed to listen to. Douglass's conduct was actuated in principle; Washington's by prudence. Douglass had no limited, copyrighted programme for his race, but appealed to the Decalogue, the Golden Rule, the Declaration of Independence, the Constitution of the United States; Washington, holding these great principles in the shadowy background, presents a practical expedient applicable to present needs. Douglass was a moralist, insisting upon the application of righteousness to public affairs; Washington is a practical opportunist, accepting the best terms which he thinks it possible to secure.[3]

With the fall of Black Power, Washington rose as the first and last black man in America who spoke for all blacks in the sense that he was a king maker. He had access to the White House, influenced political jobs, and dictated who would get them among blacks. This powerful patronage of the man from Tuskegee Institute in Alabama was sought after by whites in the South who requested his support. Given his perspective, he truly sought to give blacks a better share of the American pie. He was the preeminent black leader for thirty years. His accommodating leadership subsided with the movement North of the black masses. Though challenged by black leaders, it took the economic needs of the North and World War I, which brought the first mass migration of blacks out of the South, to topple Washington.

Between the leadership of Douglass, which demanded rights for blacks, and that of Washington, which gained opportunities through conciliation, there came forth an intellectual giant who led the new pattern of appeal to the conscience of whites through reason. This man was W. E. B. Du Bois, educated at Harvard and in Europe. A small, but influential set of black intellectuals arose at the turn of the century. Their admitted leader was Du Bois. He had deep convictions about black consciousness, supported by a lively mind and a strong will. He knew the soul of the black masses, but did not appeal to it, and therefore neither worked with nor spoke for them. His conception of a black leader was the profound conviction that there was a "talented tenth" among blacks whose responsibility was to prove themselves equal to whites in intellectual acumen and culture:

> The Talented Tenth of the Negro race must be made leaders of the thought and missionaries of the culture among their people. No others can do this work and Negro colleges must train men for it. The Negro race, like all other races, is going to be saved by its exceptional men.[4]

In this stance, Du Bois was consciously offering an alternative to the manual labor approach stressed by Washington. More than that, he was betraying his elitist standpoint and personal disappointments. Here was a scholar of the first rank who was not accepted by whites and not at home among the masses of ignorant, poor, deprived blacks. His response was to join with the few blacks, the "aristocracy of talent and character," and in a Herculean stance raise the black masses by the sheer power of reason, the strength of culture, and dedicated perseverance. He practiced what he preached and taught in Atlanta for a period. He could not grasp, however, the truth that the black bond was so strong it could only be broken through all blacks' uniting in a common effort at that point where the leaders determine the oppressor to be the weakest.

Instead of developing Black Power in the tradition of Vesey and Douglass, Du Bois chose only one aspect of this fighting pride, intellectual power, and with it launched the first civil rights movement with its emphasis upon protest. As a beginning, Du Bois returned to Harpers Ferry, West Virginia, with a group of black intellectuals with whom he had met previously in Niagara Falls. There, in 1906, the Niagara Movement was born, ostensibly to carry on the work of old John Brown in a different style. Instead of militancy, the spirit was that of a conference, and it concluded in this way:

> We shall not be satisfied with less than our full manhood rights. We claim for ourselves every right that belongs to a free-born American, civil and social, and until we get these rights we shall never cease to protest and assail the ears of America with the stories of its shameful deeds toward us. We want our manhood suffrage and we want it now. Second, we want discrimination in public accommodations to cease. Third, we claim the right to associate with such people as wish to associate with us. Fourth, we want the laws enforced against the rich as well as the poor, against capitalists as well as laborers, against white as well as black. We are not more lawless than the white race; we are more often arrested, convicted and mobbed. Fifth, we want our children educated.[5]

This statement reads like the original of those set forth by civil rights groups six decades later. If the meetings of the Niagara Movement and the time spent on civil rights complaints came to naught in 1905, this is understandable given the same reality today.

Three years later a conference was called of concerned whites and blacks, in the light of the civil rights denied blacks. W. E. B.

Du Bois and a number of those present at the inception of the Niagara Movement were present. The conviction was held that black intellectual power was not enough to achieve what this conference called for: abolition of all forced segregation, equal educational advantages for colored and white, enfranchisement of the blacks, and enforcement of the Fourteenth and Fifteenth Amendments. Out of this conference came the National Association for the Advancement of Colored People, the first interracial civil rights group. Du Bois became publicity director and editor of the NAACP's organ, *Crisis.*

The base of the NAACP is the middle-class-oriented blacks in nearly every community where they reside; this has been so from the beginning. With the leadership of Du Bois and others of the intellectual elite to follow, the NAACP continues in the throes of the "talented tenth." It is directed by the high command from the top, and if it has more members than any other civil rights group, it is also the one where the masses are led like sheep. In the beginning, the program seemed radical to many whites and their support was slow. But an elite white body of liberals came to its aid with money and community support, as well as advice. It is a nationwide organization, a familiar term in most homes. Its most spectacular dimension is that of the NAACP Legal Defense and Education Fund, which has won the major civil rights cases in this century. The head of the Legal Defense has included such distinguished Americans as William Hastie, former Dean of Howard University Law School and now a federal judge; Mr. Justice Marshall; and presently the first white head of this legally separate NAACP body, Jack Greenberg. Walter White and Roy Wilkins are the persons who gave meaning and fame to the role of Executive Secretary, the real head of the NAACP. There has never been a black man as president of the NAACP, an assurance of its intention to remain interracial.

Given the starting base of the NAACP and its stellar achievements throughout this century, there can be no doubt of its indispensable role in prodding the law of the land to return to blacks in the South the civil rights taken away by the Black Codes and white supremacy. This fantastically complex, expensive, and extensive accomplishment continues to be advanced. The combination of black and white brains backed by black and white funds early believed that the only way to make democracy work in its legal dimension was to force the issue in the courts through such efforts as opposition to lynching. The significant role of the NAACP in coming to the defense of persons involved in sit-ins and other protests is nothing short of magnificent.

Yet, the indispensable work notwithstanding, the elitist dimension of the NAACP best serves to reveal that with all the brains and money mustered from liberal whites, especially Jews, and blacks, they do not have enough power to bring the black masses into the mainstream. The effort of making democracy work better than it was thought possible resulted in the success to date of nearly all the original programs adopted in February, 1909. What has failed is the effort at equal education, followed far behind by enfranchisement, which still is not settled throughout the Deep South. Desegregation has had very little effect on the black masses. Lobbying, legal assistance, formal protests, pressure through business and governmental channels—all lead to the description of the NAACP, what Du Bois called the "aristocracy of talent and character," as the queen of the civil rights aristocracy.

For all of its dedicated effectiveness, the NAACP as queen of the civil rights aristocracy at best chips away at the block of racism. So massive is this block of petrified color prejudice that the NAACP serves only to point, attractively, if astutely, to the aged formation. Its activity shows that nothing short of the will of the people acting through the great resources of the federal, state, and local governments in cooperation with business can remove racism's triple evils of black deprivation in jobs, housing, and education. There is no expectation that such a will is forthcoming to remove these evil branches of racism, to say nothing of the color prejudice root. An axe has to be laid to the tree and coals of fire set in the remains to burn out the roots. This is not the work of the NAACP. It began as a middle-class-oriented group and has increased the number of blacks who participate therein. But it feeds on a broad mass base of blacks who at least aspire to the middle-class values, leaving untouched the real black poor who do not participate in these benefits directly or vicariously.

The NAACP increased its membership from 11,524 in 1917 to 427,434 at its fifty-ninth annual convention in 1968. The increase in participation at the level of poor blacks has been less dramatic. The organization is a tightly run ship. The rules and policies are so intricate that they serve the interests of the leadership, which does not necessarily reflect the interests of the people it serves. A serious threat to this leadership broke forth in Atlantic City in June, 1968. The youth opposed the old guard in a move to have participatory democracy through committees set up to report to the main body of 1,600 delegates. The aim was to make the NAACP relevant to the black community, as opposed to the view that the best interest of that community should be determined from the top. These committees, in keeping with this demand, would study the revitalization of the NAACP, African-American culture, buildup of black economic and political institutions, the survival of black Americans, and Afro-American or nonwhite world affairs. This move was defeated 432 to 288.

This defeat expressed the confidence of the NAACP that through its traditional methods blacks are very close to the goals set forth by the organization. The charge of the dissident youth is that the NAACP is not relevant to the black community—it is too legalistic, system-oriented. There is evidence here of a split between the solid black constituency of the South, made up of the black bourgeoisie, and the youthful blacks of the North who do not believe whites can be trusted to deal with black America. New forms to deal with the needs of the black masses other than the black elite is the cause of the insurgency.

In a word, the NAACP faces an increasing challenge from Black Power. Yesterday's radicals have become today's reactionaries. The division between Douglass and Washington is being repeated in the present-day movement of Black Power versus aristocratic civil rights. Black Power is not opposed to leadership; its opposition is to the autocracy of Roy Wilkins, who is the NAACP. The call of Black Power is for a leadership that speaks out of the masses and moves the people forward by giving its feelings sensitive direction with which they can identify. The issue is not one of frustration with the past; the NAACP in its emphases served its time well. Black Power believes this is a different era which demands new forms. The NAACP is suspect because it is not entirely dependent upon blacks. The NAACP suspects Black Power because it holds black control to be more emotive and less realistic than desired. Roy Wilkins is not so much conservative as he is the representative of the outlook and ideology of the NAACP. This was once the most important of the civil rights groups; it is still the largest. Black Power represents a new and rising group which may well dominate the decades ahead. Its perspective is that civil rights efforts have performed their function well, but they have not accomplished the job because they ignore the people and underestimate racism.

From the intellectual giant without peer, Du Bois, to the organization man *par excellence,* Wilkins, there has resulted a continuous debunking of the ability of the black masses to determine their destiny. The rise of Black Power is a return to the fighting stance of Denmark Vesey in the hope of uniting a people for the final push, a unity delayed by the singular failure of the NAACP—ignoring the masses.

In 1910, the year following the inception of the NAACP, the National Urban League was born. It perceived its function to be the alleviation of the sufferings black masses met in cities. Its method was that of social welfare and the training of black social workers. The National Urban League did not consider itself a movement in the NAACP sense of molding a people to overcome the forces which denied them their manhood. Rather, the Urban League took the more modest route of recognizing the industrial needs of blacks through study. This awareness led to a countering of inequality by training blacks to deal with industrial America. Industrial America could not be changed, but the blacks who were primarily an agricultural people could be fitted into the society and thereby minimize the inevitability of a second-rate lot.

This tactic of the Urban League required financial support not available in the black community. As a consequence, the Urban League was interracial from the beginning and received financial support from among the most distinguished names in the Northeast: Rockefeller, Rosenwald, and Stone. Within a few years after its formation, blacks moved North to fill the industrial openings created by World War I. The NAACP was the most active organization in the period with respect to citizenship rights for blacks. Although the National Urban League was not a movement of the people, even in the spurious way of the NAACP, the migration North made it the most important agency, white or black, dealing with social welfare problems stemming out of the migration waves. Its success grew and its offices expanded to every important city in the nation. The expertise in handling migrants from the South became its primary business. It served to screen applicants for industrial jobs; it served to find blacks to fill openings; it ran a service for locating housing; it provided black in-migrants with social welfare information and services.

The prime mover in bringing the Urban League into being was George Haynes, Professor of Sociology at Fisk University. His work was continued by such Executive Secretaries as Lester Granger. The chief architect of the Urban League today is the former Dean of Atlanta University's School of Social Work, Whitney M. Young, Jr. Mr. Young is known in the business world by every important corporation executive. The relationship between Young and these financiers is cordial, warm, and intimate. He is known as "a great guy." He is able to increase the budget of this social agency by millions each year. His technique, and that of the agency, is to be the best manipulator of human relations on the American scene. In this he is intelligent, forthright, honest, imaginative, and dedicated to the best interest of blacks as he sees them.

With the best technique, skill, and will in the world, the long and specific service of the Urban League has only scratched the surface. The fact is that the problems of the cities have increased so fast that this intelligent organ has been left far behind. It has promised a great deal, but the black masses have received very little. Unlike the NAACP, however, the Urban League under Whitney Young is moving to a *rapprochement* with Black Power, as is set forth in another chapter. This change may well be due to the clear recognition that a movement of the people as a whole is indispensable, that blacks intend Black Power as the means to "achieve their aims by their own efforts, not as a result of white beneficence." Charles

Silberman caught the spirit of Black Power before it began to crystallize, a spirit which Whitney Young is catching:

> Having suppressed their rage these many years behind a mask of servility or humility, Negroes must prove their new found courage to themselves, as well as to the whites. When the poor Negroes of Montgomery stopped riding the buses, and when the college students in a dozen cities started sitting-in at lunch counters, many Negroes in the United States walked a little straighter; and whites began to see Negroes in a somewhat different light. The truth is that people can gain their freedom and self-respect only in the process of fighting for it. Thus, the very militancy and stridency that whites find so upsetting is indispensable if Negroes are to shuck off their traditional dependency and become truly free and equal, if they are to learn to respect themselves, and to be respected by whites.[6]

The NAACP and the National Urban League in their historic roles serve as surrogates to Black Power. They have failed to gain or seek a movement based in the black masses which expresses their anger and develops it into a nearly solid fighting force. Their failure is not a total loss from the perspective of Black Power. They have a running start on the work to be done beyond the revolution.

This failure of Black Power in these groups was due to a lack of leadership from the beginning. As the masses of blacks moved North during the World War I era, black leaders and organizations ignored the significance of this in-migration. They followed the masses and did not lead them, for they neither took time to understand them or the conditions in which they struggled. Civil rights organizations had their minds made up in advance. Regardless of what proved to be the situation, they knew what was good for masses of blacks, and they intended to do it on their behalf whether the masses deemed it wise or not. In this respect, the NAACP and the Urban League were as paternalistic and insensitive as the white system they opposed. Blacks were powerless at the turn of the century when the civil rights groups came into being and took over from the religious and fraternal groups the leadership of citizenship rights for blacks. The judgment of this century indicates that blacks without Black Power will continue to be powerless.

It is important to recall here that the quest for freedom and equality through Black Power was stymied by white supremacy and Black Codes, the delirium in which the country, and the blacks especially, wallowed after their hopes had been dashed by the broken promises of the Civil War, Emancipation, and Reconstruction. Civil rights organizations moved on the scene at this juncture, believing that the war between the North and the South would not have to end in a war between blacks and whites to end the racism endemic in both. The problem was seen as ignorance. The task was one of education. The method was of protest with patience. Fighting pride and power were unthinkable. This illusion exploded with the mass in-migration of blacks with whom black leadership never kept pace and whose confidence they never won because it was not sought.

Between 1910 and 1920 the mass migration of blacks North was considered by many to be but a continuation of the previous black migration from the border states. What, in fact, occurred was that the black peasants from the Deep South came North. In part they pushed out of the South due to the tenancy system, the loss of crops by boll weevil, and floods leading to famine. At the same time, the need of labor in the North was pronounced, and this became the real reason blacks from the depths of the United States traveled North to the promised land. By and large, they were concentrated in Philadelphia, Chicago, Detroit, and New York. There they met with impersonal social and economic forces which limited them to a bulging section and restricted their employment to personal and domestic service and unskilled occupations.

This in-migration brought with it a sharp increase in what may be called the small black middle and upper classes. By and large, blacks received higher wages in the North when they could find work than in the South or in the border states. It was the middle and upper classes which developed the black leaders, and they responded as racial diplomats. The hope of the black communities seemed to rest with a rising middle and upper class. However, members of these classes were intent upon being accepted by whites, and the frustration gained from the persistent rejection developed into a concern with their own good life, ignoring the black masses. In fact, the truth is that the black masses were seen as the cause of the troubles that blacks who were making it had in being accepted. A guilt reaction caused black middle- and upper-class members to engage in leadership of civil rights groups and become spokesmen for the masses to the whites. But the masses were not accepted; they were tolerated as the problem. As Du Bois once put it, the black lower class produces the "submerged tenth" which throttles the "talented tenth."

In truth, the black lower class, comprising more than two thirds of America's blacks, earns a most precarious living or exists by benefit of sporadic employment or welfare. Illiteracy, shiftlessness, irresponsibility, and instability are characteristics of the black lower class. The families are disorganized and headed by women because the male cannot find economic security. Overcrowded and segregated housing by design leads to poor health and poorer education. Discrimination in job opportunities leads to poverty. Disruption of family life first by slavery, then by the Civil War, and then by Emancipation and Reconstruction finally led to widespread disorganization in the crisis of urbanization. The high rate of crime and delinquency again resulted from the social and economic status of the masses. As Gunnar Myrdal pointed out:

> Caste, especially when it operates to cause legal injustice and insecurity of life and property, prevents the Negro from identifying himself with society and the law.[7]

Faced with this overwhelming complexity of human misery, the Northern black leaders and groups frantically pursued their ways of making the black man in the image of white values. The pride and power in being black which once marked the leadership of the masses were at their lowest ebb. There were present in this urban setting common traditions, psychological and sociological conditions enough to form a solid black consciousness with a mission in the world and a historical past to draw upon. Indeed, a consciousness of being black and the meaning thereof were intensified. Only among black men of letters did there emerge a militancy with a black mission and destiny. A Black Renaissance in letters came about during this period which influenced the masses. The works of these militant writers influenced not only the black masses and shaped them toward black consciousness with enthusiastic pride, but, as we shall see in a later chapter, they have inspired Black Power. James Weldon Johnson, Langston Hughes, and Countee Cullen are among the black bards who stirred the souls of black masses. They were ready; the leaders were not.

Into this void came the phenomenal Marcus Garvey, the man with a program, a cause, a gift of leadership with mass appeal. He was the most charismatic black man of this century. Out of this urban pathos, he created a movement.

Marcus Garvey, founder of the "Garvey Movement," was born in Jamaica, West Indies, August 17, 1887. There this former printer's apprentice organized a Negro Improvement Association based upon his experiences in England and France. But to no avail! During World War I, on March 23, 1916, he arrived in New York, hoping to meet and counsel with Booker T. Washington, who had encouraged Garvey via correspondence; but Washington died prior to Garvey's arrival. The questions which haunted him were, "Where is the black man's Government? Where is his King and Kingdom?" There in the midst of Harlem, he singlehandedly sparked a black consciousness movement unequaled in its appeal to black masses throughout urban America. The Universal Negro Improvement Association, founded on July 19, 1914, which failed in Jamaica, took off in Harlem with the migration of large numbers of blacks from Jamaica. They formed the nucleus which appealed to American blacks immediately. To the question, Where is the black man's country—his ambassador, his army, and his men of affairs? he responded: "I will help to make them." Within ten years this intense, passionate, prophetic visionary had the blacks of America in his hands. After traveling in South and Central America, the West Indies, and London, he was determined that the black man be no longer kicked about. His enemies claim there were only a million followers; he claimed six million blacks, and his critics credit him with a following of four million.* On any count, no formal organization of blacks has approached any of these figures. Indeed, there is every indication that he was right in claiming more members in his organization than in all other black groups combined. The "talented tenth" opposed him tooth and nail; consequently, they showed more contempt than scholarship by ignoring the movement. As a result of their hostility and envy, with all their aristocratic knowledge and culture, we do not know today the real effects of this movement on the black masses whom he came to save. The most important black movement in history was ignored along with the masses.

Marcus Garvey knew that black intellectuals were ineffectuals. This was not because they opposed him vehemently almost to a man. This truth came to him through their endeavors which virtually ignored the beauty and pride of blackness, the very masses themselves. Thus, in counterpoint to all the other black leaders stood for, he made black pride and beauty his theme.†

* He once wrote an autobiographical defense explaining his movement: "I traveled all over the country for the association at my own expense, and established branches until in 1919 we had about thirty branches in different cities. By my writings and speeches we were able to build up a large organization of over 2,000,000 by June, 1919, at which time we launched the program of the Black Star Line. . . . By August, 1920, over 4,000,000 persons had joined the movement. . . . The temporary ruin of the Black Star Line has in no way effected the larger work of the Universal Negro Improvement Association, which now has 900 branches with an approximate membership of 6,000,000." Marcus Garvey, "The Negro's Greatest Enemy," *Current History Magazine,* Vol. 18 (September 1923), pp. 955–956.

† "We are working for the peace of the world which we believe can only come about when all races are given their due.

"We feel that there is absolutely no reason why there should be any differences between the black and white races, if each stop to adjust and steady itself. We believe in the purity of both races. We do not believe the black man should be encouraged in the idea that his highest purpose in life is to marry a white woman, but we do believe that the white man should be taught to respect the black woman in the same way as he wants the black man to respect the white woman. It is a vicious and dangerous doctrine of social equality to urge, as certain teachers do, that black and white should get together, for that would destroy the racial purity in both." Marcus Garvey, "The Negro's Greatest Enemy," *Current History Magazine,* Vol. 18 (September 1923), pp. 956–957.

He would look into the faces of blacks and tell them to worship their broad noses, nappy heads, thick lips, and black skin. The black man and woman who had been taught by other black leaders to escape their primitive past for the white culture found in this emphasis upon their natural being a new lease on life. The black masses were dissatisfied with America. Especially was this true of the many peasants from the South who had come up to the promised land and found it to be filled with hatred of blacks, inflicted with discrimination and segregation, torn by riots.

In the place of white supremacy and white heroes, he reminded blacks of their homeland. In Africa, he claimed, blacks were the inheritors of a civilization without peer in a land with abundant wealth which whites stole to build up the West. Whites were plunderers, murderers, dependent upon blacks for all they possessed. World War I was proof of this abominable white primitiveness. In this vein he despised handouts from whites in the name of progress. Self-help and self-determination were his call and message:

> Being subservient to the will and caprice of progressive races will not prove anything superior in us. Being satisfied to drink of the dregs from the cup of human progress will not demonstrate our fitness as a people to exist alongside of others, but when of our own initiative we strike out to build industries, governments, and ultimately empires, then and only then will we as a race prove to our Creator and to man in general that we are fit to survive and capable of shaping our own destiny.[8]

Clearly, he despised white people as hypocrites not to be trusted. They fought in World War I to make the minorities of Europe safe and, at the same time, oppressed the blacks at home. Whites condemned Germany for breaking treaties, and they totally ignored the Constitution of their own country with respect to blacks. Racism for Garvey was so firm in America that he found incomprehensible and intolerable blacks who advocated cooperation with whites, who appealed to their consciences and sense of justice, who taught that the whites and their system included the sense of fair play. This was no less than a direct attack upon the black leadership which actively sought white support and proclaimed that the way for blacks was that of taking on the values of whites. To his mind they were neither "hot nor cold." In fact, they downgraded blacks and sold them out for compromises. Instead of protesting with their actions, black leaders formed a grand alliance of appeasement. Black educators, religious leaders, civil rights workers, publishers, and writers, almost to a man, denounced Marcus Garvey.* This did not bother him; the masses were with him. In fact, he appeared to relish their attacks, which gave him reason to call them opportunists, liars, thieves, and traitors. They were on the defensive. Their pride would not enable them to see a little of the truth he spoke about them and the society, to say nothing of his solutions.

In this sense the opposition of the black leaders left him alone among the leaders with the common touch to work among the masses without competition. He addressed himself to the masses, particularly to the blackest among them. Blackness was not only beauty and pride; it was strength. Thus, he taught the masses to think of God and Christ as black and reject white images in religion. Thus, he stood against the otherworldliness of black churches, into which they had totally lapsed following the Civil War. He struck black hero images by giving blacks a new history of Africa and pride in their ancestry:

> But when we come to consider the history of man, was not the Negro a power, was he not great once? Yes, honest students of history can recall the day when Egypt, Ethiopia and Timbuctoo towered in their civilizations, towered above Europe, towered above Asia. When Europe was inhabited by a race of cannibals, a race of savages, naked men, hea-

* "My negro enemies, finding that they alone could not destroy me, resorted to misrepresenting me to the leaders of the white race, several of whom, without proper investigation, also opposed me. . . . I have been deprived of the opportunity of properly explaining my work to white people of America through the prejudice worked up against me by jealous and wicked members of my own race. My success as an organizer was much more than rival negro leaders could tolerate." Marcus Garvey, "The Negro's Greatest Enemy," *Current History Magazine*, Vol. 18 (September 1923), pp. 956–957.

> thens and pagans, Africa was peopled with a race of cultured black men, who were masters in art, science and literature; men who were cultured and refined; men, who, it is said, were like the gods. Even the great poets of old sang in beautiful sonnets of the delight it afforded the gods to be in companionship with the Ethiopians. Why, then, should we lose hope? Black men, you were once great; you shall be great again. Lose not courage, lose not faith, go forward. The thing to do is to get organized; keep separated and you will be exploited, you will be robbed, you will be killed. Get organized, and you will compel the world to respect you. If the world fails to give you consideration, because you are black men, because you are Negroes, four hundred millions of you shall, through organization, shake the pillars of the universe and bring down creation, even as Samson brought down the temple upon his head and upon the heads of the Philistines.[9]

This is black power in its very essence.

Convinced of the objective, Garvey set about the task. His main thrust was that blacks could never find justice and freedom with equality in an America with systematic racism advanced by white supremacy which all whites accepted, consciously or unconsciously. Thus, a great many blacks in America had to join him in his "back to Africa" movement. There they would set up an independent nation, a strong state which would become the Empire of Africa to challenge white power all over the world.* When blacks built their own nation under their own

* "We believe that the black people should have a country of their own where they should be given the fullest opportunity to develop politically, socially, and industrially. The black people should not be encouraged to remain in white people's countries and expect to be Presidents, Governors, Mayors, Senators, Congressmen, Judges and social and industrial leaders. We believe that with the rising ambition of the negro, if a country is not provided for him for another 50 or 100 years, there will be a terrible clash that will end disastrously to him and disgrace our civilization. We desire to prevent such a clash by pointing the negro to a home of his own. We feel that all well disposed and broad minded white men will aid in this direction." Marcus Garvey, "The Negro's Greatest Enemy," *Current History Magazine,* Vol. 18 (September 1923), p. 957.

leadership with their own culture, they would be strong enough to eliminate racism in America and elsewhere. His grave mistake was in believing this could not begin in America, so he pressed for a return to Africa. Negotiations were started with the Republic of Liberia. There were white entrepreneurs there he deemed it necessary to drive out. To this end he founded the Universal African Legion, the Universal African Motor Corps, the Black Eagle Flying Corps, the Universal Black Cross Nurses, the Black Star Steamship Line, and purchased ships.

In 1921 the Empire of Africa was formed, and Marcus Garvey was inaugurated, formally, as President-General of the Universal Negro Improvement Association and provisional President of Africa. Parades were held; a flag was created of black, red, and green. Africa had not begun its independence, so his movement to free blacks throughout the world and build again an African culture was laudable, even plausible. He developed to a fine art all the techniques of leaders of mass movements and used them with the most imaginable effectiveness.

In order to give his movement impetus, Garvey founded two newspapers, one of which, *The Negro World*, had a circulation of 200,000. There was also a monthly magazine. In addition, a millinery store, a publishing house, a tailor and dressing shop, a restaurant, and a chain of cooperative grocery stores were set up, along with hotels. The Universal Negro Improvement Association included branches in Boston, Philadelphia, Detroit, Chicago, and Cincinnati. Harlem was the largest. There in August, 1920, 25,000 blacks sat on the edge of their seats as Marcus Garvey spoke to them.

This was a Northern and urban movement. Blacks in the South were caught up with black churches in which being a Methodist or a Baptist was their history and heritage, not being black. The pressures of this world were not so great and opportunities so few that Southern blacks could let go of hope for a better life in the next world, following the defeat in Reconstruction. Yet, in all of this, Garvey was not anti-religion, although the movement was certainly secular. He drew on the religious heritage of blacks. In his message on entering prison, the messianic dimensions of his movement were clear, if brief:

> If I die in Atlanta, look for me in the whirlwind or the storm, look for me all around you, for, with God's grace, I shall come and bring with me the countless millions of black slaves who have died in America and the West Indies and the millions in Africa to aid you in the fight for liberty, freedom and life.[10]

His attack on blacks for their acceptance of handouts from their drive for assimilation, their credence of white people's affection for blacks, was countered by an extremism in which he opposed white liberals as phonies and praised white racists for their candor. Senator Bilbo believed in white supremacy, and he could be counted on as evidence that America would not respond to the needs of blacks; therefore, "back to Africa" made sense. White liberals could not be counted on to deliver their promises.

Marcus Garvey's ambitious program required a great deal of financial backing. In order to finance his commercial organization, he sold stock for his Black Star Line and was convicted of using the mails to defraud. In a long and tangled legal suit he would not accept a lawyer and pleaded his own case. As a result, he was sentenced to the federal prison in Atlanta in 1925. In 1927 he was released and deported as an undesirable alien. Although his movement had collapsed under the legal difficulties and counterpropaganda charges, he continued to protest unsuccessfully from the West Indies. He died in 1940 in London, a poverty-stricken, broken, and lonely man.* Black intellectuals who opposed him most strongly at the pinnacle of his success

* "Looking toward a century or two, we can see an economic and political death struggle for the survival of the different race groups. Many of the present-day national centres will have become overcrowded with vast surplus populations. The fight for bread and position will be keen and severe. The weaker and unprepared group is bound to go under. That is why, visionaries as we are in the Universal Negro Improvement Association, we are fighting for the founding of a negro nation in Africa, so that there will be no clash between black and white and that each race will have a separate existence and civilization all its own without courting suspicion and hatred or eyeing each other with jealousy and rivalry within the borders of the same country." Marcus Garvey, "The Negro's Greatest Enemy," *Current History Magazine*, Vol. 18 (September 1923), p. 957.

for his "back to Africa" theme, his courting of white racists, and needling of their motives looked back upon him with more candor. James Weldon Johnson, author of "Lift Ev'ry Voice and Sing," once the national hymn of blacks, often sung at the opening of gatherings, reflected:

> Garvey failed; yet he might have succeeded with more than moderate success. He had the energy and daring and the Napoleonic personality, the personality that draws masses of followers. He stirred the imagination of the Negro masses as no Negro ever had. He raised more money in a few years than any other Negro organization had ever dreamed of. He had great power and possibilities within his grasp. But his deficiencies as a leader outweighed his abilities.[11]

W. E. B. Du Bois put Garvey in this historical light:

> It was a grandiose and bombastic scheme, utterly impracticable as a whole, but it was sincere and had some practical features; and Garvey proved not only an astonishing popular leader, but a master of propaganda. Within a few years, news of his movement, of his promises and plans, reached Europe and Asia, and penetrated every corner of Africa.[12]

The Garvey movement came into being amidst the deep despair of black masses who had migrated North looking for the promised land. In Marcus Garvey they found a man who understood them, respected them, loved them, challenged them, and spoke their language of black pride, beauty, and power. The basic essentials of Black Power were in this man and the movement. He proved that the black masses are deeply dissatisfied and can be reached with an effective drawing upon their hopelessness into a movement of the powerless for the attainment of power. Black pride, black organization, black intelligence, black history, black cooperation, black unity, and black culture are the basics. But they are not enough. Added to this is the necessary element of imaginative leadership with a clear and single objective. Such a leader is not present in every decade, or every generation. The necessary social, political, and economic conditions which made Garvey's entrance so timely are not always present with such ripeness. The despair of black masses has been the one persistent ingredient in this century, repressed from time to time by national diversions of war, depression, and promises. Within the next several decades the social, economic, and political conditions may once again converge to produce the man and his men, or vice versa, but undoubtedly some combination of the two. Marcus Garvey was a forerunner of the right man, at the right place, in the right time. He was, nonetheless, a Black Power surrogate, though the most illuminating of all.*

Black Power is a fighting movement for freedom with justice and equality for all in America. It is the consistent hope of the black masses with deep historical roots reinforced by relentless oppressive conditions. The mission and cause of black people here are the acceptance of men as men, the measure of which is the black man himself—to the extent he wrenches freedom for himself and realizes fraternity, equality, and liberty, it will be so with other men. Black Power states that the black man must become human where he is by using all of his might in order that others may become human by right. Marcus Garvey provided all the coordinates necessary, but he misread the direction they formed. His intended universality of blacks requires the unity of blacks everywhere to make true universal humanity a reality in each locale. Although he intended the "back to Africa" movement as a first step to gain the strength that demands respect, his delusion was the illusion that a prestigious black nation or continent would inspire blacks the world over and provide an equality of ground on which to meet whites. Whites everywhere need to be transformed, to be sure, but such transformation requires power that confronts, not simply symbols that fascinate.

* "White men who have struggled to build up their countries and their own civilizations are not disposed to hand them over to the negro or any other race without let or hindrance. It would be unreasonable to expect this. Hence any assumption on the part of the negro to imagine that he will one day become President of the Nation, Governor of the State, or Mayor of the city in the countries of white men, is like waiting on the devil and his angels to take up their residence in the realm on High and direct there the affairs of Paradise." Marcus Garvey, "The Negro's Greatest Enemy," *Current History Magazine*, Vol. 18 (September 1923), p. 957.

Marcus Garvey did not hate whites and did not teach blacks to hate whites, although, for all practical purposes, his undertones and overtones produced the same results. What he taught was that blacks should be proud of themselves, for pride begets power through self-respect. Toward this end, he realistically assessed this as a white racist-dominated society not to be accepted on any terms because the society does not have the will to make necessary radical change. Only blacks can bring about the change necessary. Therefore their energy must be spent in loving blacks. If he had used his great talents toward the end of building up a people to turn this society upside down in order to turn it right side up, more than the imagination of blacks would have been stirred. In his view, blacks were not strong enough to stage such a fight and win. Redemption of the black people and the achievement of their destiny required a return to Africa. The legacy of Marcus Garvey provides Black Power with an enormous heritage and an equally enormous failure. If Black Power learns the lesson that in history men cannot return to the past but must go forward from where they are, the revolution will be anticipated here through concerted efforts toward this end that will bring forth the harvest planted by Marcus Garvey.

The Garvey movement withered away, but left its impression. One offshoot was the African Orthodox Church which began as an anti-white group, emphasizing its function as "segregated but equal" religion. Branching out in many cities, its membership has not become impressive, though it entered into affiliation with the Greek Orthodox Church and dropped its restrictions. Even less impressive in numbers were the various Islamic cults which looked to Muhammadanism for salvation through alignments in spirit with Asia and Africa. Whites were prohibited from their services, and thus they did not come to whites' attention. The Moors in Chicago was one such group which developed a harem, as well as a working religious and economic unit.

One such Islamic cult of black Moors began without spectacular expectations in Detroit in 1930 under the leadership of W. D. Fard. Master Fard was a door-to-door peddler of such yard goods as silks. In the process he initiated household meetings, much as the cottage prayer meetings of more conventional religious sects, where small groups of blacks gathered to listen to his teachings. This was the depression, and blacks in the ghettos were on the bottom of those at the bottom. They were ripe for anyone who would take the time to tell them about a way out of their poverty lot. Master Fard began by telling them of their African homeland and of his birth to an Arabian prophet. The authentic religion for blacks was that of Islam, whose God was Allah, and their proper name was Muslims. Blacks in America were the lost people from the Nation of Islam, and Master Fard was the redeemer sent by Allah to save them from their lot. There was no other world about which to be concerned; thus they had to be about making their conditions right by their own hard work and good living on the earth. Certain foods, such as pig, were forbidden, and other rituals and ceremonies were elaborately developed.

In 1931, Elijah Poole met Master Fard and became one of his first ministers with the title Elijah Karriem. In time he became the Supreme Minister, having studied privately with the Master and gained his confidence and wisdom. In this schooling there emerged a vision of the future path for the Muslims of America. The esteem with which Elijah Karriem was held by Master Fard was expressed through his being renamed Elijah Muhammad. In 1934, Master Fard disappeared without a clue. Elijah Muhammad carried on his teachings amidst running-steps ahead of the police who pursued him for ostensibly being a draft dodger. He was jailed for three and a half years in 1942. In 1946 he returned full-time to the work of the Muslims. Through the use of the press, success with convicts, the call for disciplined self-help, rituals, and emphasis on blacks as brothers, the Muslims were reported to have developed a following of 100,000 by 1960.

The Muslims under Elijah Muhammad, popularly called the Black Muslims, drew national attention and appeared to be a movement comparable in appeal to the black masses with the Garvey phenomenon. The teachings which gain widest response are not those of Elijah Muhammad as the Last Messenger of the Messiah, Master W. D. Fard, to the lost black people of North America. It is creating the white man as the victim against whom Muslims can direct their hate which electrifies. Blacks are known as brothers and sisters. "The white man is the devil," or "the blue-eyed devil white man." Whites have created conditions, and willfully glee in them, which keep the black man down, the proof of the need for Muslim teachings and their opportunity.

This constant attack on whites is complemented by the glorification of blacks. In the flirtation with the black masses, there is the fundamental call of pride and self-respect through hard work and clean living. Black beauty is independence from whites; it is black control of every aspect of life. Self-reliance and mutual responsibility for each other are reiterated without ceasing. The results have been excellent in terms of the lives of those who join the movement, especially among those at the bottom of the ladder. Converts have, however, tended to fall away after being put on their feet by Muslims. This is due, in part, to the strict teachings, to the religious twist, and to the realization of inner confidence to such a complete degree that independence from the Muslims follows.

The most important development to date from the Muslims was the rise and departure of Malcolm X. Since Marcus Garvey, no black American has had such persuasive hold on the black masses. He was handicapped by the limitations of the Muslims themselves. A puppet on the string, espousing the party line, admittedly with infectious excitement, until he severed relations with Elijah Muhammad, Malcolm X never really came into his own. The national attention which came to the Black Muslims largely centered around Malcolm X, who knew how to make it work. He died on the edge of a new career, assassinated allegedly by Muslims for religious and political reasons.

The basic difficulty with the Muslims as a Black Power movement is its lack of an authentic ring. A part of this phoniness is the religion, which, while appealing to black pride, history, culture, and manhood, at the same time is built on distortions, errors, lies, and intellectual dishonesty. Here no question is raised about the Muslims' diagnosis of white racism or their call to black glory, but the religious enterprise itself cannot withstand scrutiny. Further, there is a conviction that the earlier Islamic cults of black Moors with their harems have left their mark on Elijah Muhammad, whose teaching is the exact opposite from what is believed to be his practice. Unlike the Garvey movement, which was sincere but misguided, the Muslims give the impression of being deficient in ability and integrity.

For example, the Muslims rightly call for blacks to engage in self-help programs. To further this, their goal is complete racial, political, and economic separation. But they ask, Why cannot white people "subsidize a separate state, a separate territory, for we black people who have been such faithful slaves"? The idea is that the white society owes blacks their own land for the unpaid slave labor. The point is well taken, but there is something incongruous about demanding separation and the end of begging while, at the same time, requesting a subsidy. The Muslims oppose "humbling themselves, and begging, trying to 'integrate' with the so-called 'liberal' white man," but it is all right to beg for "some land of our own." Desperate as the black masses are, they know the difference between a Garvey, who did not beg for land, but sought to negotiate for it, and a Muhammad, who raises the hopes of being subsidized by the very people blacks should not take a quarter from.

Hate of the white man, opposition to integration, the call for separation, and the expectation of the Muslim man that he will defend himself, his brothers, and his women are all understandable in the light of the American experience. What makes the Muslims a Black Power surrogate is not these inflammable, but positive suggestions; it is rather that the Muslims are basically selfish and defeatist. They desire to give blacks a better life in which to live by escaping from their responsibility of re-creating the whole society. Black Power means direct confrontation which fights until right is ready. The American soil, indeed the whole Western world, is drenched in the blood of blacks. A place in the sun will not honor these dead, nor will it give manhood to those blacks to come. Black Power is not "The Hate Hate Produced," it is the love of freedom which dares to attain it for blacks, and thus for all, at whatever the price. Muslims pale into insignificance precisely because they take the basic elements of Black Power and bastardize them, not in the old religious escape to another world, but in the pseudoreligious escape to a separate state.

The final Black Power surrogate is the current civil rights

movement and particularly the method of nonviolence. With this program we are quickly coming to the end of the alternatives to Black Power. The revolution Black Power demands cannot be long delayed through further diversionary tactics we have seen throughout this century. Unless fundamental, radical, root changes are forthcoming soon, there will be no place to go but to Black Power.

Civil rights and the nonviolent movement were based on the assumption that if the hurt and misery of blacks could be dramatized so that all whites perceived it, they would do what is necessary. In this drama of marching blacks and whites from Montgomery to Birmingham to Selma to Washington and back again to Washington, we have run the gamut of this possibility. Nonviolence met its death when it was grasped at frantically in Milwaukee by Father Groppi, a white Roman Catholic priest. It kicked a little in the 1968 Poor People's March on Washington, and we may see a few more final jerks before it is at last buried deep in memory.

The achievements of civil rights and the nonviolent movement are among the most heroic in our American history. There is no doubt about it! What may prove its most lasting achievement is the demonstration through these efforts that this society cannot be coaxed or cajoled into coming forth with the will to do the job.

There was the expectation that the civil rights movement, and particularly the nonviolence method, would be the means by which the black people of America would save its soul and that of the whites. People, white and black, were convinced there was something rotten in Denmark. It would be nonviolent blacks, they thought, who would exterminate this rottenness. Whites and blacks truly believed nonviolence to be the way because they felt blacks to be religiously superior to whites, the proof of which was the expectations riding with nonviolence. What whites and blacks refused to accept was the reality that the black spirit is a fighting spirit, one that does not beg for freedom, but demands it at any cost. Nonviolence continues to be a direct repudiation of the Black Power dimension of blacks, which began on the slave ships and continued through the insurrections into the Civil War and Emancipation. The stranglehold Reconstruction placed on blacks only repressed the desire to win the freedom expected. So it has been with other movements in this century. So the repressed desires will end with nonviolence.

Nonviolence drew largely on the white influences upon blacks who found no outlet for their true expressions. They were forced to disguise them in spirituals, blues, work songs, religious meetings, and a thousand other daily ways. The unadulterated black spirit is a drive to freedom that is not given, but taken. Nonviolence taught the direct opposite and drew upon the Christian teachings which blacks never found to be singularly authentic. It is striking to recall that nonviolence is a Southern movement, and in the South the repression is still so deep that it can be used by religious leaders. It was the South which ignored the Garvey movement, but it was the black peasants from this same Southland who, when given the opportunity in the North, revealed their true feelings. Indeed, more than their feelings were revealed. They became aware of the true nature of the society and saw clearly the depth of racism. Technology, mass industry, urban metropolises, and all the other forces of a dynamic society are not the basic reasons blacks cannot respond in the North to nonviolence. Nonviolence never approached a soul movement in which blacks were really convinced. It did not have anywhere near the mass appeal of the Garvey movement. It would be foolish, indeed, to believe that in this day of many groups and leaders going off in a thousand different directions there cannot come forth in time the dovetailing of these currently different directions which will produce a leader whom the masses will follow. When this occurs, the medium and the message will be Black Power.

4.

BLACK POWER Subterfuge

Black Power cannot be definitively defined because it is the multifaceted emergence of a whole people with all their varied experiences and achievements into a nearly common consciousness of a single destiny. Black Power is not a slogan in the sense of being a catchword. It is at base a muffled battle cry, the subject of which will be the final chapter of this book. It is not simply an emotional concept, although it has immense emotive power. Black Power is a rallying cry of shrouded joy announcing the death of nonviolence and the trumpeting of hope in the birth of black souls. Black Power is the embodiment of one single truth: "that death precedes birth, that birth is the fruit of death, and that the soul is precisely the power of transforming an end into a beginning by obeying a new name." [1] This single truth must be held tenaciously until the final chapter. Here it is incumbent upon us to explore the Black Power controversy as a conscious and unconscious subterfuge signifying the need for time to prepare the black masses. As subterfuge, the Black Power controversy reveals itself to be a set of variations on several dynamic themes. The controversy will serve its purpose if, through this subterfuge, Black Power is brought through the set of experiences, images, presuppositions, expectations, organizations, disciplines, communities, and operations of inquiry and decision making by which black men make themselves conscious, first, of the world in which they live; second, of their own identity; third, of how they are related to the whole world; and fourth, of how they change their section of the world.

The real meaning of Black Power, to be set forth, is so compelling that many whites, especially the liberals, have taken pains to interpret and modify it to the extent that it is not militant but only a new dimension of the old civil rights. They call it pluralism—Black Power style. These expressions of hope express their deep bias but will not stand the test of serious scrutiny. Blacks have retreated into a maze of definitions and redefinitions as well. It is a question though. Did blacks realize the meaning of this theme and pull back from it out of fear, appeasement, or lack of preparedness? No doubt many blacks, as whites, latch on to Black Power because it is both popular and inscrutable and therefore manipulatable for their particular purposes. But all of these interpretations and redefinitions here set forth will be seen to be subterfuge in the light of unmasked Black Power or preparations for and instruments in the revolution which has yet to begin.

No matter what may be written or spoken to the contrary, the true feelings and intentions of Black Power are in the facial expressions and body movements of its advocates. A picture is worth a thousand words. Thus, when Robert C. Carson of Brooklyn led his fellow dissidents out of the CORE convention in Columbus, Ohio, in July, 1968, he conveyed the deep ideological split between Black Power advocates who see it as a revolutionary movement and those who see it as a reform movement within the system.[2] Such actions are no mere expressions of sour grapes or healthy differences of opinion; they are the revelation of a split in the psyche of Black Power that cannot remain forever repressed. Sometimes this split cannot be controlled in the statements of Black Power advocates. The public statements of Stokely Carmichael say that Black Power is nothing more than a way to help blacks develop black pride and use the ballot box for their educational and economic advancement:

> I have never said anything anti-white in my life. I am pro-black, I'm not anti-white.[3]

When at home among fellow blacks with soul, Mr. Carmichael is free:

> When you talk of "black power," you talk of bringing this country to its knees. When you talk of "black power," you

> talk of building a movement that will smash everything Western civilization has created. When you talk of "black power," you talk of picking up where Malcolm X left off. When you talk of "black power," you talk of the black man doing whatever is necessary to get what he needs. . . . We are fighting for our lives.[4]

Black Power is nothing less than blacks' fighting for their lives. In this chapter Black Power takes on the connotation of a pro-black reform according to the self-style of various definers and groups, a way of the black man's getting what he needs. The nitty-gritty of Black Power as a movement is either seduced or camouflaged by these sincere efforts. Nitty-gritty Black Power holds that

> the white man either wants to rid the world of us, or is laughing at us by making promises or passing laws that he never intends to keep. Some of the Congressmen must say after they pass a civil-rights bill, "Those niggers will believe anything." [5]

It is important to be clear on this matter. There is yet no revolution within the revolution because the black revolution has yet to come. We need to be careful of a "misreading of all the politicking, power playing and priority shifting—the teams and the players change but the name of the game remains the same —get this man off our backs." [6] The goal is the same for all those who identify with Black Power; it is the method which distinguishes between true believers and those who co-opt Black Power. Respectable Black Power co-opted is pluralism or powerlessness embraced. Black Power in the raw is militant and seeks more than little victories.

In this chapter I am going to review a variety of ways people have used the term Black Power, as well as the variety of positions taken at different times by the same people. Black people have always found it useful to play games with white people, and they often end up playing games with each other as well. It may be imperative to stall for time, to cloak the dagger of Black Power, but Black Power cannot be co-opted and remain Black Power in patterns like those which follow.

INTEGRATION

Black Power has been a force among blacks for some years now, but it was not until 1966 that it was named—tagged and bagged. The nation was no longer interested in civil rights and had returned to the old attitude of blacks as "the Negro problem," with which they were saturated. In February of that year, Dick Gregory expressed his bitterness about what was happening to blacks in America, "We promise instant freedom to a foreigner, but I get mine on the installment plan." [7] This single sentence summed up the feelings of the black masses everywhere who were ahead of the black bourgeoisie in their sensitivity that an era had come to an end with the all-out commitment of the United States to beat those "yellow commies" in Vietnam. Integration through nonviolent direct action was not denied:

> The 1960 sit-ins desegregated lunch counters in more than 150 cities within a year. The 1961 Freedom Rides put an end to segregation in interstate travel. The 1956 bus boycott in Montgomery, Alabama, ended segregation on buses not only of that city but in practically every city of the South. The 1963 Birmingham movement and the climactic March on Washington won passage of the most powerful civil rights law in a century. The 1956 Selma movement brought enactment of the Voting Rights Law.[8]

But despite this progress, the legislation and the promises, the black masses were as powerless as ever, and, in addition, they were being sent, all out of proportion to their numerical size, to die in Vietnam in a war for the freedom of others. SNCC was so distraught over the war and the plight of the black masses that it snubbed the White House Conference on Civil Rights. In May, 1966, Stokely Carmichael reflected on what he rightly believed to be token integration:

> I'll take an example from Lowndes County (Alabama). Last year five Negroes entered the white school. All the papers hailed this as a great triumph. Finally Lowndes County had been cracked. But all the other Negro children

> had to go to the same old schools. And no whites went to black schools, because they were in fact inferior.[9]

During this same month, Congressman Adam Clayton Powell spoke at Howard University in Washington. In this speech he praised SNCC for having alone avoided the "drug" of integration. Powell called for "audacious" power, for "to demand these God-given rights is to seek black power . . . the power to build black institutions of splendid achievement." In May, 1966, Carmichael was organizing the black people of Lowndes County in a voter registration drive, the climax of which was the formation of an all-black political party. In the midst of these efforts, in June, 1966, the one-man march of James Meredith through Mississippi was interrupted when he was shot. There followed a rally on his behalf, June 17, 1966, in which Carmichael led an electrified demonstration in which "Black Power" was heard via television throughout the nation. Thus, Black Power was a name given to what blacks asserted in response to the powerlessness yielded by integration. There was deep disappointment in the failure of integration, for as Stokely Carmichael and Charles V. Hamilton put it: "to black people, it [integration] has meant a way to improve their lives—economically and politically." [10] Yet the cry of Black Power was not idealism lost, but realism won. Things were no longer disconnected; the pieces of the puzzling restlessness fit together; integration equaled powerlessness for the masses. A little bit sadder, perhaps a bit poorer, but certainly a bit wiser, the black masses and particularly their leaders were no longer frustrated by integration. As Gloria Laney, a Field Secretary for SNCC in June, 1966, once put it:

> Today most of us have come to the conclusion that integration is not meaningful . . . what we decided to do was to move into communities and build up political, cultural and economic strength.[11]

They were not alone, even Bayard Rustin, the leading disciple of realism in the civil rights movement, said of integration in September, 1966:

> If in 1954 when the Supreme Court handed down the desegregation decision, you had been the Negro parent of a

first-grade child, the chances are that this past June you would have attended that child's graduation from a segregated high school.[12]

Integration proved its uselessness for the masses in its tokenism, but that was not its fundamental error. Of course, many white people look upon integration as "black men wanting to marry white daughters; it means 'race mixing'—implying bed or dance partners." [13] Yet this dominant theme is but a manifestation of a deeper sickness. Integration as a concept contained within it the belief that movement was only one way:

> Its goal was to make the white community accessible to "qualified" Negroes; and presumably each year a few more Negroes, armed with their passports—a couple of university degrees—would escape into middle-class America and adopt the attitudes and life-styles of that group, and one day the Harlems and Watts will stand empty, a tribute to the success of integration.[14]

The idea of bringing blacks fully into the mainstream, or assimilation of the black masses, is not what the Black Power advocates question. What is basically erroneous about integration as a goal is put this way by Carmichael:

> This concept of integration had to be based on the assumption that there was nothing of value in the black community, and that little of value could be created among blacks. So the thing to be done was to siphon off the acceptable Negroes into the surrounding middle-class white community.[15]

The few blacks who make it in integration "are of no value to the remaining black masses. They become meaningless showpieces for a conscience-soothed white society." [16] There is no doubt in the minds of militants about this matter:

> This is why SNCC—and the concept of Black Power—affirms that helping *individual* black people to solve their problems on an *individual* basis does little to alleviate the mass of black people.[17]

Further, integration has meant a society on the way to becoming color-blind, the acting today as if the society had reached this stage in maturity. Carmichael and Hamilton do not pooh-pooh this, but

> while color blindness *may* be a sound goal ultimately, we must realize that race is an overwhelming fact of life in this historical period. There is no black man in this country who can live "simply as a man." His blackness is an ever-present fact of this racist society, whether he recognizes it or not.[18]

The price of integration into the mainstream of American society in the system as it is is too high because being black is degrading. The truth is that integration

> has always been Negroes going to white schools because the white schools are good, and black schools are bad. Negroes have been made to believe that everything better is always white. If integration means moving to something better then integration is a subterfuge for white supremacy.[19]

Thus, integration errs in reinforcing among whites and blacks the superiority of the one and the inferiority of the other. Finally, as Carmichael and Hamilton set it forth in their book, integration "means that black people must give up their identity, deny their heritage." [20] The real meaning of integration is the end of the black community when "what must be abolished is not the black community, but the dependent colonial status that has been inflicted upon it." [21]

In the light of these criticisms of integration, it is to be expected that those white liberal critics of Black Power holding on to what for them is a meaningful objective find these positions offensive. James Wechsler of the *New York Post* expressed his hurt:

> "Integration is a subterfuge for the maintenance of white supremacy," wrote Stokely Carmichael . . . thereby in a sentence proposing to reverse the whole thrust of the effort for which Negroes and whites have hand in hand exposed themselves to the fire and fury of the racists. . . .[22]

Carl Rowan, the black columnist, writing in *Ebony,* described Black Power in a bad light, with the suggestion that its advocates "created a crisis of leadership within the civil rights movement" which raised what for him "is still the crucial question: does the Negro seek integration within the mainstream of American society, which admittedly will be difficult to attain . . . ?"

Given this full position of Black Power advocates on the issue of integration, little room is left to doubt their integrity, sincerity, or their judgment. What has been positively accomplished by the civil rights movement will not be undone. Black Power is about going beyond civil rights by recognizing it for what it is. If, in shrouded joy, the death of nonviolence and civil rights is announced, what is being born with the trumpeting of Black Power?

The response of Maulana Ron Karenga is the "Sevenfold path of Blackness,"

> to Think Black, Talk Black, Act Black, Create Black, Buy Black, Vote Black, and Live Black.[23]

We will be dealing with many of his presentations in more direct form subsequently. Ron Karenga is widely admired by black youth as a militant Black Power advocate in Los Angeles.* The rebirth of black people following the death of integration is for him by way of cultural revolution:

> Culture is the basis of all ideas, images, and actions. To move is to move culturally; i.e., by a set of values given to you by your culture.
>
> The seven criteria for culture are:
>
> 1. Mythology
> 2. History
> 3. Social Organization

* Ron Ndabezitha Everett-Karenga graduated from U.C.L.A. *cum laude* and holds a master's degree in languages. He has completed substantial credits toward a Ph.D. in political science. He speaks Swahili fluently, reads French and Spanish, has studied Egyptian and Zulu. He believes that 1968 is the year of political self-determination for blacks, 1969 the year of reflection upon the 1968 developments, 1970 the year of separation, and 1971 the year of the guerrillas. He states, "Everybody might not belong to the same interest group, but everybody has the same interest: self-determination, self-respect, and self-security, the ability to defend ourselves." *New York Times,* September 2, 1968, p. 13.

4. Political Organization
5. Economic Organization
6. Creative Motif
7. Ethos[24]

Mythology for Karenga, organizer of US, in 1965, shortly after the riots in Watts, is the development and promotion of black values, black pride, and black qualities which are superior and provide black people with a sense of destiny. *History* is the discovery of new black heroes, customs, rituals, festivals, parades, and events with which blacks can identify today and history continues the myth that "to go back to tradition" is the first step forward. *Social Organization* is the bringing into being a strong family life in a strong community in which the matriarchy is replaced by the male head. *Political Organization,* in essence, requires an all-black party, just as *Economic Organization* connotes black businesses, enterprises, franchises, and cooperatives. *Creative Motif* includes black beauty standards, black music, black art, the interpretation and expression of "soul." *Ethos* is the development of soul to the point of its being alive through education in a fertile soil of solidarity.

BLACK PRIDE

The major contribution of integration to Black Power was that it made transparent to all alert blacks the abyss of inferiority in which each and all are held by the system and most of its dominant participants:

> Now there's one modern day lie that we want to attack . . . and that is the lie that says anything all black is bad. Let's make that our major premise. Anything all black is bad. Minor premise, or particular premise: I am all black. Therefore . . . I'm *never* going to be put in that trick bag. I'm all black. And I'm all good.[25]

Thus, the first and vital step is to recognize this "trick bag":

> From birth, black people are told a set of lies about themselves. We are told that we are lazy—yet I drive through the Delta area of Mississippi and watch black people picking cotton in the hot sun for fourteen hours. We are told,

> "if you work hard, you'll succeed"—but if that were true, black people would own this country. We are oppressed because we are black—not because we are ignorant, not because we are lazy, not because we're stupid (and got good rhythm), but because we're black.[26]

The recognition of this reality requires that black people accept their blackness and wear it with pride, using it to their mutual advantage:

> Black people in this country are oppressed for one reason—and that's because of their color . . . their rally cry must be the issue around which they are oppressed, as it was for unions. The workers came together, they were oppressed because they were workers. And we must come together around the issue that oppressed us—which is our blackness. Unions—they needed power to stop their oppression. We need power to stop ours. So it's black power. And black power means black people coming together and getting people to represent their needs and to stop that oppression.[27]

In the speeches and writings of Carmichael, this theme of inferiority is pressed over and again, as if to make this indelible in the minds of the whites and an irritation in the minds of blacks:

> The history of every institution of this society indicates that a major concern in the ordering and structuring of the society has been the maintaining of the black community in its condition of dependence and oppression. This has not been on the level of *individual* acts of discrimination between individual whites and individual blacks, but as *total acts* by the white community against the black community. This fact cannot be too strongly emphasized.[28]

The impression that Carmichael and others have made on black youth across this country is unmistakable. Integration opened the doors to one percent or less of blacks in a great many colleges. The first arrivals in the early 1960's were pleased to be allowed entrance, just as was the case with integrated elementary and secondary schools. Black Power changed all this. In response to this new mood, black youth in white colleges has become militant instead of grateful. Demands have been made to increase the number of black students, professors, and administrators. High on the list of priorities is the demand for more courses in the history and role of blacks in America and throughout the world. In most instances, blacks have won because white institutions were guilty of the lack of earnest endeavors in seeking out black students, professors, and administrators. The view once held that they were unavailable only served to reinforce the criticism of token integration. The lack of blacks in the history books is so blatantly obvious that nothing more than the pressure of blacks sent scholars back to reorienting their texts, lecture notes, and manuscripts in preparation. Within the past two years, the number of new courses developed out of this controversy is nothing short of fantastic. Black youth in mainstream colleges and universities have heard the preachments of Black Power advocates and taken them to heart: "We must undo the centuries-old brainwashing by the white man that has made us hate ourselves. We must stop being ashamed of being black and stop wanting to be white!" Sometimes blacks respond by demanding that they be given separate housing or other facilities where the handful of soul-brothers and soul-sisters can develop a sense of community about who they are and what they are to be about, and often this soul searching turns on how to relate to the black community both now and in the future. Sometimes they are led to transfer to predominantly black institutions of higher learning in the expectation they will there be saved.

Black students who flee to black colleges and universities find, in the words of Ernest Stephens, editor of the Tuskegee *Black Thesis,* that the Freedom Movement led by students of these institutions sparked campus revolutions for freedom of speech and action everywhere but at home:

> Indoctrination is employed at the black university as a more subtle vehicle for controlling the students. The black university is plagued with programs of compulsory ROTC, compulsory religious services, and ludicrous curfew regulations. On many black campuses students are not only confined to their dormitories after dark, but they are re-

> stricted to the confines of the campus during the day. This indicates acceptance of the white mythology that Negroes are more sexually promiscuous than white people and should therefore be kept under close supervision. Black students are regimented and encouraged through the ROTC program to further the cause of American imperialism throughout the non-white world.[29]

This kind of internal criticism would have been unheard of from black participants in black colleges a few years ago. This is hard evidence of the real impact of Black Power. It had led to pride, an expectation that black communities become what they can be without glossing over their weaknesses. Mr. Stephens declares that

> the assumption made to justify the policy of rigid control is that the black student, having been "culturally deprived," is incapable of making sound decisions concerning the direction of his development.[30]

This kind of misguided restraint would be nearly tolerable were these institutions aiding students to deal with a racist society. Instead, they are "training schools for Negroes":

> In terms of the free expression of new ideas and concepts, there is not one black university in this country which functions as an institution of higher learning. The present situation within black universities is one reflective of an archaic and repressive ideology. Independent thinking is discouraged; diversity is stifled.[31]

Christopher Jencks and David Riesman in *The Academic Revolution* make clear many of these heartbreaking points in the detailed chapter on "Negroes and Their Colleges."

Black students from the North who retreat to these institutions find that

> brotherhood for black men and women has meaning only within the context of white sanction. Black fraternities, sororities, and other socially inclined groups are not only condoned but encouraged, yet black political parties, black controlled economic bases, and black controlled educational

> structures are considered out of the question. If we entertain ideas of uniting black people in an effort to attain power (the lack of which is subjecting black people to genocide in this country), we are called racists. Essentially, it is the white folks who determine the line between brotherhood and racism for black people, and their right to do so is legitimatized at the black university.[32]

Speaking of white power structure through white-dominated boards of trustees to black students in Atlanta, Stokely Carmichael was scathing in his remarks:

> Your presidents call these people philanthropists. I'll tell you what they really are—they're thieves. If you don't believe me look at how they got their money. Look at how they're getting it now. Look at their South African investments, especially through Chase Manhattan Bank.[33]

Black Power has not only struck students but professors as well in black higher-education institutions. Vincent Harding, professor of history at Spelman College, calls the schizophrenia of black institutions "that brink of madness" challenged by Black Power. Black students coming to these institutions

> find little attention being given in Negro schools to the non-Western roots of their own lives or to the black experience in America. Sometimes this is because these things are not even known, but sometimes it is because the white and Negro faculty and administration often see such roots as incidental to the life of an educated man—and absolutely irrelevant to graduate record examinations and accrediting association! [34]

Harding sees the Black Power challenge as the demand to know

> of the Negro schools if they have nothing better than schizophrenia to offer the majority of their students. Can there be no new turnings to the vast masses of their people? (Is our sanity to be found anywhere else?) Must service in the ghettos be left to white Christians, black Muslims, and other odd humanitarian types? Is black education to continue to be an education directed to the service and admiration of a

> pale, middle-class, Western-oriented society which is geared to kill black people with that unspectacular violence of economic, political, and social oppression? [35]

Black Power is strength to Professor Harding and provides him with pride in his place and work with renewed enthusiasm, so much so that he suggests the future of vital black institutions of higher learning:

> Perhaps there are a significant number of persons—both black and white—who would eagerly come to study and teach at schools where non-Western life and culture are given a major emphasis and where the experience and institutions of the Negro in America were studied seriously and unashamedly—from Benjamin Banneker to James Brown. Such renewed centers might even become gathering places for the non-white students of the world who want to do something more than copy the American Way. Perhaps there are even some persons and organizations with enough vision to help finance such a venture.[36]

This is undoubtedly what Carmichael had in mind when he spoke of pride as self-esteem:

> It is clear to me that we have to wage a psychological battle on the right for black people to define their own terms, define themselves as they see fit and organize themselves as they see fit. . . . The fact is that all black people often question whether or not they are equal to whites because every time they start to do something white people are around showing them how to do it. If we are going to eliminate that for the generations that come after us, then black people must be seen in positions of power doing and articulating for themselves.[37]

Here we see the basic relationship between blacks' having pride as a group and blacks' having power as a group. Anything less means blacks are without their humanity for manhood. It is this independent base of pride and power of the black community that brings black consciousness, the initial stage in the Black Power movement.

The Black Power message of pride has spread abroad with enthusiastic response from the black masses, black intellectuals, black middle class, and the black fringe, or marginal people. Martin Luther King, Jr., termed this "psychological call to manhood" a positive aspect of Black Power, "compatible with what we have sought to do in the civil rights movement all along without the slogan."[38] This glory in blackness is now expressed freely and openly with a zest previously unknown.

The expressions of Black Power pride indicate that the call to black consciousness through cultural developments has great psychological power. This is precisely what Carmichael is after:

> Black people can and should develop what we have in our own neighborhood and make it good and beautiful. It's time for some psychological equality. To a Negro, faith in himself plus power equals black power.[39]

The solidarity of the black community through "psychological equality" gains pride for blacks only if organization and leadership in these ghettos are the work of blacks only:

> The need for psychological equality is the reason why SNCC today believes that blacks must organize in the black community. Only a black people can convey the revolutionary idea that black people are able to do things themselves. . . . In the past, white allies have furthered white supremacy without the whites realizing it—or wanting it, I think. . . .[40]

Is this emphasis upon the development of black pride through black people doing their own thing a notion that has sprung full-grown from some mythological pandit? Quite to the contrary. Carmichael is setting forth what he learned at the roots, among the black masses. He is returning to them in the form of Black Power the knowledge and wisdom black masses taught him. Black Power is first and foremost black masses. The black masses have never forgotten, unlike middle-class blacks seeking entrance into the mainstream, that they are descendants of slaves. In remembering themselves as once slaves, black masses have stayed at the root of black culture in this country. It is this knowledge which, never far from the conscious of black masses, expresses itself in self-hatred. It does not, as we are led to believe by behavioral scientists, result from self-destructive forces feeding on the "chronic feeling of self-denigration." Self-hatred is a reflection of the reality that the black masses know to be true; they are ex-slaves, and the repressed rage concerning this fact has produced black music. This black music reveals not only self-hatred but an optimism, which combined give strength to endure creatively. It is in this dimension among these people that Carmichael learned the meaning of pride and brought it home to them in his own way. Pride for blacks is music. As Ray Charles likes to put it, all the black man ever had was his music and his woman. It is the music born of suffering which has given the black masses psychological kinship through the centuries, and Black Power reinforces this psychological kinship with community self-help for psychological equality and power.

The most expressive music of black people in any era sets forth clearly who black people are, what they think, what their situation is, their hopes, disappointment, and dreams. In the beginning there was the blues, for there have always been two Americas. Blues gave birth to jazz. Blues was born in the church and went the way of the casual in informal settings where sensual pleasure instead of religious jags was the means of locking out of one's mind the troubles of the world. Blues and spirituals both have the uniqueness of total giving and commitment; the whole self is thrown into them and for frenzied moments there is a blotting out of this world. The hard times of blacks from slavery on were endured by music—traditional blacks expressed their concern in spirituals and gospel music; others expressed these same concerns in blues. One way to get high, to blow one's mind for awhile, was to break out in song without which the spirit would not descend:

> Gonna shout trouble over
> When I get home,
> Gonna shout trouble over
> When I get home.
>
> No mo' prayin', no mo' dyin'
> When I get home.

No mo' prayin' an' no mo' dyin'
When I get home.

Meet my father
When I get home.
Meet my father
When I get home.

or

Mary, don't you weep an' Marthie don't you moan,
Mary, don't you weep an' Marthie don't you moan;
Pharaoh's army got drown-ded,
Oh Mary don't you weep.

I thinks every day an' I wish I could
Stan' on de rock whar Mose stood
Oh, Pharaoh's army got drown-ded,
Oh Mary don't you weep.

The spirit will not descend and the human spirit will not ascend without a song. Blacks who had broken from the chains of religious restrictions moved about the countryside with shouts, chants, and hollers which were born of suffering but found outlets in the pleasure of whiskey and women. Blues were intensely personal:

I don't want you to be no slave,
I don't want you to work all day,
I don't want you to be true,
I just want to make love to you.

The development from primitive to classic blues can be seen in the adjustment of blacks first to slavery, then to Emancipation, and finally to mass migration to urban centers. In all of this, the blues remained intensely personal expressions of the individual in which those who listened were involved vicariously; the singer of the blues has been down the same road. The classic blues came about when free expression of individuals moving about was commercialized for entertainment by professionals. Always the experience of the masses was the source of the blues. By the time of World War I, the mass migration to the North, the blues of the country had become urban blues:

> My baby she found a brand new place to go
> My baby she found a brand new place to go
> She hangs across town at the Monte Carlo.
>
> She likes my money, tells me she goin' to
> the picture show
> She likes my money, tells me she goin' to
> the picture show
> But that girl's been throwin' my money
> away at the Monte Carlo.

The common urban experience created a new community of oppression. Blacks oriented around the churches expressed themselves and relieved their troubles through gospel songs. Their counterparts expressed the same experience through the blues. Originally, the blues moved out of the religious meetings. So it is today with the late Nat "King" Cole, James Brown, Little Richard, and Aretha Franklin, to pick a few. Blues represent the solidarity of attitudes and experiences of the black masses. For Black Power, they are basic to the forging of a single identity. Today, blues is urban blues, and the best of urban blues is soul music. In soul music we have an intense concern with mutual self-help, a pride in being black, a concern for soul-brothers and soul-sisters which takes on a positive thrust of black consciousness and psychological equality, best exemplified in Ray Charles. Besides their common suffering, what all blacks hold in common is concern for that woman or that man, for when all else is precarious, sexual expression remains. Soul music centers on sex, the personal heights and depths, but it is primarily concerned with self-respect—this is the connection with Black Power. Soul, as Charles Keil points out in his masterful *Urban Blues,* has all kinds of components. It comprises breath, life, body, but most of all a total giving without inhibitions in speech, body movements, rhythm, action, sex, work, and play. Soul is a pure offer of oneself looking for a pure response in kind; it is the black male looking for his manhood. Manhood is the message, blues is the medium:

> American society is in the midst of a revolution, and the crisis is forcing basic cultural adjustments on the part of both blacks and whites; the black masses have only very recently been emotionally affected by the current "revolution"; most of those in the ghettos, though they read or hear about it, have yet to receive any concrete benefits from this revolution; Negro men are especially disadvantaged, from almost any point of view, and at the very bottom of the American socio-economic heap; the spokesmen for these people—bluesmen, ministers, comedians, disc jockeys—are much more interested in freedom and self-respect than in integration per se and, perhaps because of their vested ethnic interests, even a little afraid, consciously or unconsciously, of absorption or disappearance in the white mainstream. If assertions of this sort have some validity, then the soul movement readily takes on a strong nativistic and revitalizing tone.[41]

Soul music may be a nativistic or reactionary formation seeking to hold on to the past in the present as a way of making it in a hostile world where manhood is denied outside the community and can only mature within the environs. But soul has a very dynamic revitalization dimension of self-respect and brotherhood in unity for a common cause that cannot be realized by focusing within alone. Nativism leads to revitalization, which leads to fighting for the right of cultural identity for the salvation of blacks. LeRoi Jones concluded his *Blues People* with these lines:

> It is no secret that the West, and most particularly the American system, is in the position now of having to defend its values and ideas against totally hostile systems. The American Negro is being asked to defend the American system as energetically as the American white man. There is no doubt that the middle-class Negro is helping and will continue to help in that defense. But there is perhaps a question mark in the minds of the many poor blacks (which is one explanation for the attraction of such groups as the Black Muslims) and also now in the minds of many Negro intellectuals. What is it that they are being asked to

> save? It is a good question and America had better come up with an answer.[42]

Will the salvation of blacks be the salvation of whites? There is no comment from Black Power aesthetes on this question. Black Power, as the buildup of pride, is about the business of fighting for cultural identity through the solidarity of soul. Perhaps there is something which will in time change America. It will be by way of the spirit expressed by Lincoln Lynch, former Associate Director of CORE:

> We need black people to stand on their own two feet. . . . History has shown that if you're really depending on the vast majority of whites to help, you're really leaning on a broken reed.[43]

Black Power is not now concerned to prove to whites that blacks are human; its emphasis is upon capturing freedom for the black masses through a realization of their humanity in cultural identity—which may have the same results in the end. Godfrey Cambridge defines soul in this way:

> Soul is getting kicked in the ass until you don't know what it's for. It's being broke and down and out, and people telling you you're no good. It's the language of the subculture; but you can't learn it, because no one can give you black lessons.[44]

It is this reality that produces the unique culture of blacks, best expressed in music, that Black Power wants to forge into a force that cannot be absorbed by the dominant culture. Black Power as pride is the determination of black men to be free men, selective of what they accept and reject in this society. In the struggle to accept the whole past, some black militants stress identification with Africa in music, styles of dress, history, art, and hair styles. For the most part, this response to the past is symptomatic of pride that wills a unified black America on its own two feet.

BLACK SELF-DETERMINATION

An understanding of the reasons Black Power opposes integration and embraces pride through cultural identity leads to the acceptance of their truth as valid. This is not enough, however. If step one is opposition to integration, and step two is building a base of black pride, step three is self-determination. Self-determination is essential. It means political and economic organization of the black community potential into effective power exercise, without which Black Power has neither program nor strategy. Self-determination means putting black pride to work; it means movement, and at this stage of development, the definition Floyd McKissick gives Black Power takes on meaning:

> Black Power is no mere slogan. It is a movement dedicated to the exercise of American democracy in its highest tradition; it is a drive to mobilize the black communities of this country in a monumental effort to remove the basic causes of alienation, frustration, despair, low self-esteem, and hopelessness.[45]

An aroused black consciousness is not for the purpose of glorying in blackness; it is the basis for political strength, which requires that "black people must lead and run their own organizations." [46]

The values of this society must be rejected in order for "independent political action" to emerge. These values are racist in system and structures:

> By system, we have in mind the entire American complex of basic institutions, values, beliefs, etc. By structures, we mean the specific institutions (political parties, interest groups, bureaucratic administrations) which exist to conduct the business of that system.[47]

The racist dominance of these institutions means they are not essential. Blacks are not to assimilate into the middle class because it lacks the conscience necessary to the new humanity blacks are bringing into creation:

> The values of that class are based on material aggrandizement, not the expansion of humanity. The values of that class ultimately support cloistered little closed societies tucked away in tree-lined suburbia. The values of that class do not lead to the creation of an open society.[48]

In a word, to assimilate with the white middle class would mean preservation of black inferiority and white superiority, the American Way of Death. This system promotes property rights above human life, the wealth of the few at the expense of the poverty of the many. The American system is not civilized and needs to be, that is, replaced:

> Our view is that, given the illegitimacy of the system we cannot then proceed to transform that system with existing structures.[49]

This combination of soul solidarity as group power with the strategy of group power forms forces for throwing off the oppression inflicted upon the black masses.

> In such areas as Lowndes where black men have a majority, they will attempt to use it to exercise control. Where Negroes lack a majority, Black Power means the creation of power bases from which black people can work to change statewide or nationwide patterns of oppression through pressure from strength—instead of weakness.
>
> Politically, black power means what it has always meant to SNCC: the coming together of black people to elect representatives and to force those representatives to speak to their needs.[50]

It is clear that black control in this context means pluralism and commitment to participatory democracy where decisions are made by the black masses or their representatives. This means challenging all institutions not responsive to the interest of the black community. Black control of organizations is essential for the creation and preservation of group identity. Development of unique black institutions is indispensable to impress the black masses of the seriousness with which Black Power is to be taken. No other movement has promised the black masses that leadership would be responsive directly to them. The masses, if they are to achieve self-identity for self-determination, must see black-controlled or black-run groups effectively defining goals, setting strategy, and putting programs to work. High idealism is at work here:

> But while we endorse the *procedure* of group solidarity and identity for the purpose of attaining certain goals in the body politic, this does not mean that black people should strive for the same kind of rewards (i.e., end results) obtained by the white society.[51]

Given our pluralistic society, black political organization for self-determination is not only necessary, it is also reasonable and responsible. Black Power defines power as the ability to move institutions so that the needs of the black masses are spoken to. On this score, Roy Wilkins is dead wrong in his criticism of Black Power: "In a pluralistic society, the slogan 'black power' is as unacceptable as 'white supremacy.' "[52] Carmichael underscores the error of Roy Wilkins:

> The standard argument represented against independent political organizations is: "But you are only 10%." I cannot see what the relevance of this observation is, since no one is talking about taking over the country but taking control of our own communities.[53]

The control sought by Black Power politics is unassailable. It makes all the sense in the world with respect to local issues where blacks are in the majority:

> Black Power means, for example, that in Lowndes County, Alabama, a black sheriff can end police brutality. A black tax assessor and tax collector and county board of revenue can lay, collect, and channel tax monies for the building of better roads and schools serving black people. In such areas as Lowndes, where black people have a majority, they will attempt to use power to exercise control. This is what they seek: control.[54]

There is a serious question which must be faced. Blacks may soon be the majority in most major cities. The conclusion which Black Power draws from this possibility is not radical but conservative, if not reactionary. What purpose is to be served if black people seize political control of their urban misery? It is essential to have cultural and political unity, but the problems of poverty, housing, and education remain. Black political control of the ghetto cannot end the problems; they reach beyond the ghetto into the larger regional and metropolitan areas. Black Power is aware that a black mayor cannot change this reality, nor can a black city council:

> It does not mean *merely* putting black faces into office. Black visibility is not Black Power. Most of the black politicians around the country today are not examples of Black Power. The power must be that of a community, and emanate from there. The black politicians must stop being representatives of "downtown" machines, whatever the cost might be in terms of lost patronage and holiday handouts.[55]

This awareness that a black politician is limited is not added to by an awareness that the black community is limited. A black politician responsible to a powerless black ghetto encircled by problems of poverty, education, and housing, problems which emanate from the larger sphere, will not do the trick Black Power seeks. If there were regional planning, controlled by the democratic way of "one man, one vote," black people would have a meaningful context in which to organize and exercise political power. In a pluralistic setting, the kind that Black Power here assumes, this is the way to real power. But the theory of Black Power is ahead of its organization, which may mean there is time to change. Certainly, the fear of regional power is real, but Black Power could use its power to see that the direction of regional planning becomes democratic so that black masses will not be locked into the control of misery. Regional planning is also at the theory stage; there is yet time for action.

This criticism of Black Power's continuing powerlessness in reality in no way undermines its movement for organizing the black masses, but its passion must not lead to a sellout of the black masses it has come to save. A further criticism of Black Power's "independent political action" holds it to be a no-win policy because it shuns coalition politics. A. Philip Randolph, elder statesman of the civil rights movement, once was a militant pro-black leader, a forerunner of Black Power politics. With regard to the 1942 March on Washington threat, he said:

> As to the composition of our movement. Our policy is that it be all Negro, and pro-Negro, but not anti-White, or anti-semitic, or anti-labor, or anti-Catholic. The reason for this policy is that all oppressed people must assume the responsibility and take the initiative to free themselves.
>
> The essential value of an all-Negro movement such as the March on Washington is that it helps to create faith by Negroes in Negroes. It develops a sense of self-reliance with Negroes depending on Negroes in vital matters. It helps to break down the slave psychology and inferiority-complex in Negroes which comes and is nourished with Negroes relying on white people for direction and support. This inevitably happens in mixed organizations that are supposed to be in the interest of the Negro.[56]

Nearly a quarter of a century later, he condemned Black Power:

> Black Power is a menace to racial peace and prosperity. No Negro who is fighting for civil rights can support Black Power which is opposed to civil rights and integration.[57]

Undoubtedly, this half-truth about Black Power is based on the commitment of the A. Philip Randolph Institute Freedom Budget, a plan which requires white financial support. Its major architect is Bayard Rustin—the intellectual giant of the civil rights movement. Bayard Rustin seeks a coalition of liberals, trade unionists, blacks, and religious groups:

> Neither the movement nor the country's twenty million black people can win political power alone. We need allies. The future of the Negro struggle depends on whether the contradictions of this society can be resolved by a coalition of progressive forces which becomes the *effective* political majority in the United States. I speak of the coalition which staged the March on Washington, passed the Civil Rights Act, and laid the basis for the Johnson landslide—Negroes, trade unionists, liberals, and religious groups.[58]

Bayard Rustin is a strategist, a realist, one who believes in meeting a problem with a program. Thus for him, it is clear that

> Black Power not only lacks any real value for the civil rights movement, but that its propagation is positively harmful. It diverts the movement from a meaningful debate over strategy and tactics, it isolates the Negro community, and it encourages the growth of anti-Negro forces.[59]

He is basically in error in his judgment of Black Power politics, but it is important to take into account his call for coalition politics as a criticism of Black Power's independent political action. The realist Rustin turns idealist with the conviction that the liberal coalition has the power to overcome the triple evils of housing, education, and jobs which plague blacks:

> We are responsible for the growth of the "black power" concept because we have not used our own power to insure the full implementation of the bills whose passage we were strong enough to win, and we have not mounted the necessary campaign for winning a decent minimum wage and extended benefits.[60]

The fact is—this coalition was possible only in the midst of special circumstances. It was an emotional response to the marches in the South and their revelation of the depth of hatred and prejudice there. The civil rights victories made more opportunity for the small middle class of blacks, and conversation for the black masses. The fact is that this coalition broke up immediately after the March on Washington, for from this point forward, emphasis was placed on the North, and there was no comparable outpouring of conscience. Most of all, the failure of implementation of civil rights legislation was not due to the call of Black Power; it was due to the rise of Vietnam as the all-pervading focus for American resources, energies, and interest. Whites were tired of "the Negro problem." Thus while it was perfectly possible for the society to fight in Vietnam and fight a war against poverty, poor housing, and education here, Vietnam was a handy excuse for what the society really did not intend to do. The argument that it is impossible for this society to have "guns and butter" was and is without substance, although it served to support the Congress in its wish not to make available the massive federal funds necessary to eliminate the plight of the poor masses, most of whom were blacks.

Another reason this criticism of Black Power does not stand is that Black Power holds this coalition to be without the power sufficient to bring about the basic changes necessary in this society. Its victories made little headway against the real issues, and the virtual ignoring of the Freedom Budget Rustin himself set up lays to rest any questions about the intentions of this society. It is to be further noted that the position of Black Power with respect to coalitions is not that it wishes to go it alone. In fact, coalitions are recognized as important, but the significance of the coalition in which blacks are a part depends upon the strength and power of the black element. If blacks join a coalition from strength rather than from weakness, that coalition will be stronger, and blacks will have, by the measure of their strength, more to say in the decision-making areas. In order to have the strength to make a coalition successful, blacks must develop political, economic, and cultural institutional cohesiveness. Only in this cohesiveness is there power for self-esteem, self-respect, self-preservation, as well as power for changing the society to speak to the needs of blacks. This kind of vital power, which all other forces in any coalition would have, requires blacks either to take over existing institutions or to develop new ones. Most probably, both patterns are essential.

The test of these institutions will be their success in providing black control over black life, providing economic support, and in confronting other institutions on an equal footing. Black control is the only way blacks can stand on their own two feet; the only way they can enter as equal partners into negotiations. In this respect, pro-black is pro-pluralism—any other way would be antihuman, inhuman, and unhuman, given this society. Finally, it is in this light that the responses of Black Power to coalitions must be seen. Black Power is not against coalitions and will enter into them provided they show real, and not merely verbal, strength. The present task of Black Power as pluralism is to bring about real, and not merely verbal, strength among the black masses, and not just among the leadership people, who, for the most part, ignore the masses. Lincoln Lynch declared that Black Power would work with any power group, including white liberals:

> We will work with anybody, literally anybody, to achieve equality of opportunity, dignity of the individual and power in the communities of Black America.[61]

In this context Carmichael's call for black leadership instead of white leadership is not anti-white but pro-black in the sense of A. Philip Randolph's 1942 statement:

> We are not opposed to whites helping in this struggle. But they must understand that Negroes must lead. We are working to develop black power independent of white power. As I say, we will work with whites.[62]

The fact that coalitions are not ruled out is clear in Carmichael's book on Black Power:

> When Black People lack a majority, Black Power means proper representation and sharing of control. It means the creation of power bases, of strength, from which black people can press to change local or nation-wide patterns of oppression—instead of from weakness.[63]

Carmichael put the matter similarly in 1966:

> When the black community is able to . . . negotiate with other groups from a position of organized strength, the possibilities of meaningful political alliances on specific issues will be increased. That is a rule of politics; and there is no reason why it should not operate here.[64]

Finally, this early statement of Carmichael's is to the point:

> No, I don't reject coalitions; what I say is that Negroes have to realize that when you form coalitions you aim toward what people call "national interest," and national interest is never the same as Negro interest. So they have to maintain their own interest first, then certainly they can form other coalitions.[65]

In this connection a condition for joining in a coalition is the stand of the group:

> We do not believe it possible to form meaningful coalitions unless both or all parties are not only willing but believe it absolutely necessary to challenge Anglo-conformity and other prevailing norms and institutions. Most liberal groups with which we are familiar are not so willing at this time. If this is the case, then the coalition is doomed to frustration and failure.[66]

The reason for selective coalition shows forth the real intent of Black Power:

> We do not see how black people can form effective coalitions with groups which are not willing to question and condemn the racist institutions which exploit black people; which do not perceive the need for, and will not work for, basic change. Black people cannot afford to assume that what is good for white America is automatically good for black people.[67]

This position may not be readily pleasing; it is practical realism.

It is clear that it takes time to build up in the black masses an "independent political action" organization to overcome real powerlessness with real power. It also takes economic resources to be independent, to work for basic changes from the perspective of the needs of black people. This is really the Achilles heel of Black Power as pluralism. Black Power advocates have called for black-controlled economic bases to undergird the independent political base. There is no doubt that the political base is wise and sound and will increase, but not as an "independent political action." The reason is that it cannot have a sufficient economic underpinning. What Stokely Carmichael, Floyd McKissick, and others suggest is black economic enterprises composed of cooperatives organized to run houses, stores, banks, apartments, and even factories. This is unmitigated subterfuge. Black Power in the quick cannot be about pluralism unless it is a hoax or word game to cover up for its real intention.

Black Power advocates of an all-black economy are misguided and will, if they continue in this, lead black masses to a bitter disappointment from which they may not recover sufficiently to do the real business of Black Power in the decades immediately ahead. An all-black, self-contained, and self-sufficient economy is based, first, on the assumption that big business will locate branch facilities in the ghetto. But as Andrew F. Brimmer, a black member of the Federal Reserve Board, points out:

> Such establishments will never provide enough jobs to absorb the existing, hard-core unemployed, those employed outside the ghetto, and to offer new opportunities for the future residents of the ghetto.
>
> The principal underlying reason is that the economies of scale and plant location in most instances will seldom if ever tip the decision in favor of concentrating a substantial part of the output of any major firm in the ghetto—removed from its principal markets in the country at large.[68]

The second basis for this call to an all-black economic base is the belief that black businessmen could meet the challenge of the whole black market. But it was the segregation of the past that provided a "protective tariff" for many black businesses, firms, and enterprises. This "protective tariff" will not be available in the future for the most obvious reasons. Soul-brothers and soul-sisters may combine some economic unity such as is found in the Muslim movement. But this combine into cooperatives or any other profit-sharing plan will gain only one, perhaps two, at best three, drops from the thirty-billion-dollar bucket blacks pour onto the market each year:

> As the income of Negro families continues to rise (probably more rapidly than for the population as a whole), the large national corporations will find the Negro market increasingly attractive. Thus, these corporations are not about to withdraw and allow the Negro businessman to treat the Negro market as his special preserve.[69]

What is more, there is a difference between increasing the independence of blacks through their management and investment opportunities with large firms in and out of the ghetto and attempting to mount small businesses for an all-black economic base in this day, when big business drives small business to the near-breaking point. Some success can be had by individuals in small business, but not by blacks as a whole. This technological and computer age works against a black economy as surely as it prevents the black man from breaking out of the vicious cycle of poverty. At last, it is even difficult to see any "net advantage to the Negro community in chasing out the few white businessmen who are still doing business in the ghetto," [70] though it is clear that unfair practices are sufficient reasons to eliminate their business when all other alternatives are exhausted.

BLACK SEPARATISM

Black Power is the call to black consciousness through cultural identity and self-determination through political organization supported by a black economic base. An increase in black economic growth will be in the best interest of blacks in general, but will be of no real strength to Black Power "independent political action." The direction of Black Power in these respects is the shape of the future; it is praiseworthy, and an important statement of blacks in their drive for humanity.

Black Power is more than cultural and political organization, for the accomplishment of these major aims requires sufficient withdrawal from the larger white society to develop a dynamic black consciousness. This separation may not be primary in intention, but it is inevitable. It begins with black control of black organizations, which means control by blacks in all black groups. Whites can participate on the basis that blacks set forth, as only the understanding and really committed tend to stay on this basis. This approach is understandable and makes a great deal of sense if blacks are to come alive. Whites also know that Carmichael was essentially correct when he pointed out the motivation for their involvement:

> Too many young, middle-class Americans, like some sort of Pepsi generation, have wanted to come alive through the black community: they've wanted to be where the action was—and the action has been in the black community.[71]

These very clear and positive aspects of black withdrawal for unity aside, it is generally known that the best way, the surest and quickest, to build a mass movement is to be against something as well as for something. In this respect, we have seen Carmichael make very clear he is not anti-white and very clear that he is anti white racism. What is certain here is that in zeroing in on white racism there is a direct attack upon institutions and systems which are maintained by whites. Indeed, Black Power finds it impossible to be allies with any group which does not denounce and renounce white racism. Thus fundamental to Black Power is the creation of a unified black people for a new society. This task requires the full allegiance of blacks through separation from racist white systems and institutions which, in the final analysis, means the people therein engaged. It is correctly not anti-white persons qua anti-white persons; but it nearly comes to the same in the end.

The basis for this strong separatist ideology is the conviction that this society is so racist it cannot change on its own. Black people must change this society through reorientation to their African heritage because in the long run time is on the side of black people throughout the world; they are the real source, inspiration, commitment, identity, and models. Where this places whites who wish to join in the black man's struggle for a new society is clear. They are to attack racism from within their own society:

> It's important to note that those white people who feel alienated from white society and run into the black society . . . are incapable of confronting the white society with its racism where it really does exist.[72]

This social change will come about through conflict, made inevitable by blacks forming a unity and being resisted by whites who cannot make democracy work and will not allow blacks to do so. Thus, the only way out for blacks is to organize as an effective, united, political organization for self-determination and social change. Inferiority will be overcome to the extent blacks have pride in their blackness, and pride in blackness means complete rejection of whiteness.

Critics of Black Power separatism vary in terms of their validity. Carl Rowan writes of this implicit separatism:

> I recognize the old "separate but equal" argument when I

hear it. I've read *Plessy vs. Ferguson* more times than I've read Carmichael's name and I've argued enough Deep South governors and politicians who favored separation of the races, to recognize what appears to be an appeal to the Negro's pride but is in fact an effort to flatter black men into believing that the short end of the stick is really the fat of Willie Mays' bat. Generations of enforced isolation of the Negro proved that "there ain't no such animal" as separate but equal; and voluntary isolation of the Negro isn't going to produce any such animal.

Carmichael and McKissick are not the first to preach black separatism, of course. Marcus Garvey wanted to haul all Negroes back to Africa. The Communist Party once promised Negroes the whole state of Mississippi.[73]

The separation called for is not for separate but equal, it is for strength to be equal on the same footing. This does lead to the notion of black political separation, but it is not in the Garvey tradition of "back to Africa" or in the Muslim tradition of separate states, although it may be in the direction of black enclaves in the major cities of the United States—which is no dream. Mr. Rowan rightly sees separatism in Black Power, but he misunderstands completely its intention to join with whites as decision-makers and not as beggars:

The Negro has said for generations: "We don't aim to lick the white man, but we sure intend to join him—in the enjoyment of every blessing of American life." Admittedly he is having one hell of a time joining the white man at the banquet. But he's got one leg under the table. Now SNCC and CORE are saying, "If we join the white man he'll lick us." So they want the Negro to run off to what will be a crumb-laden table in a cranny off the kitchen, plaster up a sign saying "black power" and pretend that the black man has found paradise.[74]

In a word, Rowan's criticisms fall short of the target because he believes Black Power means isolation when it means separatism for direct action from strength. His source for this is Roy Wilkins, whom he approvingly quotes as having

> blasted the policies of racial isolation that the "Black Power" advocates are pushing by saying: Negroes are Americans, citizens of the United States, their identity is here, as Americans. Separatism isn't going to get us very far. It is exotic and a little intoxicating, but it lacks the reality that 99% of Negro Americans must face each day. . . .[75]

Black Power as separation does not mean isolation, nor does it mean black supremacy, although it does oppose integration and nonviolence:

> The Black Power advocates . . . created a crisis of leadership within the civil rights movement. . . . This raised what is still the crucial question: does the Negro seek integration within the mainstream of American society, which admittedly will be difficult to attain; or black supremacy, which common sense says is impossible to achieve; or a separatism that would give black Americans special enclaves in which they can exercise total power . . . ? Negroes must decide whether whites are to be ousted from the civil rights movement.[76]

We have seen Black Power successfully answer all these questions, except for the one with respect to black supremacy, which for some means black take-over. To this point Carmichael speaks:

> Black people do not want to "take over" this country. They don't want to "get whitey"; they just want him off their backs as the saying goes. . . . The white man is irrelevant to blacks, except as an oppressive force. Blacks want to be in his place, yes, but not in order to terrorize and lynch and starve him. They want to be in his place because that is where a decent life can be had.[77]

Martin Luther King, Jr., thought in 1966 that Black Power

> connotes black supremacy and an anti-white feeling that does not or should not prevail. It leaves a feeling that the Negro wants to go it alone, which he cannot do.[78]

This criticism of Black Power as a first and nonreflective response seemed to be necessary in order to nip it in the bud. The pressure of whites in integrated civil rights groups in 1966 encouraged blacks dependent upon them to criticize Black Power before it was in formation. So it was with Roy Wilkins:

> We venture the observation that such a posture could serve to stir counter-planning, counter action, and possible conflict. Moreover in attempting to substitute for derelict law enforcement machinery, the policy entails the risk of a broader, more indiscriminate crackdown by law officers under the ready-made excuse of restoring law and order. . . . No matter how endlessly they try to explain it, the term black power means antiwhite power. . . . It has to mean going it alone. It has to mean separatism. Now separatism . . . offers a disadvantaged minority little except a chance to shrivel and die. . . . It is reverse Mississippi, a reverse Hitler, a reverse Ku Klux Klan. . . . We of the NAACP will have none of this. We have fought it too long.[79]

In response, Floyd McKissick of CORE declared:

> Black Power is not black supremacy, does not mean the exclusion of white Americans for the Negro revolution, does not advocate violence and will not start riots.[80]

Black Power has not only been misunderstood as if it were identical with separatism as isolation and black supremacy, but as we have just seen in the statement of Roy Wilkins, Black Power has been charged with being racist. But Bayard Rustin made clear this difference when he pointed out that Black Power says, "If you don't want me, then I don't want you." This is its independence and separatism for pride and power, but this does not rule out contact—it only means that contact has to be on equal footing. If Black Power were racist, it would say with racists, "Whatever you do, I don't want you." [81] Black critic Samuel Du Bois Cook, political science professor at Atlanta University, has made up his mind on the basis of undertones he hears rather than probing research after the smoke has cleared:

> Shorn of pretension, hypocrisy, and intellectual dishonesty, the slogan "Black Power" does have, when words, context, and program are combined, a generic or core meaning, and that meaning is racist. It is anti-white. It is separatist and isolationist. Make no mistake about it: vigorous denial under pressure notwithstanding, the unique dimension of the Black Power myth is racism.[82]

Professor Cook goes on to set forth how he knows Black Power is racist at the core:

> The racist character of the myth of Black Power is expressed in many ways: counsel to exclude whites from positions of leadership and influence in the civil rights movement, advocacy of independent all-Negro third parties, the symbol of the Black Panther, the call for a "black takeover of political power," the declaration of the irrelevance of integration and the issue of violence, self-righteous and glib assertions of the moral decadence of white America, and the general ventilations of anti-white frustrations, emotions and bitterness.[83]

We have seen how these charges do not hold up in the clear light of what Black Power as pluralism means. The fact that Black Power rejects nonviolence, integration, and advocacy of black-white coalitions without reservations does not add up to racism. Carmichael put it strongly in a speech during the rally following the shooting of James Meredith in Mississippi:

> You must build a power base . . . the power base has to get you a black sheriff . . . white people aren't going to do it for you . . . you have to stop being ashamed of being black and don't try to be white. . . . Now that doesn't mean to be anti-white . . . but get the nappiest headed black man with the broadest nose and the thickest lips and make him sheriff.[84]

Martin Luther King, Jr., was a critic of Black Power, but he knew it was not racist:

> Black Power is an implicit and often explicit belief in black separatism. Notice that I do not call it black racism. It is

> inaccurate to refer to Black Power as racism in reverse, as some have recently done. Racism is a doctrine of the congenital inferiority and worthlessness of a people. While a few angry proponents of Black Power have, in moments of bitterness, made wild statements that come close to this kind of racism, the major proponents of Black Power have never contended that the white man is innately worthless.[85]

Black Power means separatism for strength to enter the pluralistic arena with power. In this regard, Black Power is not black nationalism either in the form of a "back to Africa" movement or the call for a separate state.* It intends to take control where blacks are in the majority, a step that is within the American political tradition.

All doubt that was left concerning Black Power as separatism, political organization, self-help, and black pride vanished with the response of Whitney Young at the 1968 CORE convention in Columbus, Ohio. As Roy Wilkins before him, he acknowledged there had been confusion about Black Power to the extent that leaders like himself had written it off. This confusion was due to the pressure to respond on the spot to Black Power statements from the press and constituents. Then he went on to embrace Black Power and urged blacks to "obtain the power that America respects." Acknowledging the reversal of this stand, he said that "for an organization to change is painful" but "not to change is fatal." Addressing the delegates as brothers and sisters, Mr. Young said that he

> wanted to make it clear that the Urban League believes strongly in that interpretation of black power that emphasizes self-determination, pride, self-respect, participation and control of one's destiny and community affairs.[86]

* It is true that the third National Black Power Conference, Philadelphia, August, 1968, formulated plans aiming at achieving an independent black nation within the United States. Milton R. Henry, first vice president of the Republic of New Africa, stated that his republic was the only viable alternative because "the 10-year failure of non-violence proves the white majority in the U.S. does not want to change the status quo and cannot be made to do so by the black minority." *New York Times,* September 2, 1968, p. 13. In this respect, Mr. Henry is a latter-day Garveyite, or perhaps a neo-Garveyite.

This candor and forthrightness from the most influential leader of the civil rights groups is testimony to his stature. He previously would not talk of Black Power, saying there was only one kind of power: "green power." This is in perfect keeping with the success of the Urban League, attested to by Carl Rowan.

> Young had been so shrewd at making whites feel guilty about the Negro's plight and worried about the future that the foundations and big corporations had pumped more than $2.8 million into the 1966 Urban League budget, as against $300,000 in 1961.[87]

Of course he had been under some criticism for his success with green power, which did not penetrate to the black masses and made his stand against Black Power suspect:

> The Urban League's Whitney Young, Jr., is off on an Eastern European tour sponsored by a major magazine while Urban League affiliates are getting more and more foundation and antipoverty funds. The A. Philip Randolph Institute, with Bayard Rustin at the helm, got a big chunk from George Meany and is hoping to get more from Walter Reuther. Will the real Negro organization, supported by "Negro green power," please stand up? [88]

But Mr. Young's response is cogent: "What we did yesterday and the way we did it is not good enough for today." [89] Mr. Young said he no longer sought integration but "an open society where people have a choice." He agreed that blacks were "no longer enchanted with being near white people," and affirmed that blacks discovered white institutions were "not all they were put to be." So, the position of the Urban League is clear:

> We support as legitimate and historically consistent a minority's mobilization of its economic and political power to reward its friends and punish its enemies.[90]

He rejected the black nationalist notion of a separate state: "We do not intend to let white people off the hook that easy." Since America "does not respond to people who beg on moral grounds," blacks must use their organizations to build "the power that America respects." [91]

IN SELF-DEFENSE

The case for Black Power as a pluralistic thrust in the American political scene is clear. Yet, the movement from pride to political and economic organization to separatism is never apart from the affirmation of self-defense. Black Power has pervaded the black community from top to bottom. The black community is just beginning to be mobilized and unified around Black Power. The process is that of an uptight black consciousness which takes the form of the black ingroup in opposition to the white outgroup. The objective is radical or root changes in America, which it is anticipated will be resisted, and conflict is expected as the new form of black-white encounters. Separatism provides the cohesive strength in the escalation of conflict. In preparation for conflict, the initial step is defense of the right to enter into mobilization and unification. The movement is from debate about protection of black people from violence by the white society to a demand that blacks act in self-defense.* Self-defense is not intended subterfuge, but it necessarily leads to defense of riots as the eruption of frustration among black masses, the movement of creative disruption to creative violence.

Liberated from the inhumanity of nonviolence, Black Power is bold to reveal the vulnerability of black people:

> In Talahatchee County [Mississippi] last winter [1964] a Negro shot a policeman. The policeman was messing with him and he shot him. Now he went home, and immediately they organized a vigilante group, maybe a hundred people or more. They had machine guns, rifles, automatics. . . . They went to this guy's house and they shot up plank by plank and they dismembered him. They started at the bottom plank and they went all the way up. You have to ask yourself, "What happens to A Negro who considers arming himself to do violence to other whites?" [92]

* Dr. Nathan Hare, chairman of the 1968 Black Power Conference, told a news conference that black people are opposed to violence but they would no longer tolerate police brutality. He declared that "when black people arm, it is to stop violence against black people." *New York Times,* September 2, 1968, p. 13. This is Black Power subreption.

Such revelations as this one by Robert Moses Parris while with SNCC not only raised the question of self-defense but forced hitherto completely nonviolent spokesmen like James Farmer to come to its verbal defense. Mr. Farmer underlines

> the resentment Negroes feel over the way whites swarm over them with criticism the moment they abandon pure love and merely consider the notion of self-defense. The hypocrisy of this criticism is galling. The Negro sees analogies everywhere. There was silence in the press during the years in which hundreds of thousands of Congolese were being slaughtered; but then there came huge headlines: FIFTY WHITES KILLED IN CONGO. Why not an airlift to Mississippi, they ask? [93]

In response to this growing debate, Bayard Rustin calls self-defense versus nonviolence a "false issue" which detracts from meaningful debate and action. Yet we have seen why his objections are part of the old politics and do not fit into the new politics of Black Power:

> The reasoning here is that turning the other cheek is not the way to win respect, and that only if the Negro succeeds in frightening the white man will the white man begin to take him seriously. The trouble with this reasoning is that it fails to recognize that fear is more likely to bring hostility to the surface than respect. . . .[94]

Black Power self-defense is not a threat; it is the expectation that hostility is necessary and inevitable to bring change. Hostility is not to be feared but countered.

The debate over self-defense continued on NBC's *Meet the Press*. The very fact that this occurred marked self-defense as the coming consensus among blacks. Although the spokesmen were the lone wolf James Meredith and the charismatic Stokely Carmichael, they were not speaking only for themselves:

> *Mr. Meredith*. . . . now you take Mississippi, for instance —I know the people that shot in my house years ago. They know the people that killed all of the Negroes that have been killed. The community knows them, and I am here to

say that these people have to be removed from our society. White supremacy will not allow itself to remove these people from its society. If they don't find a way, the Negro has no choice but to remove these men, and they have to be removed. You can't have killers running around in the society killing people themselves.

Mr. Spivak. Are you suggesting then that if several Negroes are killed or any white men are killed and the law does not punish them, as happens very often in the case of white men too, that people ought to organize as vigilantes and go out and take the law into their own hands and commit violence? You are not saying that, are you, Mr. Meredith?

Mr. Meredith. That is exactly what I am saying. Exactly.

Mr. Carmichael. If you don't want us to do it, who is going to do it?

Mr. Meredith. I know personally the man who tried to kill my family when I was at the University of Mississippi, and everybody in the community knows him. I know that in all of the other communities in Mississippi—and you have read about all these killings—during the march they killed this 65-year-old (Negro) man, shot him 16 times, shot his head off.

Mr. Spivak. But you didn't pick up a gun and go out and try to kill that man because the law hadn't taken care of him; you don't believe in that, do you?

Mr. Meredith. This is what we are going to have to move to. If the law doesn't take these men, then we've got to stop this. We cannot tolerate this. Now I know why—

Mr. Spivak. Mr. Meredith, do you mean to tell me that you believe the Negroes in this country ought to organize, take up guns and if the law doesn't take care of the wrongs that the white man or other Negroes commit against him, they ought to take the law into their own hands?

> *Mr. Meredith.* This is precisely, and I will tell you why, because the white supremacy system—
>
> *Mr. Spivak.* Mr. Meredith, this doesn't even make sense against 180 million people. If you do it, they are going to do it.[95]

Mr. Spivak ably represents the position of whites in this society. There is no understanding that blacks have endured a most outrageous fortune and have called for this to stop. The debate on *Meet the Press* was a call for whites to bring law and order and, at the same time, a statement that they would not. Backed into a corner, a man has only one way to come out and that is fighting. Mr. Meredith has made public his intention never to move in the South again without a gun on his person. This kind of singular model of manhood discloses the new consciousness of black America, consciousness that will not be put down by the threats of the President of the United States or Mr. Spivak, who baldly reminds blacks they are only 10 percent:

> We have been forced by statements in this country, which remind us of the 90 percent and what they can do and the 180 million and what they can do—as if they say to us, "Now, if you don't do exactly as we want you to do, if you don't follow what we prescribe for you, then we have the power to wipe you out." That threat is not going to stand in my mind as a black man . . .[96]

In this respect, Stokely Carmichael was not speaking simply about retaliation for the sake of revenge, he was drawing upon the experience in Lowndes County, where he started the Freedom Party under the banner of the Black Panther. The threats were so constant that he was forced to draw upon political processes in the American tradition to support his promise:

> We're out to take power legally, but if we're stopped by the government from doing it legally, we're going to take it the way everyone else took it including the way the Americans took it in the American Revolution. And we've seen the way the federal government protects us, or rather doesn't protect us. If one of our candidates gets touched, we're going to take care of the murderers ourselves.[97]

The issue of self-defense arose in the South, where blacks have been intimidated and exterminated for generations, but only recently have they begun to organize for self-protection and given notice to the public. The real response to self-defense has come from blacks in the North who are unified around the issue of police brutality and other less spectacular crimes of violence inflicted by whites upon blacks in the ghettos. Civil rights leaders have done all in their power to divert blacks from the snowballing effect. They diagnosed what was happening and its probable results. Roy Wilkins spoke as sharply as any:

> There has now emerged, first a strident and threatening challenge to a strategy widely employed by civil rights groups, namely non-violence.
>
> If carried out literally as instant retaliation, in cases adjudged by aggrieved persons to have been grossly unjust, this policy would produce—in extreme situations—lynching or, in better-sounding phraseology, private vigilante vengeance.
>
> Though it be clarified and clarified again, "Black Power" in the quick, uncritical and highly emotional adoption it has received from segments of a beleaguered people can mean in the end only black death.[98]

All the arguments of common sense, reason, and patience were to no avail. The summer riots of 1966 and 1967 were spontaneous eruptions of mass frustration, and they were fuel which fired the rise of self-defense from debate to action.

The riots are black rage in mass response to the accumulation of undue suffering and unfair treatment. Blacks have been punished out of proportion when, in the South or the North, they have expressed their anger toward whites. The dethroning of Muhammad Ali, the unseating of Congressman Adam Powell, the tear gas inflicted on rioting black students, the unwarranted shooting into bands of black students demonstrating on their campus—these are the actions which fan the rage of blacks. In the past, blacks repressed their rage through being docile, being forever smiling, competing in sports, or striving to enter the mainstream. If such forms of repression have been acceptable in the past, they are no more. The Black Power political process movement is an acceptable way of organizing rage with meaning and relevance, but it has been fought all the way, and, indeed, many blacks believe the system is so intransigent that the political process cannot advance apart from violence. Thus, the disorganized and unacceptable expression of rage through riots is perceived by blacks as a healthy response which precipitates a more positive aggressive action that is organized. Black Power does not start riots; it gains impetus from them. Riots are not an expression of generic black pathological conditions but of rage running over.

Riots have driven Black Power advocates to condone these actions as rebellions. The tendency was to write off black militant leaders as rabble-rousers and to seek to confine them, on the theory that if the few were isolated, the majority of blacks would not be contrary. This theory has been exploded by whites themselves. It has been assumed by whites that blacks agreed with them that riots are criminal activities and defeat the cause. Research on the 1967 riot participation, conducted for the National Advisory Commission on Civil Disobedience, showed conclusively that riots are widely justified by the black community, although they are rarely recommended. The contention of whites has been that only the riffraff engaged in riots, which gave whites the confidence that only a handful of blacks who were the criminal element participated, and this minority could be discounted. Whites also believed that riots were not white against black but poor people looting. The study found that the overwhelming majority of the rioters were employed; that more than two thirds of those arrested were adults over eighteen years of age; that most rioters apprehended were males, but females were less likely to be arrested; and that most participants were persons who had resided in the area for some time. The conclusion of the report is that the 1967 riots were carried out by a "small but significant minority of the Negro population, fairly representative of the ghetto residents," and "tacitly supported by at least a large minority of the black community." [99]

This means that a substantial minority of blacks have lost faith in America, to say nothing of the fact that the riots can be dealt with only by radical changes in this society and not by more and more oppressive force.

Black Power advocates do not start riots even if they are gleeful about them as spontaneous disruptions. What is certain is that Black Power advocates perceive in the increasing support for a direct venting of rage through riots the opportunity for a more organized display of anger. The trouble with riots is that they are not controlled. Blacks are maimed and lose their lives without lives being given up in a concerted cause. The lesson learned from riots is that such violence does not advance the cause of self-defense. There is no question about the fact that the people have been assaulted and provoked, but their response lacks effectiveness. As a consequence, to protect blacks from themselves as well as from whites in riots, the very separatism of Black Power forces it to escalate in planned self-defense in the black community.

Eldridge Cleaver, the gifted writer and exiled Minister of Information for the Huey P. Newton-organized Black Panther Party in California, indicates this new emphasis in resisting white authority—"from now on we niggers have got to stop killing other niggers and start killing police."[100] The entire program of the Black Panthers appears to be focused on the police:

> It just happened that we learned by experience that when you challenge the police and their behavior and the tradition that they are operating out of, you have little time for anything else.[101]

This focus was triggered by the October 28, 1967, encounter between police and Huey P. Newton. The police stopped a car with two men in it, and one of the policemen said that the driver of the car was Newton. The first policeman told Newton he was under arrest and began to escort him to a police car. Shooting began. The second policeman was wounded and has said he did not see Newton shooting. He fired at Newton. The first policeman was killed.

On April 6, 1968, another incident increased the determination of the Black Panther Party to zero in on the police. Eldridge Cleaver writes for *Ramparts* magazine and is the author of *Soul on Ice.* He has spent most of his adult life in prison for possession of marijuana at eighteen and conviction of assault to kill and rape. In prison he was converted into a Muslim and took as his hero Malcolm X. It is the understanding of the Black Panthers that the police have been out to get Cleaver and others. This feeling was reinforced by the April 6 encounter in which two Oakland police were shot in the back and received minor injuries. Two Panthers were wounded, and seventeen-year-old Bobby Hutton was killed. Cleaver was wounded in the ankle and was sent back to prison, later released on a habeas corpus hearing. He claims he did not carry a gun that night. In any event, the incident described by him bears upon the incitement to police resistance. Cleaver and seven other Panthers were indicted. The story of the police is that after the two officers were shot, they traced Hutton and Cleaver to a basement. Cleaver comments:

> While we were inside that house, I got shot in the foot, you see. I got hit in the chest with a tear gas cannister, which knocked me out. Bobby thought I'd been shot. He took all my clothes off to try to find where I'd been hit, to feel for the blood in the dark.
>
> When the cops allowed us to come out, I couldn't stand very well and Bobby helped me out. I put my arm around his shoulder and he carried me out. As we came through the door, I think it was a kind of step down on a high threshold or something, and we tripped and we fell down.
>
> Then all these cops came in from the street and they started, like, hitting and kicking us. With guns and their feet, you know. Cursing at us and a lot of stuff. For two or three minutes.
>
> [They were told by the police to run to the police car. Cleaver said he would not run because of his ankle wound. He stated that the police shoved Bobby Hutton who was blinded by tear gas.]
>
> So Bobby was just like stumbling from that shove and they shot him. They try and say that he was running and all that . . .

I think they would have shot me, but there were a lot of people who were attracted to that scene, hearing all that shooting. When they shot Bobby, then these people started screaming and yelling at them, you see.

We say we'll go down with Huey and we mean that. We will not allow them to murder Huey. And that means doing anything within our power to see that it does not happen.[102]

This kind of defiance cannot be written off as the lunatic fringe.* We have seen how the Black Power movement has moved the moderate civil rights element more and more toward its position. The Black Power center groups can be expected to be pushed further toward violence by the most militant groups. The rage of black people, like that of the legendary genie, cannot be forced back into the bottle at will once the lid is off. Misdirected rage will at times border on sheer madness. Such was the case in Cleveland on July 23, 1968. Fred Ahmed Evans, a black nationalist, was reportedly upset by the refusal of a white to keep her word with respect to the rental of a building he had cleaned and painted up. Evans made African clothes and wood carvings and was director of a $10,300 summer program to train black youth in these crafts. Mr. Evans had received an eviction notice several weeks prior, but not for nonpayment of rent. When the lady backed down on her oral agreement, Mr. Evans, having spent time and money on fixing up the vacant liquor store, allegedly told his friends, "All I wanted was a little piece of land—if I can't make it, looks like I'll have to go to war." The result was that this man, whom psychiatrists had previously treated in the U.S. Army and termed hostile under pressure, led an attack on police in which three were killed, along with eight black people. The Reverend Mr. DeForest Brown, president of

* Huey P. Newton, convicted of manslaughter of a police officer in Oakland, California, and engaged in an appeal, declared, "We feel it necessary to prepare the people for the event of an actual physical rebellion." The Black Panther Party helps blacks with social complaints and "at the same time prepares them for what we feel is inevitable to come and that is armed rebellion. . . . I hope some day to be a revolutionary." His teachers include Ernesto ("Che") Guevara, Mao Tse-tung, Ho Chi Minh, and Jomo Kenyatta. *New York Times,* September 8, 1968, p. 32. This is Black Power, not subreption.

the Hough Development Corporation of Cleveland, an antipoverty organization, made the contact for Mr. Evans:

> Ahmed and his friends went in there and cleaned up the place and painted. I paid $45 to have two truck-loads of trash removed out of the place after they cleaned it up.
>
> After agreeing, the landlady changed her mind. Every black man knows the frustration of being absolutely helpless and at the mercy of some white person's whim.[103]

Mr. Morrie Thornington, black owner of a beverage store a few doors away commented:

> You should have seen it when it was empty for two years. People used to dump garbage in it and throw bottles in it. Ahmed cleaned it up—for the first time in his life he was really interested in something legitimate. This was his whole life.[104]

The Reverend Mr. Baxter Hill, head of the antipoverty project PRIDE in Cleveland, whose members were credited with keeping peace and cleaning up after riots in Cleveland, pointed out that

> this was no insurrection. The brother was mad and decided to fight. When an insurrection comes everybody'll be in it and we'll all know about it.[105]

Being a black nationalist, Mr. Evans was constantly harassed. He apparently was loaded with ammunition and had sufficient drawing power to induce a number of his associates to join him in an ambush which wounded thirty-six policemen. He was subsequently tried and sentenced to death.

Phil Hutchins, program director of SNCC, commented that a black mayor means black visibility and not Black Power. The mayor, Carl Stokes, was accused of being a part of the traditional system that is basically oppressive; he simply could not "begin to deal with the problems black people have." Mr. Hutchins was far too eager in his claim that the rage in Cleveland was "the first stage of revolutionary armed struggle. . . . It starts at resistance, and is beginning to move to armed struggle as shown in different stages perhaps in Paterson, Akron and now Cleveland."[106] The mainstream response is not fundamental change but the call for law and order. John Hope Franklin notes that in the first sixty years of this century whites were on the offensive in more than fifty race riots: "It is interesting that they never were followed with cries for law and order."[107] Dick Gregory puts this sentence of the Chairman of the History Department at Chicago University in the language of the masses, summing up their feeling by declaring that " 'law and order' is just the new way to yell 'Nigger'!"[108]

NATIONAL BLACK PANTHER PARTY

In this chapter we have spelled out at length many of the fundamental thrusts of Black Power. In doing this, we have also shown that Black Power is by its very nature and fundamental intent a movement in escalation, the pace of which is speeded up or slowed down by the social, political, and economic conditions of the society. It is on the ascendancy as the dominant mood of black America and as its authoritative voice. The distinguishing feature at the heart of Black Power is the determination to bring about very radical change in this society in the interest of blacks' becoming full men and full women, and this interest is seen as being in the national interest. Black Power is nothing if it is not complete commitment to this objective. In this regard, it is widely argued that Black Power is pluralistic, and much of the writing of Black Power advocates supports this belief. But no other major element in the American pluralistic system is dedicated to a new system, to a new order, to radical change for the sake of blacks, and thus for the democratic experiment to approach its promise. In the final analysis, Black Power as pluralism is subterfuge, misunderstanding, or co-option. The basis of this argument has been the burden of this chapter. That is, Black Power was the cry of new birth with the death of the nonviolence and civil rights era. Black Power follows an inevitable progression. It begins with a call for black people to pride in their beautiful black selves. This pride has to be expressed in self-determination through unified political and economic organization of blacks on the basis of full acceptance of themselves, their history, and their culture. Black consciousness as group identity requires group power for survival and the creation of a new society. To cohere, blacks are required to be separate as a way of being unified and mobilized, which means being pro-black institutions and anti-white institutions. Black people and institutions must be protected and allowed to express themselves freely and grow without fear, which means self-defense.

This realistic approach to power, which speaks to the needs of the black community, carries with it the rejection of separatism as the return to Africa or secessionism in separate states. What Black Power is after is political equality in the American context as regards its pluralistic dimension. The process of political equality through separation is to organize for maximum strength and, on this basis, compete for the interests of the black masses. The logical conclusion is for blacks to create an all-black political party. An all-black party means that the conflict between blacks and whites would be heightened because it would often mean blacks against whites. This would not be fatal, although the situation would be very hostile.

Thinking along the lines of a third party or all-black political organization was begun by Stokely Carmichael and others several years ago.* The Republican Party has given its clear indication that blacks are not wanted if they wish to be black in consciousness. It is the Democratic Party which has wooed blacks by promises which are not delivered. Thus, loss of faith in this party is one reason why a third-party alternative seems as necessary as it is logical, given the Black Power intention. Carmichael addresses himself negatively to the failures of the Democrats:

> The Democratic Party in this country is the most treacherous enemy of the Negro period. We've got to split it so Johnson and all the king's horses and all the king's men can't put it together again. The only way the Negro in Alabama will get justice is to smash the Democratic Party.

* The ousting of Stokely Carmichael, Mr. Black Power, from SNCC in 1968 and his alignment with H. Rap Brown in the Black Panther Party is indicative of the ideological division among SNCC members and the revolutionary intention of the spokesman for Black Power.

And the national party is opposed to the interests of Negroes. The Daley machine in Chicago is the same thing as the Wallace machine in Alabama. The Negroes in Watts are all loyal Democrats, and they're not going to get anything until they get out of the Democratic Party. And we've got to start tearing up the Democratic Party in Harlem.

We're trying to get power. The power structure doesn't want black people to have power. I'm not talking about George Wallace, I'm talking about Bobby Kennedy. They don't want black people to have power. It's in the interest of Robert Kennedy and Washington to squash the Lowndes County Freedom Organization because it will spread. And that's all we're working for. A national alternative, when Negroes will be organized independently, neither Republican nor Democrat. So it's in their interest to stop us.[109]

Carmichael made a more positive statement in 1966:

> The single aspect of the Black Power program which has come into the most criticism is the concept of independent organization. This is represented as third-partyism, which has never worked, or a withdrawal into black nationalism and isolationism. If such a program is done, it will not have the effect of isolating the black community, but the reverse. When the black community is able to control local offices, and negotiate with other groups from a position of organized strength, the possibility of *meaningful* political alliances on specific issues will be increased. This is the rule of politics, and there is no reason why it should not operate here. The only difference is that we will have the power to define the terms of our alliances.[110]

In 1968 Phil Hutchins, the program chairman for SNCC, stated that the major objective of the organization would be to form a black political party nationwide with the black panther as its symbol:

> It will not be the traditional political party giving you a choice between the lesser of two evils, but a party defined by black people and filling the needs of black people.[111]

The structure of this party was, in the view of Hutchins, to take the form of grass-roots response to grass-roots problems, needs, and directions. Candidates in these highly individual communities may be run or not, but the major aims of the party would be to give blacks control of black areas, to provide links between American blacks and nonwhites around the world, and to seek to end racism, capitalism, and imperialism here and in other parts of the world:

> We don't necessarily want a political party to win elections, but for black people to live better.
>
> Politics as Americans practice it—as well as this law and order and parliamentary rule, is designed to keep some white people on top and black people and poor whites on the bottom.
>
> Once someone robs you, he must find a way to keep what he stole.[112]

Whether or not an all-black party can be effectively organized is one problem. It ought not to be dismissed as an idle dream, for we have seen the early castigation of Black Power and its gradual winning of its original critics to at least some significant aspects of the program. If it does come to pass, there will be obvious conflict strictly along black and white lines over some issues, while in others selective alliances may be entered into. It is possible that the black minority would be relegated to a permanent minority. This very real possibility, if a third party is realized, would drive blacks to creative disruption in the cities, which would be effective in gaining some concessions.

However, racism is so intransigent in this society—and it is this Black Power is committed to eliminate—that the most fantastic combinations of alliances and selective disruption of the society conceivable will not bring about this radical change. Therefore, if Black Power is really dedicated to a new order, it will come in time to this: the escalation from a stepped-up political process to sharper conflict or creative violence.

Regardless of the diagnosis or hope to the contrary, Black Power advocates in all of their frenzied activity within the system now are fundamentally opposed to it as racist through and through. There is a deep and unshakable suspicion among them that there is no way out. This feeling is expressed by Whitney M. Young, Jr., but for him violence is not practical:

> Let me make it real clear—I'm not a pacifist. I am not a nonviolent person. I am a very violent person, particularly as it relates to self-defense for myself and my family. And I'm not at all sure that I would not be an advocate of violence if I thought I could win. If the situation were reversed and we were in Nigeria or in Ethiopia or somewhere, I might well be an advocate of violence. But looking at the hard realities, unless somebody shows me something that I haven't seen yet, by way of superior weapons, then I at this point do not see this as a very sound tactic. And so we are against violence. But I think the responsible Negro community has gone about as far as it can go in saying to its constituency be patient, be non-violent, be loyal.[113]

We have seen that Mr. Young's mind was changed once by Black Power. What if the issue were not one of winning? What if the issue was so real that blacks were willing to go down that others might rise up? At this time, Mr. Hutchins' position is, "We want to put something in his head before putting a gun in his hand, as Chairman Mao said." [114] Yet, he called the Cleveland, summer 1968, disaster the first step in an uprising. Speaking to this situation, Eldridge Cleaver said, "It shows psychologically blacks are not only prepared to die but to kill." [115] Stokely Carmichael stated, "We are only at the beginning of a revolution—the armed stage. We must create the maximum damage with a minimum of loss of black people. And that is through guerrilla warfare." [116] Despite the many interpretations of Black Power we have seen in this chapter, it is still my view that Black Power is revolution. Black Power may be co-opted for purposes of the civil rights movement, the Negro movement, the freedom movement, but I submit the co-opters cannot use Black Power for their own purposes forever, and perhaps not for long.

5.

BLACK POWER
Theology

Since the advent of Black Power, few black church leaders hold that outside the church there is no salvation. Strange things are happening. Four years ago black church leaders were so defensive that any criticism of the black church was viewed as sour grapes. Black churchmen used the same arguments as Southern white racists when criticized for their obvious weaknesses. They would reply that you don't understand us, and this disdain of criticism was revealed in the putting down of *Black Religion: The Negro and Christianity in the United States,* a book in which I attacked the hypocrisy of both white and black churchmen with equal fervor. Today, this work is readable among blacks and whites. This recent willingness to engage in honest controversy is a result of the impact of Black Power. And for that very reason, Black Power, the newfound vitality among black churchmen tends to be suspect. In *The Politics of God,* researched and written prior to the cry of Black Power, I advanced the idea of the unique role of black people as a "chosen people" or a "suffering servant people" and the supporting role of black churches therein for radical changes in the society. These very concepts are now being explored and exploited and extended in the name of Black Power by black churchmen. The "protective tariff" of segregation permitted the black churches to exist and, indeed, forced them to be separate. Could it be that the enthusiasm for Black Power is but the will to black church life as viable pluralism? Could it be that a theology of Black Power in the form of separatism gives our black churches a new basis for independence and a new lease on life? Is the "protective tariff" of Black

Power separatism a subterfuge for the continuance of black churches as a "nation within a nation" for purposes that are antithetical to Black Power? Could it be that under the guise of renewal of the church and the society, black churchmen have co-opted Black Power to serve integration through the technique of pressure tactics? Could it be that black churchmen simply miss the message and meaning of Black Power?

It is the powerlessness of the black masses that Black Power has risen to change into power. Black churches and churchmen have looked at themselves in the mirror of Black Power and have seen clearly for the first time their powerlessness. As a result, they have become open to criticism in the expectation that through Black Power they might yet realize their past promise in an even more dynamic and privileged sanctuary. From this time forth the privileged sanctuary of black existence in separation will be used to obtain power to play the game of power to its logical end, but this time blacks will be on the offensive among their white brethren in the larger society. In a word, black churchmen are committed to pluralism, to equal power, and to a balance of power, which may be neither possible nor the intention of Black Power. Arnold Toynbee observed in his *A Study of History* that the black man

> may have found spiritual salvation in the White Man's faith; he may have acquired the White Man's culture and learned to speak his language with the tongue of an angel; he may have become adept in the White Man's economic technique, and yet it profits him nothing so long as he has not changed his skin.[1]

By what stretch of the imagination or innovative process do black churchmen come to believe they can, through pluralism, change this situation? Their answer is that through the battering ram of the combined power of all blacks in all areas of the society, America can be driven toward its promise of an open society in which diversity will be cherished as enrichment.

There is no doubt about the sincerity of black churchmen. In fact, a very interesting development is taking place. Black church leaders and Black Power advocates have found a new *rapprochement*. The most vehement critics of black churches have been the dissident and disaffected blacks who rise out of and speak for the black masses. They have been the hard core blacks on *Tally's Corner* who have known their own failure and thus have perceived more sharply the failure of the black churches, which results from the same educational, social, economic, and political conditions. Now many of these Black Power advocates are, in some instances, returning to black churches. In the ten-week CORE 1968 summer training program for leaders there were visits on Sunday to local churches. The reason is put clearly by VanDike Johnson, a group leader in the program: "It's not so much to pray as to try and figure out why the churches had been the one constant black activity that doesn't crumble." [2] Black religion people and Black Power advocates are surprised to find each other; as the people put it —"the brother has come home." But it could be that each brother has returned to a very different home than the one he left. Black religion people share the same kind of soul music as their Black Power brothers, but the words set to the same music are different because the mood expressed is different. Black religion people look to Black Power for salvation, and Black Power looks to black religious leaders for technical guidance. T. S. Eliot's dictum that the greatest treason is "to do the right thing for the wrong reason" may not fully apply to the mutual congratulatory response of black religion and Black Power, but that Black Power has been found by black religion leaders is right and good and real and necessary and hopeful. The suspicion lingers not because black churchmen, in the creatism of Black Power, no longer hold that there is no salvation outside the church. It lingers because outside of revolution, there is no Black Power. That is, black churchmen misunderstand or misuse or mistake Black Power. Black Power is not faith in equality of power, nor in a balance of power, nor in a balance of error, nor even in a balance of terror. These alternatives may be tried, but they are not really live alternatives, for the task of Black Power is radical change in the society to "smash racism." Outside the revolution, there is no Black Power.

Revolution is the fundamental intention of Black Power, based on the realism that there is not the will in the society to bring the changes necessary to end racism. Black religion leaders shuffle or shy or run away from potential Black Power as if it were the truth. The radical theology of Black Power is revolution. Do we find black religion leaders in integrated, segregated, discriminated, or just plain separated institutions developing this theology of revolution? Black identity, black music, black literature, black self-defense, black history, black pride, black styles, black politics, black economics, black separatism, black beauty —are these ingredients for a continued idolatry, or are they knowledge about God's stirring in the world, calling man into responsible revolution? If there is no Black Power without revolution, then it is, like a rocket, in the first stages of takeoff toward the projected target. If black religion is but the booster of the projectile, it too will be left behind. If the radical theology of Black Power becomes for black theologians their development as technologists and not as revolutionaries, they will be compared with Pope Paul and his pronouncement on birth control in response to the expectation of a new departure, a new teaching, a new freedom. For Pope Paul, birth control did not mean birth control but traditional control. In the coming theology of black churchmen vis-à-vis Black Power, will black control mean traditional control of black institutions for black participation in the old pluralism with new verve? Will there emerge a theology of revolution?

Presently, black theologians all too often manipulate Black Power as a means to force White Power to do what it should have done long ago, in the apparently honest belief that more than tokenism will result. Why? Why? Why? Undoubtedly, it is because they believe power in the black community is the last chance before revolution. Is it wise to place all the eggs in a weak basket? Black theologians know that Black Power is not to be equated with riots and revenge, something John Howard Griffin does not understand. He writes of Black Power militancy: "Finally there comes the decision simply to destroy, to wreck, to take down as many whites as they can before the end." [3] Yet, the distinguished chairman of the steering committee for the 1967 National Conference on Black Power, Nathan Wright, Jr., writes about "Power and Reconciliation" as if he can neither endorse nor defend the aims or the means of black revolutionaries:

> However difficult the task of developing black solidarity and black pride and power may be, it is consistent with the path by which a securer place in American life has been achieved by all other rising ethnic groups. If this is, in fact, the path that must be taken now, black Americans must take the immediate initiative. They must also cease blaming white Americans for at least their present plight and devote their energies to the saving tasks that must be done in the days ahead.
>
> Bound by a yoke of a shared need for penitence basic to reconciliation, black Americans and white Americans may yet face a new day of personal and corporate freedom. This, it seems, is a significant part of the potential legacy of a reassessment of power relationships at this stage in the life of our nation and our world.[4]

Indeed, reconciliation is not a thing of the past but of the future black-white relations. But reconciliation in Black Power does not come on the other side of power; it comes on the other side of revolution and redemption. Black Power is a demand for a theology of revolution that includes reconciliation after conflict, not just after separation. Black Power holds that White Power will do precious little of all it should have done long ago. Therefore the disaster is not to be averted, nor the reconciliation thereafter. Is there a black theology of reconciliation growing out of revolution comparable with the fragments growing out of pluralism? At the heart of the Christian faith is redemption out of revolution and through reconciliation.

Black theologians have all the sounds and emotions of revolutionary Black Power but none of its substance. They are fully aware that the conclusions of the polls concerning the majority of black people supporting ministers, civil rights leaders, and other marginal men of the middle do not reveal the whole truth, and, certainly, they hide the real feelings. Perhaps it is true that most blacks are opposed to revolutionary leaders, but this is largely due to their belief that they cannot pull the revolution off. Black religious leaders know full well the truth that a small, dedicated, passionate, determined, disciplined, intelligent, and trustworthy element among the black masses could bring about a violent revolution. Its quality would depend upon black theologians and others to give it real direction. Black theologians have chosen to ignore this hard core in the fantastic hope that the lion will lie down with the lamb in peace and harmony because the lamb happens to be black, which gives it power to counter the power of the lion. Black theologians do not see Black Power as a means for a few more blacks to enter into the affluent mainstream. They see it as a few more blacks gaining positions of economic and political strength within and without the mainstream and expect that these blacks will use their power to strengthen the power of all blacks. Black theologians say all the right things about the black masses being locked in with all the other blacks without their humanity and about the poverty of education, jobs, and housing which has to be eliminated by black unity sharing in decisions. Black theologians stress the need to become human through self-identity and pride in action. What black theologians have done to this point is call for rapid social change, by which they mean revolution. In this regard, they continue to be Martin Luther King's children. They are not Uncle Tom's children by any stretch of the imagination, but neither are they Malcolm X's children. Black Power is the calling into question of the basic structures of our society, our political, economic, and cultural order. This demand for justice means *dis*order and the creation of a new order. In the Black Power sense of revolution, black theologians are not providing the blacks of America with the leadership needed for them to engage responsibly in their primary vocation as a people, the creation of a new order.

Black theologians are of the mind that Black Power put to maximum use as pluralism in the present system will bring about the change needed for blacks to be fully human. We hope with them that they are right, but there is precious little indication that the will of America is sufficient to the task. Thus, black theologians should plan on success through co-opting Black Power; they should not bank on it. If it is the case that the vocation of blacks is that of revolution, then black theologians should have a hand in its guidance. Black theologians were engaged with their brothers in the Abolition Movement, which is precedent enough. The small band of dedicated revolutionaries which provide Black Power's real impetus should not be isolated or ignored at their roots for the sake of their fruits. To do so would be to treat them the way black churches have treated the alienated of the community all along: write them off. The task of the theologian is to discover what God is doing in the world and to rally around to further his intention. What God is doing is discovered in what men are about who are doing God's work without awareness, perhaps, and often without wisdom.

It is the responsibility of black theologians to develop a theology of revolution for several reasons. First, black people have as their unique function in this world the vocation of revolution, whereby all people through them become human and attain their manhood. The second reason that black theologians ought to develop a revolutionary theology is not only as preparation in the event it becomes necessary but as their own special achievement. That is, Black Power is the creation of black people. So far, black theologians have followed its lead in terms of taking up and supporting the themes of pride, mutual support, organization, etc. But all of the action, the leadership, the initiation, the innovation have been developed outside of theology, if not outside of black religion. If the revolution is the vocation of blacks, and Black Power is the spirit held in common, then the benefit and resources thereof ought to flow from, as well as to, theology. To this point, black theology has simply joined the movement like a stray dog wandering into a parade at the tail end, and in some respects seeks to be the tail that wags when it should do the reverse.

The third reason black theologians should develop a theology of revolution is a realistic appraisal of the situation. The 1968 Republican Convention virtually wrote off blacks on the assumption that the white majority could have their society of law and order on their own terms. The convention called for peace and expressed a desire to use peace as a means of bringing into being a new future for America and the world. But the peace was not based on a common goal for whites and blacks; the peace envisioned was one that whites alone would determine. If the Republican Party truly represents the average American and the dynamics of the society, there will be no revitalization of America as perceived by Black Power pluralism. In that eventuality, a theology of revolution is required which gives direction to black America instead of wishful thinking.

Drawing upon the reality of Black Power as revolution beyond pluralism, the future of Black Power and the future in Black Power, I want to suggest some elements of a theology of revolution. These are but suggestions offered in the hope that black theologians will work out such a theology.

ELEMENTS OF A BLACK POWER THEOLOGY OF REVOLUTION

In a society which is as intractable as Black Power claims this society to be, practical politics will not suffice. In such societies a break with past traditions, systems, and structures has been the historical pathway toward the future. This constitutes a hard saying, but insofar as Black Power contains truth, its conclusions will be hated and vilified by good men in the name of the good society. Yet, responsibility before God requires irresponsibility before good men and good systems that are nonetheless unjust and evil *and* revolution against good structures. Whatever good forces control or restrict unjustly a human being, and thereby deny his freedom to act in responsible self-determination, must be broken.

All men are good, and all men are evil, and this paradox results in the most evil acts being perpetrated by good men in the name of goodness. Thus, it is the case that all men are sinners who fall short of the intention of God. And it is also the case that all men are saved by the gracious mercy of God. Consequently, between birth and death on this earth, man, who is both good and evil, sinner and saved, requires the process of political equality to approximate as nearly as possible the norm of social justice. This paradoxical nature of man often takes the form of pride as lust for power and its exercise for what he deems his own interest singularly. As a consequence, men have devised some form of central government to prevent anarchy and institutionalized power for its more equitable dispersion. In a word, government comes into being as the creative instrument for the positive apportionment of justice and order. Those who function well in a society place their emphasis upon order as having priority over justice; the dysfunctional perceive the priority in reverse. The American creed of justice and equality for all men except black Americans has been upheld by both those who operate out of the democratic creed alone and those who include as well the Christian faith. The belief that neither of these perspectives will bring about the fundamental changes necessary, as well as the belief that both of them *should,* provide the believer with sufficient grounds to lead them both to the logical results of their own names.

Revolution in the terms of Black Power is the bringing about of any real freedom for blacks and whites. Black Power means White Power must be brought to an awareness of its true self, political equality and power distributed responsibly. The historical and religious precedents for revolution are ample. Theologians need but recall the Protestant revolution for a clear-cut theologically based calling of structures and systems into question. The power of Protestants came into being as a result of action in the name of freedom and in opposition to evil or unjust control which denied Protestants their individuality under God. For five hundred years Protestants and Roman Catholics have been separated without any steps, until recently, toward reunity. The basis of reunity, if it comes, will include the assurance that the Protestant belief that nothing is sacred in and of itself. There will also be the demand that the uniqueness of Protestantism developed in separation from Roman Catholicism be the contribution brought to union. Indeed, it is evident that only through revolution against evil forces that act to control unjustly does responsible freedom or the power of self-determination become authentic and a new and better order result. Other revolutions which readily come to the minds of theologians need only be mentioned: for example, the Exodus led by Moses and its resulting wars of liberation, the early Church against the Roman Empire, the American people against the British Commonwealth, the French Revolution, and the Cuban Revolution.

Black theologians need only to read the Bible in the light of the Cross to discover that its central message is about freedom and power. In the Cross freedom and power are available as the grace to counter all that keeps us from responding to the source of all freedom, power, and truth in its light. Black Power speaks of war and revolution amidst insensitivity and noninte-gration. It is the Cross which reveals war and revolution as the life-giving means to counteract the misuse of freedom by men with absolute power who tend to use it irresponsibly to abridge freedom of the powerless. The Cross reveals that there are times when no other sacrifice but that of life has the power of defeat-ing evil in the name of new life. It is from the Cross that the black theologian knows all things and from that perspective all events are understood. In the light of the Cross all fundamental change takes place, change which destroys the old order and brings forth the new order of peace. The Cross declares that a just war is as much of a risk as an unjust peace, but no more so. It is the Cross which has demanded that the responsive being become a soldier for truth, to sacrifice his life for it. To be a vitalist is to view the human condition from a perspective other than that of the Cross.

Integration has meant the pathway of progress for a dominant majority of whites and a minority of blacks. But the minority of blacks have not gained their humanity. In this respect, integra-tion means the entrance of more and more black Americans into the mainstream dominated by the white culture. This might well have worked if whites were able to let down all of the barriers. But the failure of integration provided blacks with the opportu-nity for the salvation of their soul. Now integration will come after the revolutionary beginning anew in which black and white will contribute each to the other. The outcome cannot be known from this vantage point. This revolutionary new beginning is inherently bristling with tension and conflict, one sign that it is genuine. Another is that the traditional ways of relating no longer suffice; the situation is rapidly reaching the molten stage. The very expectation and anticipation lay to rest all arguments about whether there is available to all the American dream Rich-ard Nixon put forth in his 1968 acceptance speech at the Repub-lican Convention. The looking forward to the revolution by those who have been shut out at various levels brings to naught the old argument that through peace and the orderly processes all good things come in time, if you work hard enough. The madness of the American system vis-à-vis black Americans de-mands the heroic response that will risk it from ruin.

In *The Politics of God* I pointed out that the irrational is a third force other than reason or anti-reason, and the most certain form in which the holy discloses itself:

> By irrational we mean a persistent, pervasive, and effective force which is neither unreasonable nor in conflict with reason but one which governs human intercourse on a more elementary level than reason. It is other than rather than opposed to or in conflict with reason. This elemental force of the irrational is given expression in religion.[5]

On the edge of what Charles E. Silberman prematurely described as the *Crisis in Black and White* we perceive the injustice of racism and rampant injustice. The civil rights movement of integration responds through the call of "Come now, let us reason together." On these terms reason means treason. The response of Black Power is irrational; it takes the form of repudiating love and pledging hatred of white supremacy and the racist society; it expresses itself in righteous black rage and manly self-defense; and it believes its cause is on the side of the will of God.

The key to understanding the world and the responsibility of man is suffering:

> While the Negro is insisting upon "freedom now," he has not yet understood the price of freedom to be his responsibility of living this passion, chosen for him and all by God. The Negro's suffering will be creative only when he accepts "Negro consciousness" and learns that his destiny is true freedom, which is not possible for some individuals or groups apart from all individuals and groups. Friedrich Engels once pointed out that "freedom is the knowledge of necessity." If the Negro people can soon accept the fact Negroes will always be black and objectionable to whites and thereby the necessity of their role as the "suffering servant" in the Kingdom of God, this knowledge will be the black hope upon which the freedom of all men is possible sooner than later.[6]

Black Power understands the mission and meaning of suffering; its knowledge attracts our attention because in it we perceive that the suffering of blacks is not a vicarious experience. Thus,

Black Power is able to stand in the face of those who cry that violence has no place in a civilized society based on order and justice, and is able to point out that blacks' suffering did not take place in another country, nor is violence inflicted upon blacks by hands other than Americans'. It is from the Cross that Black Power sees that suffering is the result of violence, that only through violence does suffering come to full meaning and fruition in redemption. The Cross of sacrifice, once for all, does not mean there should be no more suffering, no more violence. The suffering of the Cross makes clear that the redemptive power of suffering comes only through violence which is unleashed in the spirit of the Cross. If suffering is endured from pride or violence let loose as revenge, there is no support here from the redemptive meaning in the Cross. If suffering takes the form of violence and the sacrifice of life for the good of a whole people and through this people, all people, then it is atonement, in attunement with the Cross. Death on the Cross does not mean the end of all dying, suffering, and revolution. It means the end should come to all meaningless dying, suffering, and revolution. The light in which revolution is judged to be meaningful is the extent to which life is given as a sacrifice to make real the freedom and power the Cross states is the gift of God and his will for all men. The passion, excitement, and will to suffer for freedom and manhood are a deep part of Black Power, which black theologians would do well to draw on and to draw out as a counter to those all around who say, "Keep it cool!—Don't get excited!"

It is from the Cross as well that another implicit theological spur in black theology cries out for theological treatment. Black Power holds almost fatalistically that that which is worthy comes only by rebirth after death. That is, real life comes only through the agonizing pain of creativity at the hands of death, which gives a backhand to the past and its ways. Intrinsic in this perspective is the sound view from the Cross that it is not the length of life but the quality of life which brings forth creative new life. The center of the Christian faith moves from death to resurrection, from Good Friday to Easter Sunday. That is, from the Cross the Christian looks forward into the future and makes way for it in the present. Death does not simply mean the end of life for a given individual. Death means the end of the world that is a persistent reality for individuals, communities, and societies. The end of our little kingdoms, groups, power exclusions is not a reality to be feared but one to be grasped. We come to ourselves only through the death of that to which we hold so tightly that there is not room for living. Only in the death of that which is not in our best interest can we come to life through the birth of that which is. The future in and the future of Black Power lie precisely in the knowledge that the end to this society's dysfunctional systems and structures is the way to new ones. That there are some things which must die to make way for the life they are choking out—can this be denied from the Cross? The end of our little worlds is the way to the birth of new ones. What in the world is God doing? Through Black Power he is driving home the truth that all our little systems must die, that nothing created by man lasts forever or is good forever. Indeed, nothing on earth is good, is sacred, is beyond criticism, is without need of rebirth. The very acceptance of death by Black Power as a way to new life has elements within it of the deepest affinity with Christian teachings from the crucial center of the Cross. Was it not the Cross which made clear once and for all that no man or no people should submit to any prejudice or racism or exclusion or inhumanity or tradition or order for fear of death? Indeed, the Cross holds forth the reality that only the quality of that for which one is prepared to die illuminates the living. Black Power is prepared to die for a black people.

The contagion of Black Power is its dream of a new world and a new order born of the old world and order where men are not divided up by the accidents of history, but by the accidents of history are brought into a unity of enrichment through diversity. Is there not some direction for black theology in this unity vision, in this will to universal mankind? Isn't Black Power that willingness to live by the end for the sake of the present? And isn't this living from the end of this time the process by which new time becomes present time? What else does the Christian perceive creation to be from the Cross? Black Power calls into question the disabling aspects of our systems and structures and dares to claim that the end of this way of life is not far off. Is this not the only way to creation? Is this not the revolutionary gospel that comes breaking in upon us at the depths from the height of the Cross? To be sure, this will to bring an end to this disabling rather than enabling aspects of our society is a threat, but it need not be feared. In fact, the Christian message is that the end of our little worlds is the only sign of hope, the only sign we have that the Kingdom is about to break in a little larger. The power of Black Power is its central belief in the victory of black people by way of egress, not ingress. So it is from the Cross we know this truth to be self-evident, that the Holy One comes to us in fullness only after death.

Black Power is a call for an open society in which all men share and find their contribution acceptable and accepted. That is, this drive for an open society is a drive toward the future. Black Power holds that the future of black people is crucial; it depends upon an open society, but an open society will not come automatically. Blacks have to make that future be open; they have to storm the doors of the traditional and *status quo* and re-open the future by death if need be so that life may come to millions of blacks who follow. It is this knowledge of truth through its living which gives Black Power that authentic ring. If theologians co-opt only, if they do not work out the meaning of this lived truth, we may not benefit from the new humanity into which Black Power is leading. Black Power is trying to change the world. Black theologians know the necessity of this change. But precisely because they are theologians caught up in the tradition of Christianity through the institutional church which has never sought so bold a scheme as to change the world, theologians may fall back into the usual organizational pattern. In fact, this pattern of reform or renewal, never revolution, is already hardening among black theologians.

When will black theologians begin to read the signs of the times and respond to them as realities, rather than subverting them? There never was an opportunity for black theologians like the one given to them by Black Power. Theologians of all people teach, and hopefully believe in, the fatherhood of God, yet, as we shall see, they act as if the belief in the one God demands one capitalistic or one pluralistic belief. Black Power contends only that the cause of black people is right and that if any system denies them their rightness, black people are more important than that system. There are some elements here of the teaching about the Sabbath versus man that black theologians can develop.

It should be very clear by now that Black Power has declared war against racism. This is a holy war, a religious war, the only kind of war that is indispensable from time to time, unlike the wars in Korea or Vietnam. The test of a religious or holy war is whether or not the declared enemy uses power to keep human life inhuman, to prevent men from coming to manhood, to prevent the unity of all men in the diversity which enriches. The test of Black Power is the fruit it produces; so far it has been abundantly rich. It behooves black theologians not to be satisfied with picking a few underripe pieces from an underdeveloped fruit tree. The proof of Black Power is its growth. It has yet to come to maturity, but black theologians are already frantically picking away at its fruit because it is so tempting. In this, black theologians are less faithful than are the Black Power advocates. Black theologians take the premature growths of Black Power to serve the time in which they live. But the mature Black Power does not serve this time; it is an idea whose time has not yet come.

The freedom which Black Power says black Americans must wrench from White Power is, in essence, the gift of God for humankind. The fact that this freedom to be a people who contribute with pride as a group and as individuals of the group is denied, and manhood withheld, results in racism. Black Power is consistent with the Cross in its demand that freedom be a reality, that blacks fully express the liberating power of freedom, for this power is the only human force for the creation of a new community of new men and women. The youthful militants of this generation are engaged in a war on racism which is altogether unprecedented in its objective, if not in its philosophy. They are convinced that change is their *raison d'être*. So, they are committed to fight as soldiers in this war against racism. The war is not the end; it is the means which justifies the end of a new future which will not be built upon the past crises of credibility. Black theologians must not gag the youth, must not compromise their work, must not inhibit their passion, must not attempt to curb their idealism by reasons of practicality. The heroism of youth is fed by soul food and soul power, that consciousness of being black by which they think and act and dare to question radically the current condition. So far, black theologians have countered the passionate feelings and impulses of militant black youth with a practical wisdom of traditionalism. When black theologians match in theological thought the depth reached by youth in their passion, Black Power will come to maturity, and there will be reinforcement enough to be open to the future.

So far black theologians have been largely interpreting their respectable version of Black Power to the world. Black Power is about changing the world.

The most illuminating way to perceive the need for a revolutionary theology developed by black theologians is to understand Black Power as

> the embodiment of one single truth through the ages: that death precedes birth, that birth is the fruit of death, and that the soul is precisely this power of transforming an end into a beginning by obeying a new name.[7]

It is of significance for us to pursue the extent to which black theologians have developed this substratum of Black Power and found meaning therein because their contribution to the movement depends upon their responding to the root of the movement and not simply being satisfied with "a piece of the action."

STANDPOINTS OF BLACK THEOLOGIANS

Just before the turn of this century, W. E. B. Du Bois wrote that

> the Negro Church is the only institution of the Negroes which started in the African forest and survived slavery.[8]

It was the contention of Du Bois that the development of black churches with overwhelming response from the black masses needs to be understood in the light of the African priest or medicine man who

> early became an important figure in the plantation and found his function as the interpreter of the supernatural, the Comforter of the sorrowing, and as the one who ex-

> pressed, rudely, but picturesquely, the longing and disappointment and resentment of the stolen people.[9]

The records yield very little evidence of any connection between African religious practices and the black churches which erupted in America. It is true that in 1822, during the Denmark Vesey insurrection, Vesey's religious persuasion did not cause him to inhibit his lieutenant, Gullah Jack, the sorcerer, from using superstition to give confidence to the slaves. Gullah Jack used the fetish beliefs and practices of the slaves who were responsive only to this kind of motivation to provide the necessary moral solidarity needed to rebel. Yet, the breakup and destruction of African tribes and kinship groups and clan organizations were so thorough that even the religious cults and myths of the past lost their meaning in the New World. This devastation of the African heritage prevented any organization along African religious ideas such as those which developed in Brazil. This did not mean blacks were unresponsive to their past; it meant that white masters were ever on guard against the reemergence of African religious patterns and stamped them out wherever they were found for fear their continuance would lead to revolts.

We do know, however, that in times of crises men tend to revert to their past and anchor their moorings there. It is not surprising, then, that before America heard of the Black Muslims, a goodly number of similar religious cults had previously paved the way. There was the Prophet F. S. Cherry, who formed the Black Jews on the belief that Jesus Christ was a black man and that the "so-called" Jews were impostors. Prophet Cherry taught that black people were the first inhabitants of the earth, that God and his prophet Jacob are black, that the Talmud is the authority of Black Jews, and that their task was to become leaders in society as proof of their superiority.

Another example of this never-completely-severed tie from African religion in the American environment is the Moorish Science Temple of America. The founder of this religious body was Timothy Drew, born in 1886 in North Carolina. Somehow he came upon writings from the religions of the East and created out of his knowledge of the Holy Koran the Moorish Holy Temple of Science. Drew was certain that wholeness for blacks in this country could come about only through the rediscovery of their native origin, religious practices, and the renaming of themselves as Moors. He changed his name to Noble Drew Ali and became the leader of hundreds of blacks. These Moors formed an aggressive cult fashioned out of Islam, with a star and crescent as their banner for unity under Allah. Their basic teachings were love, truth, peace, freedom, and justice, the latter two becoming dominant. In fact, the group became extraordinarily aggressive and hostile toward whites who did not respect them as men and women of Allah. The movement was thwarted when one of the leaders was killed and Noble Drew Ali was apparently falsely arrested for the death. Noble Drew Ali died under mysterious circumstances, and the Moors split up into a variety of independent cults. It is worth noting that Jesus was an important but not dominant figure in this cult. Noble Drew Ali was Allah's main prophet, sent to lead blacks out of their darkness and to return them to the great Empire of Egypt. Blacks were to rename themselves Moorish-Americans since the term Negro meant death, and colored meant something painted. January 5 became the date for Christmas, a celebration of the anniversary of Noble Drew Ali's reincarnation. Rituals were adhered to, such as greeting the fellow members with "Peace" or "Islam," and disciplines such as being forbidden to eat meat and eggs, drink intoxicating liquors, or straighten hair were developed.

The emergence of these groups does not document the assertions of Du Bois, but they do reveal the persistent need among the black masses to express their blackness and identify with it through religious organizations. Of course, the number of blacks who do so respond are in the minority, but their presence throughout the centuries is indicative of a real need. For the most part, this identification with the African past and blackness through religious mediums has taken the form of non-Christian religion.

The new perspective of what it means to be black in the crisis of our time has taken an extraordinarily interesting direction within one congregation. The Reverend Mr. Al Cleage, Jr., Minister of the Central United Church of Christ in Detroit, has been deeply influenced by Black Power:

> It was impossible in the past for black people to think of Jesus as black, because they hated themselves and their color. But now it is becoming impossible for black people to worship a white Jesus, and historically they are right. Jesus definitely was non-white, and the whole teaching of the New Testament deals with a non-white nation's struggle for power against a white colonial oppressor, the Romans. Now it is for us to evolve a theology and a black church that speaks to black people in this twentieth century, and that is what we are evolving here.[10]

Mr. Cleage had declared himself a black nationalist Christian minister. In so doing, he removed the images of Jesus as a blue-eyed white in his church as well as expressions of the white Madonna and replaced them with a black Jesus and a black Madonna.* We are told that the response was immediate and overwhelming; the average attendance of fifty increased to nine hundred in a few short weeks. Whether or not he preaches a new doctrine of separatism or merely sets forth a new separatist strategy is difficult to determine:

> I don't have to work for separation. The white man has done too good a job. I was separated from the day I was born. Every area of my life has been separate. Church? I always went to a black church. They were acting white but it was a black church. Essentially all the people I know are black.
>
> You can't ask me if I'm advocating separation. I don't know anything else. I know all about separation. But I didn't do it. I just inherited it.[11]

Mr. Cleage believes in blackness as the basis of black identity:

> Black consciousness. Black pride. The search for black identity. This is a people seeking mental health. We've been sick a long time. We lost our identity when we were brought to this country as slaves. We were told we were inferior.

* See Albert B. Cleage, Jr., *The Black Messiah* (New York: Sheed and Ward, 1968).

They cut us off from each other and from our African traditions.[12]

His church is attended by professionals and ADC mothers and black militants. With respect to black militants, he told an interviewer this:

Yes, we welcome black militants. By militants I presume you mean black people who are tired of oppression and who have given up on the assumption that you can talk white people into changing. Those black militants who are committed to change and who want to do something about it—activists—we welcome them. And Central is about the only church in Detroit where respectable black militants can come without shame.[13]

With respect to violence, he does not advocate it, or preach it, or condone it:

I think any black person—militant or non-militant—except the extreme Uncle Tom (and there aren't many of them left)—is ready for violence if it is necessary. Just like any white person is ready for violence if it is necessary.[14]

On the occasion of the death of Dr. Martin Luther King, Jr., Mr. Cleage declared that he was not a disciple of nonviolence or of Dr. King's movement, yet held him in the highest regard. There is in his statement a respect for the preparatory work of both Dr. King and Malcolm X, a kind of acceptance of the revolutionary dimension of Black Power:

Nobody would have listened to Brother Malcolm if Dr. King had not created the situations in which we began to learn that we could FIGHT and that we could WIN. Our victories did not consist of the pitiful little civil rights which we won but the changes which took place in us as we struggled.

This was Dr. King's basic contribution. Even as he was saying "We Shall Overcome" and "I Have a Dream," he was systematically destroying all our myths and dreams about the goodness and invincibility of the white man. . . .

> Every little prod, every fire hose, every jail, every violent cruelty inflicted upon us by white people revealed to us the real nature of the enemy we face. Now the final violence of Dr. King's murder has severed the last link in the chain of illusions which bound us in second-class citizenship.
>
> Dr. King laid the foundation for the emerging Black Nation. White people will never admit it but they created the Moses who led us out of bondage and pointed us in the direction of the Promised Land.[15]

We have yet to see just how Mr. Cleage will develop the theology he promises is being worked out in his church. So far, the rhetoric of the Black Power movement is accepted, the forms of worship and preaching influenced, but no new substantial theological depths have been mined. A good deal of what he says and does has been finely worked out in earlier contexts by non-Christian blacks who were nationalists. He is not to be ignored—because he is trying to find a way to express black consciousness in a Christian context, for which we have few if any historical precedents.

The Reverend Mr. Archie L. Rich, Minister, Berea United Methodist Church in Detroit, is a very young and dedicated pastor who, in response to the riots and the troubles of black people, has gone to Black Power in his ministry. He sees the riots as rebellions in response to the subtle lawlessness of which the ghetto residents are victims. Therefore he reaches this conclusion:

> The revolt must continue, and we as Christians must become a vital and active part of it, not as looters, burners, and snipers, but as persons dedicated to the Christian concept of fullness of life for all men. Our dedication to this cause must have priority over our own personal comfort and security. We must plunge into this struggle without delay, and the plunge must go far deeper than it has in the past.[16]

He sets forth the task of white Christians to be the correcting of the system of racism which excludes blacks from the mainstream of the society by "changing attitudes that feed the system." He warns:

> If this is not done, the dreadful next step will be violent revolution.[17]

Mr. Rich seeks no wider war and suggests ways it can be prevented by the black middle-class, churchgoing Christians becoming participants rather than mere spectators in the struggle, for it is as much their own as that of those cast lowest in the caste of racism:

> Churches in the Negro community must take a greater concern in the day-to-day needs of persons in the neighborhoods. We must give peaceful but firm articulation to the needs and problems that face all of us who live in the community. Middle-class Negroes must not become so delighted over the crumbs that are thrown down to them that they ignore their black brothers who have been denied even the crumbs. Neither must middle-class Negroes allow themselves to become brainwashed into thinking they have received the whole loaf, when in reality all they have gotten are crumbs.[18]

Mr. Rich sees his role as being an activist amidst the religious community, which in his judgment has been too aloof from struggle. He accepts all of the Black Power forces for pluralism as the means for the black community to unite and achieve "the great American dream or the potential of America's demise." He is not sure which it will be, but he is at work for the one hope. Nevertheless, we are not led to see how the churches are more than another instrument captivated by Black Power. What do churchmen bring to the movement besides their commitment, their buildings, their organization, their energies? That is, what is their theological contribution?

Some theological explorations are set forth by the Reverend Mr. Leon Watts, Area Program Counselor for the New York City Presbytery. In an article entitled "A Modern Black Looks at His Outdated Church," Mr. Watts states that black Pietism manifests itself as the idolization of the outrageous.

> Its adherent seeks to point toward the pervasive dishonesty of the professional Christian by showing himself to be a brutally frank, cursing, swearing priest. In his attempts to say to the world that "I am first a human being with all of the emotions, frustrations, anxieties of any other human being," his honesty becomes at once outrageous and dishonest. Placing himself in such a position, he is compelled to overact. The white churchman is not satisfied with any mediocre playing of the role which he has cast for the black churchman. This does not meet the white man's needs. Therefore the game becomes; "How bad can I appear to be?", "How many nasty things can I say?", "How salacious can I be?" and finally, "How can I lose my own integrity?" For ultimately such a black man ceases to be himself. For this is what *they* want. It must be given. Not only for their satisfaction, but for mine as well. And he, like his white brother, goes back to his community to business as usual—melting away before his own congregation.
>
> Another aspect of the black Pietism is expressed in an over-emphasis upon his blackness. It says to the world, "See, how black I am." "See, I celebrate my blackness." And this may very well be necessary. For even the church has made the world feel that there is something ominous, unhealthy, sinful about blackness. The black man in times past, because of this feeling, tried to be as white as he could. The more white he was, the better his acceptance among white as well as black. Often, in changing directions, it is necessary to move to the other extreme. But black men must not resort to the worship of black skin as white men worship white skin.[19]

Mr. Watts espouses the Black Power call to self-identity and dignity, but as to separation, it is a necessary transition:

> I only perceive separation as an interim strategy whereby the black community gains power, integrity and self-identification. The white liberal's task at this point in history is in his own community. . . . To be the white nigger not in SNCC or CORE but in the Rotary or Kiwanis.

> It is his responsibility to hear the word, see the judgment and catch the vision of the resurrection; to use his resources in the black community through black men and to allow black men the privilege of being. For power is all about the ability to be.[20]

In these theological fragments, Mr. Watts comes close to agreeing with Tom Wicker's judgment:

> Black power theorists believe that the black church, which has been let alone to thrive and grow in its own way, is as a result the strongest of all black institutions. . . .[21]

The Reverend Mr. Henry H. Mitchell, Minister of Calvary Baptist Church, Santa Monica, California, is in sympathy with Black Power and Malcolm X. He sees in it a new opportunity for integration to gain positive meaning. For this to be so, integration "will have to be redefined to denote completely unrestricted acceptance for black people." For another thing, integration will have

> to be absolutely two-way, but the emphasis will have to be on the white-to-black phase. To compensate for the generations of brainwashing the Negro has undergone and to validate the equality of identities and cultures in a dramatic way, the white man will have to become integrated into black culture. . . .
>
> A second demand of the new integration is that the white man shall go to the other side of the two-way street to *receive,* just as the Negro has done when he has joined the whites. He must not patronize; he must see that the black church has something he needs. . . .
>
> A third demand contradicts the clever dictum of Martin Luther King, Jr.: "I don't want to be your brother-in-law, just your brother." This is a bald evasion, as legislators from the south have always known. If you are not willing to be both brother-(or sister-)in-law *and* brother (or sister), just forget the whole idea of a raceless church. Acceptance of black folk must be totally without reservation, and commitment to the cause so complete, as to out-

weigh all rejections by the white peer group. This is not to say that most blacks want intermarriage, but simply that any reservations at this point sour all efforts toward integration. They must be eradicated by whatever long or short, painful or painless process we can devise.

> The final demand is that we seek to spread and even to universalize the practice of multi-cultural and multi-identity approaches. . . . The white ego can't imagine that he should *be* black in the manner that he has required the black man to *be* white.[22]

It is Mr. Mitchell's position that the task of the Church in the face of Black Power is to increase efforts to bring whites to an intelligent and honest acceptance of blacks in eating, actions, interests, and worship. In a word, it is to take the white tradition and to stretch whites to the point of power, which is blackness. Blacks are to find acceptance in white structures, and whites identity in black structures toward the goal of a "raceless, classless, but colorful" church. Thus, among some theologians Black Power is co-opted to further integration on this side of the change Black Power calls for in the society. The message such a theological position contains for black masses is spurious at worst, ambiguous at best.

Vincent Harding, who heads the Department of History and Social Science at Spelman College in Atlanta, has grasped some of the basics for a Black Power theology in his article, "Black Power and the American Christ." It is his conviction that "there is a strong and causative link between Black Power and American Christianity." [23] He points to the experience of Christ and the response of white Christians and concludes that ambivalence between Black Power and Christianity is not a new situation for black Americans:

> When we leaped from the decks to be seized by sharks we saw his name carved on the ship's solid sides. When our women were raped in the cabins they must have noticed the great and holy books on the shelves. Our introduction to this Christ was not propitious. And the horrors continued on America's soil. So all through the nation's history many

> black men have rejected this Christ—indeed the miracle is that so many accepted him. In past times our disdain often had to be stifled and sullen, our anger silent and self-destructive. But now we speak out. Our anger is no longer silent; it has leaped onto the public stage, and demands to be seen and dealt with—a far more healthy state of affairs for all concerned.[24]

It follows then that Mr. Harding perceives the involvement of this "American Christ and his followers" in the emergence of Black Power, and therefore God is both alive and just:

> May he not be attempting to break through to us with at least as much urgency as we once sensed at the height of the good old "We Shall Overcome" days? Perhaps he is writing on the wall, saying that we Christians, black and white, must choose between death with the American Christ and life with the Suffering Servant of God. Who dares deny that God may have chosen once again the black sufferers for a new assault on the hard shell of indifference and fear that encases so many Americans.[25]

Here we have some fundamental theological rudiments of Black Power as pluralism, but are they elements of a Black Power theology of revolution? Black Power is the embracing of Black identity; it is a return to and a search for roots; it is unity of blacks; it is the renouncing of the "American Christ" insofar as his followers are paternalistic, condescending, engaged in keeping blacks separate, poor, illiterate, intimidated, and restricted. The call to humility by white Christians and their attempts to put down the responsive rage of black youth in the name of love, as well as sending them off to war without providing them with equal employment at home, leads to a rejection of Jesus by these black youth:

> Their rage cries out: "Give us no pink, two-faced Jesus who counsels love for you and flaming death for the children of Vietnam. Give us not a blood-sucking savior who condemns brick-throwing rioters and praises dive-bombing killers. That Christ stinks. We want no black men to follow

> in *his* steps. Stop forcing our poor black boys into your legions of shame. We will not go."
>
> "If we must fight," they say, "let it be on the streets where we have been humiliated. If we must burn down houses, let them be the homes and stores of our exploiters. If we must kill, let it be the fat, pious white Christians who guard their lawns and their daughters while engineering slow death for us. If we must die, let it be for a real cause of black men's freedom as black men define it. And may all the white elders die well in the causes they defend." This is Black Power—the response to the American Christ.[26]

From Mr. Harding's perspective, this response is not blasphemous. The blasphemy is that of black and white Christians who take in vain the name of Christ and lead others to perceive only a phony Lord. The judgment is not on the heads of Black Power advocates primarily then, but upon Christians:

> This may be God's message for the church—through Black Power. It is a message for all who claim to love the Lord of the church. If this reading is accurate, our tears over the demise of the civil rights movement may really be tears over the smashing of an image we created or the withdrawal of a sign we were no longer heeding. Therefore if we weep, let it not be for the sins of SNCC and CORE but for our own unfaithfulness and for our country's blasphemy. And let us begin to pray that time may be granted to us to turn from blond dolls to the living, revolutionary Lord who proclaimed that the first shall be last and the last, first.
>
> If this message can break the grip of self-pity and nostalgia on us, the power of blackness may yet become the power of light and resurrection for us all. Has it not been said that God moves in mysterious ways his wonders to perform? I can conceive of nothing more wonderful and mysterious than that the blackness of my captive people should become a gift of light for this undeserving nation—even a source of hope for a world that lives daily under the threat of white America's arrogant and bloody power. Is that too much to hope for? Or is the time for hoping now past? We

> may soon discover whether we have been watching a wall or a curtain—or both.[27]

The threat Black Power holds for us all is very clear in Mr. Harding's writing, but the impression is unshakable that for him it is only a threat. In his very excellent article on "The Religion of Black Power," he turns to phenomenology to elucidate the connections between the two subjects of his work. Black Power for him is the new man, the new community, the new messianism, new glory, new power—but it is not revolution. He approves of Black Power's squarely facing evil racism in America and calls for new experiments for hope, but hope which is also prepared for defeat:

> For if racism rages as deep into American life as it appears and if violence is its closest brother, then a black revolution will no more solve the problem than a civil war did (even if Rap Brown gets his atomic bomb). So it may be most responsible to ask if it is more than despair to speak of a long, grueling battle with no victory—and no illusions—this side of the grave. Has it been important and necessary simply to learn that there are no large citizen armies of white deliverers? Was it not absolutely necessary that all trust in courts and troops and presidents be shattered? Is this part of a black coming of age, a coming which eventually reveals that even the black God of the ghetto is dead? [28]

Black Power examined phenomenologically instead of theologically is descriptive and clarifying; it does not give the black theologian a theology, but it does provide a direction in which to hammer one out. Mr. Harding comes up to the edge of Black Power as revolution and then backs away, failing or fearing to see the holocaust as a final plunge of cleansing action. Nonviolence for him is still a faith; it alone is the hard reality. Black Power is thus heading for the "Beloved Community" of black and white together without real revolution, "but it probably needs some new and stripped-down coming of Martin King's most fervent hopes to accompany its path." [29] Black Power does not here become radical theology; it does not go to the roots of Black Power and its meaning for black theologians. What does occur is that Black Power is co-opted in the hope of some very general religion, which is extremely suggestive, but equally frustrating because it cannot choose between tender-mindedness and tough-mindedness. The result is a dilemma in which neither horn is fully grasped.

The clearest prophetic or theological statement produced to date on Black Power has been set down by my colleague who taught religion at Adrian College, a few miles down the road from where I am writing, presently at Union Seminary in New York, the Reverend Dr. James H. Cone.* He is explicit in his purpose, "to examine the concept of Black Power and its relationship to Christianity and the Church." [29] In the best prophetic tradition, he does not back off from the subject or merely encircle it with intriguing, but finally empty, hypotheses:

> It is my thesis, however, that Black Power, even in its most radical expression, is not an antithesis of Christianity, nor is it a heretical idea to be tolerated with painful forbearance. It is rather Christ's central message to 20th Century America. And unless the empirical denominational Church makes a determined effort to recapture the Man Jesus through a total identification with the suffering poor as expressed in Black Power, that Church will become exactly what Christ is not.[30]

Professor Cone asserts that nothing less than the Church's faithfulness to its Lord is at stake, whether or not it launches a "vehement attack on the evils of racism in all forms." This is dangerous, given the complexity of man as portrayed in the doctrine of sin or pride, but "obedience to Christ is always costly." In a word:

> The time has come for the Church to challenge the power-structure with the power of the *Gospel* knowing that nothing less than *immediate* and *total* emancipation of all people is consistent with the message and style of Jesus Christ. The Church cannot afford to deplore the means which op-

* See James H. Cone, *Black Power and Black Theology* (New York: Seabury Press, 1969).

> pressed people use to break the chains of slavery because such language not only clouds the issue but also gives comfort and assistance to the oppressor.[31]

There is here a clear appeal to the gospel—a commitment without reservation is demanded—and an indication that even the radical approaches are to be upheld. This latter point is made even stronger, for Mr. Cone nearly takes the root meaning of Black Power seriously:

> Unfortunately, many well-intentioned persons have insisted that there must be another approach, one which will not cause so much hostility, not to mention rebellion. . . . These men argue that if progress is made, it will be through a careful, *rational* approach to the subject. . . . Black Power, in this respect, is by nature "irrational," i.e., not denying the role of rational reflection, but insisting that human existence cannot be mechanized or put into neat boxes according to reason. Human reason, though valuable, is not absolute, because moral decisions—those decisions which deal with human dignity—cannot be made by using the *abstract* methods of science. Human emotions must be reckoned with. Consequently, black people must say "No!" to all do-gooders who insist that they need more time. If such persons really knew oppression—knew it existentially in their guts—they would not be confused or disturbed by black rebellion, but would join black people in their fight for freedom and dignity.[32]

Mr. Cone puts forth Black Power as a kind of holy impatience with accommodation, injustice, inequality, and even love. This means the black man

> will protest, violently if need be, in the interest of absolute emancipation. Now! Whenever one group breaks the human covenant of mutual respect for human freedom, the seeds of rebellion are implicit in that act.[33]

Here the voice of the prophet is unmistakable; there is no attempt at cleverness or obscurantism which seeks a public, but the kind of forthtelling or prophetic "telling it like it is" which is always the mark of the prophet. The prophet is always the least acceptable because he is understood, he is the man who can hurt and therefore becomes the man to hurt:

> When we make Jesus' message contemporaneous with our life situation, his message is clear enough. The message of Black Power is the message of Christ himself. To be sure, that statement is both politically and religiously dangerous. It is so politically because Black Power threatens the very structure of the American way of life. It is theologically dangerous because it may appear to overlook what Karl Barth has called "the infinite qualitative distinction between God and man." But if Luther's statement, "we are Christ to the neighbor" is to be taken seriously, and, if we can believe the New Testament witness which proclaims Jesus as resurrected and thus active even now in the midst of human misery, then he must be alive in men who are where the action is. If the Gospel is a gospel of liberation for the oppressed, then Jesus is where the oppressed are—proclaiming release to the captives and looking askance at those Christians who silently consent to their discomfiture. If Jesus is *not* in the ghetto, if he is not where men are living at the edge of existence, if he is somehow ensconced in the split-level hypocrisy of suburbia, then the Gospel is a prevarication and Christianity is a mistake. Christianity cannot be alien to Black Power; it *is* Black Power! [34]

In these standpoints of black theologians, there is evidence of a variety of perspectives and many attempts at a theology of Black Power. To date, no one has come forth with a full statement about the theological implications of radical Black Power, perhaps because no one has yet completely given up on pluralism, or better still, no one has seen beyond Black Power as pluralism to its fruition in revolution. The Reverend Dr. Nathan Wright, Jr.'s, *Black Power and Urban Unrest* deals with every facet of this movement except its theological significance for black theologians and churches:

> Black Power, in its simplest terms, speaks to the nature of humanity. The greatest problem before the churches, and

> before every institution in our world, is some form of the human problem. What is the human goal? Toward what end should every aspect of human life be directed? The answer given by the current impetus toward Black Power is the one word fulfillment.[35]

The newfound activism among black churchmen and churches as signaled in Dr. Wright is real and vital, but from whence cometh the power for critical evaluation and strength to move ahead? Historically, this has been the function of theology even among the most radical church movements, for example, "the social gospel." The greatest opportunity for black theologians and churches is Black Power. So far, Black Power, which took its cohesive form outside the Church, has contributed vastly to the Church with very little return in kind.

The nearly universal defense of Black Power, through one interpretation or another, by black religious leaders is proof of the impact it has made. The black church has always been the fundamental expression of the black community. As goes the black community, so goes the black church. When the black community changes, the black church will change. The solidarity behind the black church is indisputable and inscrutable. No other institution and no other organizational leaders in the black community are subject to such constant criticism and constant favor. The black church is the black community in all of its complexity. The black church as the organ of the black community has been prevented from unity by competition among the various classes, denominations, status symbols, educational attainments, and life-styles. This has resulted in the black church's being atomistic and highly individualistic in its various expressions, and unable to form a singular organization of commitment to action amidst diversity. Black Power is at bottom a move to unite the *lumpenproletariat* in appeal without deference to the churches. The overpopulation of black churches is a witness to the enthusiasm for religion among black folk, a religion which is basically a center of belonging, but it is rivaled by policy stations and other nonreligious ways of life. The push of Black Power has awakened blacks at every level; the result has been an overwhelming response from black churches and churchmen. The significance of this is that the black churches have been a potential power organization. Black churches have the masses organized and therefore could line up the black masses behind a program if they were of such a single mind. The fact that the black churches have not united into an organization for collective power, but have rather been passive in the sphere of power as an instrument to raise the position of blacks, is one very clear difference between black and white churches. In this century, the black churches have been the heart of the black community inasmuch as the churches are places where black people can have "a good time." The fact that church news is no longer central to the pages of black newspapers does not mean black churches are on the way out; it does raise questions about the black church as a power institution.

The *rapprochement* of Black Power and black churches indicates an awareness on the part of Black Power advocates of the real potential of black churches, and the reverse is equally true. The churches, as places where respectable black people have a good time and as refuges from exclusion amidst the daily mainstream of life, were in the process of slippage prior to the call of Black Power. In turning support to Black Power, there may be more than just a methodical attempt to stay next to the people and be their expression; black churches may be about uniting from top to bottom, from class to class, across denominational lines, into a union of real power from the grass roots up. If black churches turn their potential power into real power, they will do more than keep alive the consciousness that oppression is evil and the hope that a good life is in the plan of the just God. Real power will then face the reality of the need for new structures. A real solution for black people can come only through new structures of political, social, and economic life. Beyond the task of mobilization, the churches must contribute the theological, spiritual, and moral resources without which success is not possible. If these very radical changes in the structures and systems are forthcoming, theological resources will be essential to detrack Black Power from its headlong race to revolution. If these root changes are not forthcoming, theological resources will be necessary to give the revolution direction and bring order and justice out of the chaos. In either event, a theology of revolution is indispensable. It is not enough for churchmen to be engineers of social progress; there are others equally adept, and perhaps more so, in these special fields calling for technical competence. There is no other source for strength and insight of theological revolutionaries. If black theologians line up with Black Power as pluralism and selectively accept or reject certain of its ideas and leaders, and it fails, will black people be left without hope, without vision, without resolve?

Theology begins and ends with the affirmation that man's origin and destiny transcend human existence. Theology lives the task of giving meaning to the human condition out of this affirmation. The work of theology is the enrichment of human existence in that period between birth and death where man alone is responsible for the quality of personal and interpersonal living. Theology is concerned with the deepest relations, the deepest concerns, the deepest apprehensions of all men, none of which is arbitrarily ruled out on the grounds of social or political or economic or practical realism. Theology asks fundamental questions and questions every fundamental of the human condition. The necessity of questioning provides the possibility for radical criticism and radical newness. Black Power's theological radicalism springs from the drive of black Americans to call into question the power structures of the Western culture and system. Theologically, Black Power is a set of variations on several themes within black consciousness and unity. Its task is to reveal the reality of the world amidst a revolution of color, to reveal realistically the meaning of self-identity and possibility of self-determination, to reveal how black people are related to the world of America and the larger world, and to reveal how the world can be changed in light of a just God.

The task of the black theologian is to be clear, open, and fluid about his maturing perceptions of himself, his God, and his world. With respect to black people, he is concerned with the individual's understanding of God and of his actions in the world. His primary task, however, is to clarify and motivate a people to become God's people within the context of his time, and the present time is dominated by Black Power. Black Power perceives American life as racist, counterrevolutionary, antihuman, pro-property, imperialistic, and militaristic. These are indeed ethical questions, and theology is more than ethics, living the truth, but not much more. The theological response begins with the conviction that the correct perception of Black Power about this society means that the society directly contradicts what black Americans hold to be the truth about God, man, and community. Where the grace of God is thwarted, the grace or power of God is present in the demand for integrity, authenticity, newness, and confrontation on the way to reconciliation. This means that grace is a gift of God, and such power is not ruled out of revolution. If revolution is Black Power, the total energies now given by black theologians and religious organizations to the movement without a theological understanding lead to the conclusion that either Black Power is not about revolution or that black theologians are not about Black Power, that is, revolution.

Have black theologians and churches become so drunk with the new wine of Black Power that it leaves them busily, dizzily shoring up the old way of life instead of building anew? Perhaps they do not feel the need of taking seriously the statement of James Baldwin at the Fourth Assembly of the World Council of Churches because they believe it was not directed to them:

> If you are born under the circumstances in which black people are born, the destruction of the Christian churches may not only be desirable but necessary.[36]

Their hope may be that the Christian church still has the power to transform America, or other areas of the world for that matter, with a conviction comparable to Mr. Baldwin's:

> I believe that the Christian church still has power to reform the Government of South Africa and to stop my Government from dropping bombs in Southeast Asia.[37]

Such a position is more an appeal to conscience than a statement of hope. The suspicion of black theologians' intentions vis-à-vis Black Power remains, basically because they do not take the revolution seriously enough. Samuel L. Parmar, an Indian economist and a member of the Church of North India, has pointed out that the very quest for justice creates disorder, for order camouflages injustice:

> If we believe in progress and development, let us not flinch at disorder or instability.[38]

In fact, he said, "disorder and revolution are the new name for peace":

> Our task is to imbue the revolutionary movements of our time with creativity and divest them of their anarchic content.[39]

There is a growing tendency of conservatism in America and a growing neo-isolationism in the world:

> We are also beginning to realize that if the West and the East come together, as they seem to be doing, they could maintain their economic prosperity, technological superiority and military strength completely independently of the "third world." [40]

If "have" nations or classes of the world have not "willingly given up any of their privileges" in the past, what leads black theologians to hold that this can be done in America outside of revolution? Could it be that the black church as the heart of the black community is a fact of the past and not of the present and the future? Could it be that Black Power is turned to as a means of attracting the youth without which the black church cannot have social usefulness? Could it be that Black Power is really co-opted because it is the authentic spirit of black people, the archenemy of black religion, and therefore its archrival, which can only be reckoned with by taking it over through taking it in? James Baldwin does not suspect black churches so much as he holds a different view of their importance from that of black theologians. In an interview in *Esquire* of July, 1968, Mr. Baldwin evaluated the black church in terms of social progress:

> You must consider that the fact that we have a black church is, first of all, an indictment of a Christian nation. There shouldn't be a black church. And that's again what you did. We've used it. Martin Luther King used it most brilliantly, you know. That was his forum. It's always been our only forum. But it doesn't exist anywhere in the North anymore, as Martin Luther King himself discovered. It

> exists in the South, because the black community in the South is a different community. There's still a Negro family in the South, or there was. There is no Negro family essentially in the North, and once you have no family you have no church. And that means you have no forum. It cannot be used in Chicago and Detroit. It can be used in Atlanta and Montgomery and those places. And now since Martin is dead—not before, but certainly since he is dead—that forum is no longer useful because people are repudiating their Christian church in toto. . . .
>
> Let me rephrase it. It does not attract the young. Once that has happened to any organization, its social usefulness is at least debatable. Now that's one of the great understatements of the century.[41]

Black theologians could not disagree more. They are convinced by Black Power that their institutions are essential. As a consequence, neither the revolutionary depths of Samuel L. Parmar nor the criticisms of James Baldwin are reflected in the response of black churchmen to Black Power.

BLACK CHRISTIAN ORGANIZATIONS AND BLACK POWER

In the face of powerless love and loveless power, black theologians have organized behind Black Power in the search for power and freedom, power and love, power and justice, and power and truth. The National Committee of Negro Churchmen wrote a defense of Black Power in a widely circulated statement which took up a full page in the *New York Times* on July 31, 1966. This conciliatory and reconciling message was a call to cooperation among all people in the drive of black people for organizational power. In a direct appeal to black people to get themselves together, or in the words of the statement, "be reconciled to ourselves to recognize the resources we already have and upon which we can build," the chord was struck for pluralism without any doubt about its attainment. The unshakable confidence in black institutions, not the least of which is the church, is clear:

> "Black power" is already present to some extent in the Negro church, in Negro fraternities and sororities, in our professional associations, and in the opportunities afforded to Negroes who make decisions in some of the integrated organizations.
>
> We understand the reasons by which these limited forms of "black power" have been rejected by some of our people. Too often the Negro church has stirred its members away from the reign of God in *this world* to a distorted and complacent view of *an other worldly* conception of God's power. We commit ourselves as churchmen to make more meaningful in the life of our institution our conviction that Jesus Christ reigns in the "here" and "now" as well as in the future he brings in upon us. We shall, therefore, use more of the resources of our churches in working for human justice in the places of social change and upheaval where our Master is already at work.[42]

This same kind of response is called for among black social and professional organizations, a clear indication of the middle-class dominance and perspective of these churchmen with little regard for, if not suspicion of, the black masses as leaders with power as well as resources—at least this is the case from the perspective of Black Power which begins among the masses. Power is needed "to participate more effectively at all levels of the life of our nation," thus it is necessary "to be reconciled with the white majority" on "the firm ground that we and all other Americans *are* one." Instead of "ill-tempered explosions without meaningful goals,"

> we must work with the remainder of the nation to organize whole cities for the task of making the rebuilding of our cities first priority in the use of resources. . . . We must move from the politics of philanthropy to the politics of metropolitan development for equal opportunity. We must relate all groups of the city together in new ways in order that the truth of our cities might be laid bare and in order that, together, we can lay claim to the great resources of our nation to make truth more human.[43]

On November 3, 1966, the National Committee of Negro Churchmen made a statement on "Racism and the Elections," which was less conciliatory, in response to the backlash threat of that election year:

> Let us try to be very clear about one thing, America. Black Americans are determined to have all of their full human and constitutional rights. We will not cease to agitate this issue with every means available to men of faith and dignity until justice is done. . . .
>
> We submit that the resolution of the crisis which is upon us requires a change in the nation's priorities. The welfare and dignity of all Americans is more important than the priorities being given to military expansion, space exploration or the production of supersonic jet airliners. To this end, we of the Negro church call for a massive mobilization of the resources in the Negro community in order to give leadership in the fulfillment not only of our own destiny but in order to help produce a more sane white America. . . .
>
> Again, we say: America is at the crossroad. Either we become the democracy we can become, or we tread the path to self-destruction.[44]

The Committee sees clearly the possibility of revolution, but has yet to come up with a statement calling for direction in the light of this possible eventuality. Instead, it concentrates on the pluralistic contribution it can make. The Board of Directors, meeting in Chicago on April 5, 1968, declared their

> conviction that the black church is the most viable and durable institution in the central cities of most of the major metropolitan areas of the nation.
>
> We believe it would be a tragic mistake for predominantly white denominations to choose to bypass this institution in an effort to relate to and invest in urban ghettoes. The black church has a physical presence and a constituency already organized in these communities. It is available as a means by which the whole Christian community can deal

substantively and effectively with the urban crisis, the sickness of body and spirit which we see in the metropolitan centers of America today.

> We, therefore, call upon the white churches and churchmen to take with utmost seriousness the black church as the only, though imperfect, link with inner city life for the mission of the church and we insist that the mission structure of the national denominations must identify with and be led by the black churches if their efforts are to have either credibility or reality.[45]

This unmistakable riding of the coattails of Black Power flies in the face of the judgment placed on these institutions by James Baldwin. It is an interesting fact that Black Power has emphasized the organization of black economics among black people on their own and encouraged black people to stand on their own two feet. Black churchmen here call for the channeling of white resources into the hands of black churchmen

> so that the rich potential of the black churches can be fulfilled with the excellent by-products of mutual respect, comradeship and ecumenical development resulting therefrom.[46]

In return for the financial support of white churches and their mission in the ghetto under the direct control of black churches, there is no call for mobilization of black resources but a defense for the plea:

> Because of the depressed economic situation in most black communities the black church has seldom been adequately staffed to perform its task of Christian education and mission. Accordingly, priority must be given to providing the necessary staff, financial resources, equipment and property, educational materials and instrumentalities for use among black people. Both black and white denominations should reorder priorities and reallocate their resources toward these ends.[47]

This is a very new and very bold move, but is it Black Power co-opted? In effect, black churchmen are asking white churchmen to support them in keeping and improving black institutions for black people on the Black Power assumption that only black people can work effectively with black people. It is a serious question. Will such a move increase the standing of black churches among black people via a strong purse and return the youth to this institution, or will it do the job of remolding the urban ghetto? How will such a move differ from the results of the National Urban League with all of its millions from corporations and its recognition that the old way of doing things is no longer good enough? Black churchmen are convinced the job can be done, and so they propose, in return for support, a new style of black churchmanship. The real question is, can the National Committee of Negro Churchmen pull off "this new style of mission" among black churchmen? Perhaps the revitalization of the black church will ultimately serve as a conservative force against the revolutionary dynamic of Black Power, although it might be the best preparation of black churchmen for the revolution. Does a revitalized black church on the basis of Black Power's momentum mean it has captivated Black Power for its own interests, that it is in tune with Black Power, or that Black Power has captivated it? One thing is clear; in return for economic support, the black churchmen speak not of their commitment to radical change or revolution, but to renewal. In church circles renewal has become the conservative word best embodied by the Roman Catholic Church, which opposes the idea of revolution; it does not need to change; it only needs to put in modern form its old ways that have been so successful. The renewal promised by black churchmen in return for financial support is one of mission, and the issue is whether this mission is for the church or for black people:

> The renewal and enhancement of the black church in terms of its liturgical life, its theological interpretation, its understanding of its mission to itself, to the white church and to the nation.
>
> The development of the black church, not only as a religious fellowship, but as a community organization, in the technical sense of that term, which uses its resources, influence and manpower to address the problems of estrange-

ment, resignation and powerlessness in the political, cultural and economic life of the black community.

The projection of a new quality of church life which would equip and strengthen the church as custodian and interpreter of that cultural heritage which is rooted in the peculiar experience of black people in the United States and the faith that has sustained them for over two centuries on these shores.

The contribution of the black church, out of its experience of suffering and the yearning for freedom, of that quality of faith, hope and love which can activate, empower, renew and unite the whole Church of Christ.[48]

If the black churchmen and theologians remain suspect vis-à-vis their intention and that of Black Power, it is because the institutional mileage gained out of Black Power takes a different turning than that which dominated the 1967 National Conference on Black Power in Newark, New Jersey. The Reverend Mr. Clayton E. Hammond, Minister of Whatcoat Methodist Church in Dover, Delaware, participated and reported:

The conference began to revolve on its base of black nationalism, militant radicalism, and black muslimism, which at the outset took control of the conference.[49]

Mr. Hammond came from the conference convinced that it was about "a revolution, a movement that was righteously black." Mr. Hammond is for racial integration:

Whether integration can retain its viability and value for Negro Methodists depends on how much attention, action, and momentum Black Power's separatistic goals receive and generate. Separatism is contrary to everything our integration goals stand for.

SEPARATISM is the ultraradical goal of the movement, and hopefully is the least likely to prevail. But it may be the point from which the movement will move to more reasonable and realistic pursuits. Separatism and virtually all other goals that were adopted made the conference a veritable summit meeting for rebellion. This rebellion against The Establishment would preclude the Negro's participation in the Christian dimension of the white man's world. From this position, Methodism is not only a religious "cop out," but a social anomaly as well.[50]

The Black Power Manifesto of blackness allows for less radical goals than separatism, which Mr. Hammond and presumably all others committed to the view of the National Committee of Negro Churchmen wish to capitalize upon:

> "It is evident that it is in our interest to develop and propagate a philosophy of blackness as a social, psychological, political, cultural, and economic directive." This means self-determination, dignity, cultural expressions, valuations, economic power, political structures, and also ethnic unity stand as racial challenges to every Negro. These are less radical goals than separatism, but they are radical in that they can inspire a new Negro thrust for recognition.[51]

The renewal Mr. Hammond calls for draws upon black church resources in a way that contradicts the National Committee of Negro Churchmen:

> This calls into question the way our Negro churches are utilizing the vast reservoir of resources they control in the Negro community, both human and financial. It is quite possible that the human resources could be better used for a more direct role in the Negro's "creatism" on the local and national levels. Financial resources could be pointed more toward community need. In too many cases Methodist churches represent a source of resource drain rather than a source.[52]

Mr. Hammond holds that black churches are also handicapped in Methodism because they must support the larger Church's program, and thereby ignore the immediate problems of the community. The demands of Black Power on black churches are very harsh and may not at all be about black churches' coming to life, but Mr. Hammond prefers to interpret this judgment as Black Power's "subconscious plea for Christianity to rise to its potential through the Negro church." Whatever Black Power is about, Mr. Hammond seems to be saying, let us make the most of it so that we do not lose to Methodism the low-income black masses forever:

> To avoid this, the new United Methodist Church must place itself within the struggle for the minds, souls, and allegiances of the distressed, dispossessed, disinherited Negroes who are confused and frustrated as to what their commitment should be. In many cases we will be challenging the Black Muslims, the Black Nationalists, the Communists, and all other anti-Christian movements that offer panaceas and rebellious ways out of the Negro's psychological and sociological trap.[53]

Instead of the spirit that unites, Black Power comes down to a force which must be dominated even at the expense of dividing the already fragmented black community. Is this the way black theologians tend to deal with Black Power, to strip it down? Black Power is here baldly rejected; the savior of the black community is to be the United Methodist Church. It would be difficult to conceive of the theological justification for such a strategy. To be sure, competitive Methodism has nothing to do with revolution, nothing in fact to do with Black Power. Mr. Hammond is a traditionalist, a Methodist who believes in using the church as a vehicle because it has some inherent superiority:

> Only those of us who shared in the Black Power conference can fully appreciate what it was saying to America by its extremism, its anti-Americanism, its rebellion in general and its black revolutionism in particular. It made we ministers feel as one that Christianity has its work cut out for it, because few of us want to see our people go the way the conference declared black America must go for its salvation.[54]

So, as Mr. Hammond puts it, there can be no cooperation with Black Power; a choice is to be made between Methodism and Black Power. Perhaps the churches are rightly suspect, and maybe it is clear why no theology which fully explores Black

Power has yet to surface among black churchmen committed to black churches:

> The Black Power movement, with all of its frightening pronouncements, irrational separatism, senseless negativism, racial degradation, and the Negro's cry for help, has spoken to The Methodist Church. How shall we answer? [55]

One answer has been set forth by the National Committee of Negro Churchmen. Yet, this kind of repudiation of Black Power has significance for the renewal of the church, if not of the society. The National Committee of Negro Churchmen has established a National Economic Development Corporation into which all Christian ghetto-bound funds of white denominations can be deposited:

> The basic purpose of the corporation is to provide a means by which the Negro community can more effectively participate in and control for their own self-development the vast financial resources which are being expended by the federal and state governments for community development projects including urban renewal, slum clearance, medical and health facilities, housing for the elderly and myriad of other programs and projects too numerous to be catalogued in this presentation.[56]

In September, 1967, a conference sponsored by the Division of Christian Life and Mission of the National Council of Churches met in Washington, D.C., and divided into black and white caucuses to gain strategy for effective involvement in urban affairs. The black caucus called upon the black church to commit itself to the following:

> To the establishment of freedom schools to offset the degradation and omission of a white-dominated school system.
>
> To workshops fostering Black family solidarity.
>
> To training lay leadership in community organization and other relevant skills.

To massive effort to support financially Black groups for self-determination.

To the removal of all images which suggest that God is white.

These very important developments by churchmen do not entirely remove the questions concerning their motivation. The feeling runs deep that black churchmen in all-black or integrated denominations are about the upstaging of Black Power and the running of their own show, independent of the other forces in the black community—especially the Black Power forces. Black Power simply gave black churchmen a new opportunity, but having taken its shot in the arm, black churchmen are off on their own in black caucuses.

Those of us who met with the black Methodists in Cincinnati, February 6–8, 1968, received working papers and other background data for what was initially called the National Conference of Negro Methodists, which was given its very spurious name during the conference of Black Methodists for Church Renewal. One of the working papers was entitled "The Black Methodist's Response To Black Power." The paper began:

Perhaps the greatest opportunity in this century for black Methodists and the greatest gift to white Methodists is the concept of Black Power. Through the creative and responsible application of Black Power, both white Methodists and black Methodists will begin to see themselves and each other in an entirely new perspective. In the new relationship which the dynamics of Black Power could create, there hopefully may develop a new humanity in which the special uniqueness of every man may be joyfully given and received.

The Black Revolution is a fact. It is a call for black people throughout the nation and the world to stand on their feet and declare their independence from white domination and exploitation. The mood of the day is for black people to throw off the old crippling myths of white superiority and black inferiority. The old myths are being re-

> placed by black pride, black solidarity and black self-determination.

The paper went on to suggest that in working together as black Methodists we were instrumental in bringing about the intended goal, racial inclusiveness as a working principle, and not as a future goal. To do this, we need to have power:

> If the purpose for the power we seek is to enable black people to contribute significantly to the Church, the society and the world, then we should embrace it and throw ourselves fully into the struggle. When our vigorous support of Black Power on the one hand is met by responsible white power on the other, the Methodist Church will truly become itself and may thus open the door to a glorious new age.

The high point of the conference was the session with Methodist layman Stokely Carmichael. This kind of confrontation between Black Power and black Methodists led us to believe that cooperation was possible, that black Methodists were concerned about radical change in the society through harnessing their efforts with all brothers in the black community. But it turned out that Black Methodists for Church Renewal proved a singularly apt title. The General Conference of the United Methodist Church met in April, 1968, in Dallas, Texas. As a result of the forces of black Methodists, a commission on religion and race was set up, paralleling the National Council of Churches' similar commission, with an operating budget of $700,000:

> Among its proposed functions: supervision and administration of a general church fund set up to assist mergers of predominantly white and Negro annual conferences; counseling and encouraging local churches seeking to become inclusive fellowships; cooperation with various "prophetic movements" for racial and social justice; working to assure participation by members of Negro and other minority groups "on every level of the church's life and ministry." [57]

The first Black Methodists for Church Renewal Newsletter *NOW* was overjoyed with the decisions at Dallas:

> It must be remembered that BMCR is committed to the

> renewal of the whole church, under God, that it may be one in life and ministry and structure—as well as in word. There is no question that BMCR was at work, along with other renewal agents, in paving the way for somewhat of a "God-happening" at the Uniting Conference. This conference was, indeed, confronted by change and the mandate to be a new, honest and more relevant church.[58]

We must await the developments, but one thing is certain. The initial newsletter did not carry the words "Black Power" or develop the concept on any of its eight pages. A great deal of stress was placed on renewal of the churches: "BMCR is committed, however, to new styles of renewal of the whole church." The total impression of the newsletter was that BMCR is committed to gaining positions of power for black Methodists. This is a legitimate undertaking, but it is not the objective of the new society that Black Power focuses upon. James Lawson, chairman of the BMCR, wrote:

> Cincinnati was necessary in order to say to our church that we reject tokenism. We refuse to tolerate a cheap, meaningless fellowship not rooted in Christian acceptance, dialogue, and mission. We will settle for nothing less than a church where the love of Christ rules and where a man is a man not by race, or blood, but by the will and power of God.
>
> Plainly this is a different day. Our hope is that Black Methodists for Church Renewal will soon be out of business. For years we have hungered not only for the end of the Central Jurisdiction [black Methodists segregated from whites] but for the end of segregation in all its forms—explicit or implicit. Perhaps now we can so move in obedience to God's demand that we be one in life and ministry and work and structure—as well as in word. If Cincinnati somehow enables us to see this need and to commit ourselves with courage to His task, then the conference may prove to be the most exciting and historical event in American Methodism.[59]

It is true that Methodists have made as many adjustments as, and perhaps more than, any other denomination in America. If BMCR succeeds in bringing about basic changes within Methodism, that will be miracle enough. But in this fundamental thrust to give blacks an equal partnership in Methodism and the bringing into being of a truly inclusive church, BMCR is all about integration, which is not on the agenda of Black Power. It is most difficult to determine how black Methodists can effectively cooperate with Black Power in the community, to say nothing of developing a theology. But Black Power for black Methodists may simply mean the power of blacks in Methodism, an example for the rest of the church and the society. BMCR is definitely about renewal of the church. Is this Black Power? Is this organizational adjustment Black Power theology? Will the power of blacks in Methodism increase the power of blacks in the society at large, particularly among the black masses?

The most impressive impact of Black Power on black churches was the organization in Dallas in November, 1967, of the National Committee of Negro Churchmen. Since then, nine black caucuses in predominantly white organizations have sprung up to make demands upon these institutions in a pattern similar to that of black students in mainstream institutions of higher learning. These black caucuses are the Black Methodists for Church Renewal, the Black Affairs Council (Unitarian Universalist Association), the Union of Black Clergy and Laity (the Protestant Episcopal Church), the American Baptist Convention Black Caucus, the Black Lutheran Caucus (American Lutheran Church, the United Lutheran Church, and the Missouri Synod Lutheran Church), Concerned Presbyterians (the United Presbyterian Church, U.S.A.), the Black Caucus of the Presbyterian Church in the U.S., the Black Clergy United (United Church of Christ), and the Black Caucus of the Roman Catholic Church. If these caucuses are primarily about renewal in the denominations, perhaps there can yet come forth black caucuses in black denominations primarily concerned about their relationship to Black Power and the development of Black Power theology.

Black Power erupted in the 99 percent white and liberal Unitarian Universalist Association in October, 1967, and resulted in the Black Unitarian Universalist Council's creation of a permanent Black Affairs Council with a $250,000 funding for the 1968–1969 year at the seventh General Assembly in Cleveland in June, 1968. This power move for a reordering of priorities with respect to the Association's financial involvement in black communities under largely black leadership may prove to have more of an effect within the Association than outside of it. The Union of Black Clergy and Laity of the Episcopal Church was founded in February, 1968

> to remove racism in the church and in the community by any means necessary to achieve full participation on the basis of equality in policy making, decision making, program and staffing on the parochial, diocesan and national levels.[60]

A New York metropolitan chapter was formed for more direct participation in the three-million-dollar annual budget for three years which the Episcopal General Convention allotted to combat poverty in slum areas. Specifically, the New York chapter charged that the administration of the program failed to involve or assist the black congregations "in any meaningful and relevant way." Apparently officials of the Episcopal Church deposited funds in slum-area banks across the United States with the intentions of strengthening black businesses, as well as those of other minorities, and of improving living conditions in ghetto areas. The black leaders of New York held that their congregations were not being supported in line with their expectation:

> The clergy and laity of the black congregations, in particular those who had been striving for years against injustice and discrimination in the church and in the community, expected that the new Urban Crisis Program and Fund would help them in their community efforts.[61]

Culbert G. Rutenber, Philosophy of Religion Professor at Andover Newton Theological School and President of the American Baptist Convention for 1968–1969, reported that the Annual Convention in Boston, May 29 through June 2, 1968, gave a proper response to the demands of black members. Their demands included

> (1) the right to clear all appointments to committees, boards and commissions; (2) employment of additional black administrative staff personnel; (3) creation of a new post, Associate General Secretary for Urban Ministries, to be filled by a black; (4) hiring of blacks as executives of state conventions and city societies and calling of qualified pastors irrespective of color; (5) a program to double black enrollment in Baptist schools, with enlarged financial aid to such students, and to encourage administrators to hire black faculty members; (6) a complete overhaul of the denomination's news media and employment of black staff at decision-making levels; (7) financial support of such organizations as the Southern Christian Leadership Conference and the Opportunities Industrialization Center; (8) turnover to the S.C.L.C. of all funds raised in memory of Martin Luther King, Jr.; (9) placing under black leadership all A.B.C. personnel working in black communities; (10) withdrawal of A.B.C. funds from financial institutions which practice racial discrimination; (11) pledging by the A.B.C. of 10 per cent of its investment portfolio as a backstop for a line of credit for developing and capitalizing black businesses; (12) election of a qualified black churchman as president of the convention.[62]

It is difficult to perceive how Black Power could have a greater impact upon the internal workings of most black churchmen in mainstream denominations. They have been chafing at the bit of integration for a long time, and through the diffusion of Black Power they have managed to divert it in their own employment. This is a proper and strategic use of Black Power; it is also the kind of move that can only be made once. Hopefully, this one shot will be enough; if not, the enervation of Black Power will prove perverted. What is clear in all of these moves is that black churchmen are as concerned about integration as they are committed to forcing their denominations to back fully black self-determination, self-help, and self-identity.

If not in the short run, do power plays of black churchmen support or undermine Black Power in the long run? If Black

Power is deployed, will it be destroyed? Will skillful manipulation of Black Power only increase tokenism, or will it bring about a fully inclusive church in practice and in principle? Will a fully inclusive church mean further splits in denominations or a leadership of the society in its direction? Are black churchmen the future of Black Power and the future in Black Power? Is not Black Power integration a contradiction of the concept, and if not, how will black churchmen in predominantly white denominations relate with black churchmen in black denominations? Are black churchmen the prophets or profits of doom; that is, can they be trusted to serve the interests of Black Power, or is Black Power subservient to their interests? Is Black Power a mere extreme appeal to white consciences? Is Black Power on the wane? Is Black Power an extension of middle-class drives initiated in civil rights, or is it about the emergence of the black masses into the good life, or is it about radical changes in the structures and systems of the society? In addition to putting their bodies on the line, using Black Power as a slogan, diverting funds in support of black communities, what contribution is specifically made to Black Power via theology by black churchmen? Will Black Power boomerang on black churchmen? Have black churchmen divested Black Power of its essentials or of its unessentials? Are black churchmen Machiavellians, or opportunists, or innovators, or imaginators? Is Black Power denied, or applied, or perverted by black churchmen? Has Black Power a future? Are black churchmen Black Power's children of future?

The situation is confusing at best because black people are supposed to be about black religion and not about Black Power. Arnold Toynbee summed up the hopes of white Christians with respect to black Christians. Are black Christians through a black church about the bringing of dead Christianity to life, or are they about the rebirth of a civilization through black people as a whole?

> The Negro has adapted himself to his new social environment by rediscovering in Christianity certain original meanings and values which Western Christendom has long ignored. Opening a simple and impressionable mind to the

Gospels, he has discovered that Jesus was a prophet who came into the world not to confirm the mighty in their seats but to exalt the humble and meek. The Syrian slave immigrants who once brought Christianity into Roman Italy performed the miracle of establishing a new religion which was alive in the place of an old religion which was already dead. It is possible that the Negro slave immigrants who have found Christianity in America may perform the greater miracle of raising the dead to life. With their childlike spiritual intuition and their genius for giving spontaneous aesthetic expression to emotional religious experience, they may perhaps be capable of kindling the cold grey ashes of Christianity which have been transmitted to them by us until, in their hearts, the divine fire glows again. It is thus perhaps, if at all, that Christianity may conceivably become the living faith of a dying civilization for the second time. If this miracle were indeed to be performed by an American Negro Church, that would be the most dynamic response to the challenge of social penalization that had yet been made by man.[63]

6.

BLACK POWER —Before Its Time?

In the clear light of white power failure previously set forth, is it meaningful to speak in terms of black power failure?

Power is a matter of energy, the energy of dynamic change. The direction of energy is a matter of organization, the intelligent application of technical competence.

Black is the contagious spirit or soul of persons who accept their paradoxical African and American heritage. This African and American experience has evolved a people whose touchstone is deeply religious, a universal interest in actual freedom and equality for all, beginning with their own. This sense of purpose is religious—it is intuitively understood to be the responsibility of infectious black spirits, "the soul of black folks." It is for and within this religious drive toward freedom and equality for all that power is to be organized. Power without religion or the black spirit is negative, a destructive activity without purpose. Religion without power is frustration buoyed up by superstition.

The phenomenon of Black Power may be defined best as follows: Black Power is the energy and authority by which freedom and equality happen beyond isolated happenings.

The spirit of black folks provides the constructive motivation and gives meaning to the energy and authority by which their power occurs. This enabling, enlightening spirit integrates the organized energies of black souls: the ceaseless drive for change, with the equal demand for concerted direction. Black Power makes sense because it serves the meaning and direction of the only reality, the brotherhood of man.

A theological interpretation of Black Power means that this phenomenon is an instrument of the divine purpose, the brotherhood of man and the fatherhood of God. Black Power then means that black persons are to engage in this divine purpose with a single will to its realization in the land where they are born. Thus, there can be no separatism, no escape to another section of the world, or from the painful realities of this world. Further, black people are not to dwell upon past inequities. Rather, with power and purpose they are to move from the present realities to the new possibilities and necessities in the struggle against injustice.

The problem of Black Power is not one of its necessity or value. The problem of Black Power is the problem of America; it promises more than it delivers. Black Power is here; it has yet to come. Black Power has raised the hopes of black people to a new height. Will it dash them against the stones of verbiage? Black Power is not simply precarious; it is primarily precocious.

The problem of Black Power may be best illustrated through the retelling of a familiar parable.

A chicken farmer owned a large acreage, some of which was extremely hilly. It was the farmer's habit each morning to walk over a portion of his acres and survey the rest from the hilltops. One morning as he arrived at a hilltop he discovered a baby eagle. It appeared lost, hungry, and alone. The farmer picked up the eagle and placed it in the barnyard's chicken coop, where it could gain food, water, and shelter.

As the days passed, the eagle discovered his basic problem was an inability to discern the pecking order in the chicken coop and the barnyard. When it came time to eat, the eagle would always get enough to eat, but he was always the last to eat. When it came time to drink, his thirst was quenched, though he was the last one to drink. At night he received shelter, though he was the last to gain it and just squeezed in under the ledge. The eagle did not know the pecking order, nor could he find the key to it.

One day as he was playing around the barnyard some eagles circled high over the chicken coop and let out a scream. The scream increased the heartbeat of the eagle, an experience he had not previously known. After a moment of adjustment, he continued to peck away in the barnyard.

Moments later the eagles circled lower and let out a scream which knocked the eagle back and forced him to stretch out his wings. A few seconds later the eagles swooped down low and let out a scream which awakened the eagle to himself. He looked up and in that moment discovered who he was, what he was about, where he was going, and he took off.

When Black Power first electrified the nation in the summer of 1966, Stokely Carmichael appeared, leading his people in a frenzied, responsive chant. The black people of Lowndes County, Alabama, were being organized by the then chairman of the Student Nonviolent Coordinating Committee. The black people of Lowndes County were without voting power, industrial employment, adequate housing, and human respect. Blacks outnumbered whites four to one, but they were without voice or representation. Carmichael set out to change this by forming these fellow blacks into a viable political organization. Between the enthusiasm of building this initial black panther party and the failure of the movement to gain control, Black Power became a household slogan in America.

All across the land Black Power became a scream that was no mere slogan for black people. It was the siren of self-discovery, a call to be about the business of freedom and equality, a light in their darkness that gave direction, a signal to take off. Briefly, the call of Black Power was a call to revolution, to rise up against their sea of troubles and by opposing put them to an end. But the scream of Black Power was a failure; it soon became lost in charges and countercharges, interpretations and reinterpretations. Although it struck a responsive chord among the majority of blacks who are militant, Black Power failed because the ground for its realization has yet to be prepared. The spirit was willing, but the energy and organization are weak.

Black Power in the quick means violence, the fight to overthrow the systems and structures of oppression. Black Power as violence is not the call to riots, separatism, anti-whitey—it is a call to unity for direct action in the belief that all other alternatives are no longer available.

It is not of concern here to set forth the ramifications of Black Power beyond its quick, immediate understanding in the black community. Stokely Carmichael once declared that "For racism to die, a totally different America must be born." [1] The former SNCC chairman turned it another way as well: "In movements, you decide either to be guerrillas or you decide not to use violence. We are aggressively nonviolent. But if we are attacked, we are certainly going to move to destroy the persons who attack us." [2] On another occasion Carmichael put it this way:

> The question is whether or not the majority of people in this country, who are white Americans, are they ever going to make this country a real democracy? 'Cause that's where the problem really lies.[3]

Black Power as violence is very clear in this utterance:

> While we may be ten percent inside the country . . . we want to make it crystal clear that we are well located in cities across the country and that if in fact 180 million people just think they are going to turn on us and we are going to sit there, like the Nazis did to the Jews, they are wrong. We are going to go down together, all of us.[4]

The real intent of Black Power is unmistakable in these lines by James Baldwin:

> As far as I am concerned, when my countrymen can set dogs on children and blow children up in Sunday School, the holocaust is not far off. And, more than that—if I'm to be honest—one can't but feel, no matter how deeply one distrusts the feeling, that the holocaust, the total leveling, salvation by fire, "no remission of sins save by the shedding of blood," may be the only hope.[5]

Central to the real thrust of Black Power is the demand for change now, which pessimistically or realistically assumes that there will be little change without blood and death. Stokely Carmichael and Charles V. Hamilton are contentious:

> Those of us who advocate Black Power are quite clear in our own minds that a "non-violent" approach to civil rights

> is an approach black people cannot afford and a luxury white people do not deserve. It is crystal clear to us—and it must become so with the white society—*that there can be no social order without social justice.* White people must be made to understand that they must stop messing with black people, or the blacks *will* fight back! [6]

The disclaimers to this immediate understanding of Black Power are many, but they are but sober reflections on the fact that Black Power set off a false alarm. The conditions are not right; the match has not been struck. At issue is not the integrity, but the precocity of Black Power.

It is the claim of this chapter that Black Power is a precocious call to revolution through violence to attain freedom and equality for all. This is not a defense of Black Power at its heart. The intention is to describe the perspective of black people, their eagerness for Black Power. The premature birth of the idea of Black Power means that its time has not come. At this moment Black Power is the voice of the God who failed. But there is remaining the expectation of rebirth.

Black Americans in the mass are certain that their liberation, and that of all Americans, must come in the way of violence. The need for a fundamental change in conditions of black people is spelled out in their daily life. It is resisted by dominant whites who know this change must come and fear it will come only through violence. At bottom, blacks do not fear violence; they are its product.

Black Power, the actualization of freedom and equality, is nothing if it is not the turning of the social order and the social system with its structures upside down. This is only possible in murderous combat between blacks and whites. This is a reality into which blacks are born and one which they intuitively know. It is not necessary to win this war between blacks and whites to bring into being a new humanity, a new society, a new system. A decided black people molded into unity could revamp this country with the loss of ten of their twenty million.

It was this precocious call of total commitment to a total program for real humanity that black people sensed briefly at the first shoutings of Black Power! Black Power! Black Power!

Black Power! Black Power! Black Power! It is a wholly understandable, if precarious, dream, and not an idle one for the occupants of the American concentration camps called black ghettos. The black ghetto reeks with cheap wine, exposed garbage, tracings of vomit. At every turn there linger street-corner men, dope pushers, pimps, hucksters, prostitutes, homosexuals, thieves. Men are without work; children are without fathers; women are without the fullness of home. Hunger is everywhere; disease is rampant. Youths are ill-fed, ill-clad, ill-educated, ill-led. Whites are perceived as gouging shopkeepers, brutal policemen, sneaky social workers, ineffective inspectors, ineffectual intellectuals. It is the power of these passing whites and their life in the white-noose suburbs that blacks wish to wrench by violence.

The violence upon which blacks in the ghetto have been bred breeds violence. To bring white power, white people, white systems, and white structures to their knees is not an occasional thought among blacks. It is their dream, awake or asleep. Only the call of nonviolence is unnatural in the ghetto. The destruction of this society in order to create a new one is illogical from the perspectives of whites. It is the necessary end for blacks, the only sufficient means whereby white violence can be eliminated forever. The lot of black masses has been abominable from the arrival of blacks on this land: there is no experience which can suggest any way out of the mire other than a fight to the death. There can be no doubt that these feelings run deep and permeate the black masses. There can be no doubt they are right in their conclusion. In this depth of despair, blacks of the ghetto mistook for a moment Black Power as the unification of blacks on a racial basis for the express purpose of fighting as long as necessary for freedom, and until equality is taken. There is only one objective, the end of racism. This is a simple and clear demand that no black can misunderstand or dispute, regardless of age, sex, education, income, or privileges.

Not only blacks, but white Americans understood Black Power as a call to gain manhood through wresting humanity from white dominance. Whites took comfort in the belief that the 10 percent would not attempt a massacre against the 90 percent. Black intellectuals, black believers in the system, blacks who have an economic stake in the system, even though they have no status in the society—these blacks were equally quick in condemning Black Power as misguided racism in reverse. The margin of comfort for whites and blacks making it in the society, or aspiring thereto, is the conviction that blacks cannot pull off a revolution in America unless they tie in with a worldwide revolution of blacks. It is believed that although the political self-determination which has taken shape in the Third World has sparked American blacks to flex their muscles and gives them every incentive, the Third World is still under economic colonialism. This economic tie so binds that the Third World would be of no benefit to the black minority here in any attempt to pull off a revolution.

A different perspective is held by militant black youth. To them Black Power was a call to manhood and the creation of a new humanity in this country. For the most part, these youth are not caught in the vicious circle of poverty. Nevertheless, they feel trapped in the vicious circle of racism. College-bound, college-educated, or college dropouts, these black youth were awakened by the emotional impact of Black Power. Their dream is that of a united black front in America engaged in guerrilla warfare on such a wide scale as to tie up this country. Simultaneously, an extension of this dream is the belief that America is very dependent upon the Third World for both exports and imports. The combination of direct action by blacks in America and passive resistance through refusal to engage in trade by members of the Third World is held to be power enough to initiate a successful revolution. What is important to recall here is not whether realism abounds in this dream of youth. The fact is that these ideas are abroad throughout the nation. Youth still hold certain teachings of previous generations to be true. One of them is that ideas have consequences. There is another one: youth are convinced that truth is their ultimate weapon. In the cause for freedom and equality, revolution toward this end is even termed righteous.

The Kerner Report affirmed what blacks knew to be true in the wake of Black Power: this nation is rapidly moving toward a black and a white one physically, as well as economically and sociologically. This visible division is the final conclusion of the

American system. The black man has a place he must stay within, South or North, East or West. The physical ghetto of the black masses serves to illuminate the psychological ghetto in which all blacks are contained. The in-migration of blacks from the South throughout the nation has made clear that the ghetto cannot be shaken except as it is torn down by blacks' becoming men and overthrowing their condition. Cornered in the ghetto, blacks see white people as the enemy. Black and whites must have it out. If the system cannot be changed, it can be ground to a halt by putting black bodies on the line.

Black Power sums up the black determination to set this society on the right track of real humanity once and for all. Black Power does not mean a take-over by blacks. It does not mean mere self-determination in black enclaves within cities. Black Power does not mean just an awakening of black pride and the end of self-hatred. It does not mean black people with black money and black politics. These are only ingredients for the unity of black people in what is believed to be an inevitable and indispensable war. The electricity of Black Power is its call to aggresivenesss without apology. The intent of Black Power is perfectly clear and right; the timing is not. There may be other false alarms before the revolution comes; the call may not even be that of Black Power. When the trumpet does sound, the meaning of Black Power is that there will be a fight for the right.

In seeking to explain why Black Power has made such an impact upon black and white Americans, I have set forth its visceral meaning. The inner logic of the situation cannot be explained away because whites and blacks both find this demand for change now by whatever means necessary to be the shape of things to come. It is admittedly precarious, even precocious. It is the belief of black militants—and they are becoming the majority—that the Black Power failure is a temporary one. The context in which it arose merely produced a cry of anguish, not unlike "Freedom Now!" or "My God, my God, why hast thou forsaken me?" Like the eagles circling above the barnyard where the lost eagle was attempting to find the pecking order of the chicken coop, Black Power produced the initial scream which made the heart beat faster.

There are some grounds for the whites who are taking to arming themselves in unprecedented numbers. It is understandable, their immediate reaction. Common sense dictates that the conditions under which blacks continue to exist in this society combined with the rhetoric of "Get Whitey" demand that men will seek to revolutionize the pattern. Whites know that were they in the place of blacks, they would seek to be the precipitator, the prosecutor, the judge, and the executioner. There can be no denying these elements in black people. The time of reckoning has been put off, but not forever will three centuries of patience endure. Yet, when the showdown comes, it will not be determined by so limited a perspective as revenge. If millions of blacks are to die, it can only be in the cause of a new society, a new humanity, a new earth. Black people are fundamentally religious. Their unity into a fighting mass will be dependent upon nurturing a single eye to the divine will of brotherhood, a society in which all participate as men and women. Nothing less is sufficient for the shaping of a unified black people to strike out for their well-being, which is the well-being of whites as well.

The more reflective whites indicate to their white brothers that there is no cause for alarm. After all, blacks are just children crying for attention. Provide them with some token appeasements as if they were babies, and the results will be the same. When a baby has a temper tantrum, you do not slap it in the face, lock it in a room, kick it in the stomach, or choke it to death. You give the baby in this state something which will turn its attention away from the momentary fixation, and then train it to find satisfaction in what you deem its best interest. To be sure, babies grow up to be men, and in some spheres move from temper tantrums to rebellion; this is clear in the increasing youth culture. But black people are still children who take it out on themselves or their peers when they do not have their way. They do not take it out on those responsible for their condition.

For instance, as white intellectuals remind their more emotive brethren, blacks hardly ever attack whites. If you look at what happens in the black ghetto of your town, you will find that blacks cut each other. They shoot up each other. Their crime rate is extremely high, but this crime is largely self-destructive. Even the riots we have witnessed have been the burning of property, which largely destroyed black families without insurance. Black Power has not changed this reality so that blacks take out their aggressions, grievous though they may be, on whites.

There is no doubt of the accuracy of this observation. The perspective that is missed is that this mutual self-mutilation is but the prelude to what is to come. The extension of Black Power into "Burn, baby, burn" has already moved to "Learn, baby, learn" and this is not meant as "Earn, baby, earn." This shout for a riotous response was arrested in the awareness that an attack on white property is injurious to black people and only inconvenient for white people. The riots did serve the purpose of illustrating to blacks what is possible in a concerted effort where burnings are not combined with lootings but with strategic armed attacks and disruption of business as usual. The black man's need of physical confrontation still is expressed in the frustration of self-destruction. Even in this action there is a certain sense of freedom and release of power. It is potentially much more than this. If these actions appear stupid from one point of view, they are from another the necessary preparation for a war in which personal death is given without question to the cause. White people have termed black people all along to be irrational, passionate, dumb animals. The work of Black Power yet to be begun is to attune this assumption into a force of reality so that when the time comes to fight, blacks will be fearless and selfless in the struggle. Black Power effectiveness means convincing blacks that their struggle against each other is a trick whites have put them in. It further means making clear to the masses that the only way they will become men, and not animals, is to use their animalness to grab for themselves their humanity. Humanity, manhood, is not given in a society where power is up for grabs—it is grabbed. Black Power has yet to make clear to the black masses that there is no way for them to gain acceptance as men in this American system. Whites will not believe blacks are men until blacks show through force they demand white acceptance of their manhood.

In the meantime, blacks who are set up as spokesmen and models will put off reality and twist Black Power to mean more opportunity for individual blacks. The improvement of the lot of a few blacks will not change the condition of the black masses.

Moderate reforms and slightly better conditions can in no way change the fundamental condition of the black masses. Tokenism will not change the white view of blacks as nonentities, no matter how high blacks may rise. Nothing short of radical newness will bring into being the new humanity. Only after death is there rebirth which brings into being a fundamentally new possibility for a new condition. In a word, the black masses must be led to see that insofar as Black Power advocates shout slogans which make the masses feel good, they are but a modern form of the old religious jag. Violent words not backed up by radical programs which build a people for revolution cannot be trusted as the true voices of Black Power. The separatism of the Black Muslims has neither the energy nor the authority of Black Power. The self-determination of the Black Nationalists is a foolishness which comes very close to the old Indian Reservation death camps. Nonviolence is dead as a concept and a movement. Civil rights is amelioration. Integration can come about only on the other side of the revolution. Assimilation is the process which follows freedom and equality, where a new humanness inaugurates a genuine acceptance of men as brothers in deed.

The individual and his achievements are of no account in the fresh burst of Black Power. All are to make it by direct confrontation, or none are to make it. The shiftless, lazy, knife-wielding, crap-shooting, sex-laden, tar-black man is to be turned into an irresistible force, in which his past exploits will serve all blacks. This no-good dastardly black is the culmination of generations who will use his talents and experience in the only spirit that will bring success. It is the spirit which knows that death is nothing, for life has been nothing. Nothing from nothing in the cause of justice leaves the hope of starting for the first time without centuries of handicaps. These black men everywhere can be led to unified action because they already see the price of liberation is deadly violence in full force. Black Power strikes the chord; violence itself can counter violence. Violence is the only way to power for the good. Every and any means is justified; if the end does not justify the means, nothing does.

This really creative dimension of Black Power suffers from lack of intelligent organization and lack of education of the masses. It is a work that has to come. It is the quiet, dedicated, and unspectacular work which draws no attention to itself. It is not a defensive movement like the Deacons for Defense and Justice. It will mushroom as an underground movement without concern for public exposure in the press, on the radio, and the television. When the movement, real revolution, takes place, there will be no warning sounds! Its preparation will have been unapologetic.

Black Power in the nitty-gritty is immediately communicable to all blacks. Presently, its authenticity has been betrayed. Black spokesmen, including Whitney Young of the moderate Urban League, have accepted their interpretation of Black Power. These leaders of the black bourgeoisie do not support violence. In the wake of violence, they are the first to run to the power structures and say, we can stop this violence if you will only give us some victories—more jobs. These leaders are the first to claim that they have nothing to do with violence, do not condone it, give no quarter to it. Some go so far as to say that violence must be understood in its larger context, whereby the violence done to blacks precipitates violent reactions. Their goal is the system of giving more blacks economic rewards. The verbal blacks who are more militant through their grass-roots work of political organization are believers in the system and optimistically believe that only if blacks can take power will they turn the tide. In these and other ways Black Power is subtly taken over, reworked because it has mileage. The final hypocrisy of the leaders of the black bourgeoisie is that they do not believe it is true; in their depths they know the system will not work. So, they attempt to make Black Power reformist, respectable.

Perhaps they could put Black Power down for a few more decades and replace it with programs which in the end spell patience. The trouble is that Black Power is a burning desire on the eve of being born. It is kept alive as an emergent, revolutionary zeal through the heroism of such as Huey P. Newton, a leader of the Black Panther Party of Oakland, California. He was tried for shooting a patrolman to death. The Black Panthers believe policemen were out to get Huey because of the militant stance of the party he created for self-defense. Such a trial is but another instance of black stupidity for most whites. It is another story for the more than two hundred and fifty Black Panthers in Oakland.

The defensive offense of Huey is for them a glimpse of the new day. They are convinced that black people are chained in bondage by whites who are directors of an "oppressive, colonialist mother country—epitomized by white policemen." [7] Blacks who are militant identify with Huey P. Newton. He is an indicator of things to come, a forerunner of the full-blown action. He is on his way to becoming one of the real heroes of black militants.* There have not been many in the past who are looked to with pride as folk heroes because of the rebellions they led. Among them are Nat Turner, Denmark Vesey, and Gabriel. Revolutionary rebels in the cause without compromise have been rare. In the next decade or so the division between blacks and whites will be nearly rigid. This cleavage will increase violence, and with it the emergence of folk heroes whose use of force will be a strange combination of a defensive offense.

The mystique of Black Power, then, which strikes fear in whites and hope in blacks, is its not so veiled threat of attack. Nothing unites a people like the call to arms to defeat a common enemy. When it is clear to a people that the enemy is the very incarnation of evil and must be stopped by violent conflict, their response is overwhelmingly uniform. It is this truth about America that the black masses feel keenly. In this period before the internal feeling of violence is turned externally against the foe, there is some need to make the connection between the feeling and the will to action. So far, Black Power has only increased the frustration, giving it no real outlet. The potential of Black Power for destroying the nation lies precisely in its hidden meaning of forceful encounter, which is the cohesiveness black people alone require to become as one. Very little instruction is needed to remind blacks they have been raped, robbed, and ravaged. This is dynamite when strategically set forth because it is

* The Black Panther Party of San Francisco–Oakland has joined with a white peace party in vital areas of mutual interest, without merging. This cooperative venture indicates the commonality of white and black radicals; they seek power and do not disregard unity. Huey P. Newton, founder of the Black Panther Party, states his acceptance of radical whites: "With the young white radicals in general there is a change in attitude because of certain objective changes in conditions for them. For instance, they are beaten and brutalized and now they are changing their values." *New York Times,* September 8, 1968, p. 32.

the simple and unmitigated truth no one can deny. This reality finds its extraordinary expression in the preaching of violence and the arming of extremists, both under the guise of self-defense. The critics of these instigators are quite right; violence as self-defense is beside the point. This is the very point these groups are making in city after city.

The small beginnings of extremists do not arise out of despair. Extremists are the ones who at this stage are convinced their fate can be changed only through violent action. Their numbers are growing. Just where the tip point comes when this fatalism takes hold is not clear. It is like a pitcher on a hot day; his stuff suddenly goes without warning. So it is with a change in men from despair to fatalism, from revolutionary talk to revolutionary action.

The men most open to violence beyond the vanguard are those at the bottom who live a life of lechery. A few of them have been reached by the Black Muslims and lifted out of their tommyrot. But once on their feet, many leave the Muslims because Muslims can lift only single individuals. When this is accomplished, they have nothing else to offer but the idle dream of a separate state or reservation. Only a racial war can unite black masses and pull them up as a whole, giving them something to die for and if they survive, a new society in which to live and grow.

Presently, Black Power advocates do not speak in terms of violence. A great to-do is made about building black pride through black institutions, organizations, culture, and self-determination. Many are indeed earnest about this mode, which others see as a big put-on. In and of itself, black pride is a desperate effort to participate in the system on what are believed to be independent grounds. Black Power is added to by these experiments insofar as they are not taken too seriously as the way, or the end. In the end, these developments are either diversionary or supplemental to Black Power. It is the central spirit of Black Power which declares that the only creative source for blacks is in and through violent encounter with whites. It alone is creative because it alone can harness black spirits into a movement of liberation, the essential first step for free expression.

The best portrayal of this cleansing unity of violence through

Black Power was depicted in the 1950 movie, *No Way Out.* The film lived up to its title and made unmistakable the truth that however exceptional a black man may be, there is no way out of white violence through success. Sidney Poitier, Richard Widmark, and Linda Darnell star in this story about an ideal black intern caught up in racism. Sidney Poitier has the highest rating among interns in a metropolitan hospital, but applies for an extended year because of personal feelings of inadequacy. Two brothers are caught in the midst of robbing a filling station. They are shot and brought to the prison ward of the hospital and placed under Sidney Poitier's care. Both men were shot in the leg, but the younger brother has a loss of direction and sense of balance. Sidney Poitier diagnoses it as a brain tumor and proceeds to help him by administering a spinal injection. The young hoodlum dies following the injection, although he was nearly dead upon arrival. His brother, Richard Widmark, was "Nigger baiting" all along, and the death of his brother at the hands of a black man is called murder. The picture describes Richard Widmark as a very sick racist who vents his spleen on Sidney Poitier through the uninhibited and uninterrupted use of "Nigger," "Coon," "black rat," "black bugger." His hatred and will for revenge are so strong that in the end he uses his ex-sister-in-law to set up a trap for Sidney Poitier in which he intends to kill him. He is foiled, and Sidney Poitier winds up saving his life with one arm maimed by a bullet from Richard Widmark's gun. The final scene describes in a nutshell black and white relations, from which Sidney Poitier has been suffering all along. Blacks must be twice as good as whites; thus a black man in extreme pain from a fresh bullet shot can with one arm save the white man. As Richard Widmark breaks out into tears of pain from his gunshot wound, the film ends with Sidney Poitier saying, "Don't cry Whitey boy, you're going to live." Although he had the opportunity and the legal motive in this final scene, Sidney Poitier could not "kill a man because he hates me." Somehow white people can do this as the film made clear, but not black people. Black people are to be above violence where whites are involved. In a word, this film showed the futility of nonviolence, its lack of cleansing relief, its dependence on the system.

Yet, the film had a wonderful contradiction in it which set

forth Black Power in a favorable light. At the same time that the central character displayed a superiority which put him above violence, there was a scene in which violence among the masses was permitted and even sanctioned. As a part of his vindictiveness, racist Richard Widmark worked on his dead brother's ex-wife so effectively that she consented to go to "Beaver Town" and tell the whites that her ex-husband was murdered by a "Nigger doctor." It worked; the whites were so upset that they decided to gather in the junkyard to arm themselves for a raid on "Nigger Town." One of the blacks who passed for white was in the section and relayed the information back to his black brothers. The blacks gathered together and armed themselves. Instead of waiting for the whites to tear them apart in their section of the city, they encircled the whites in preparation at the junkyard. The scene is not shown. It is simply reported at the hospital that an unusual emergency upsetting the whole hospital routine is taking place because "Nigger Town" lowered the boom on "Beaver Town." The interesting thing about this black victory over whites is that no moralizing about it followed. One is left with the impression that it was justified, a work well done. Blacks have their confidence restored, their self-respect heightened, and, for a while, their sense of inferiority is relieved. Apparently, whites accept this kind of defensive offense as necessary in extreme situations, even for blacks. Such acts are not only understandable; they are fair play as well. Whites have sensed this to be the meaning of Black Power on a grand scale, and they despair because all will be involved, not just poor whites and poor blacks in an isolated gang war.

The thesis of this chapter is that Black Power in the quick means violence. It is a call to manhood, to shape the destiny of blacks by reshaping the nation. A distinction is here made between violence as rioting, or even the limited horizon of violence as rebellion, and violence as revolution for the rebirth of black people and therefore of white people. Black self-interest coincides with the best interest of the American people. There is no way for the black man to get the white man off his back, unless he is thrown off. The way in which white people have bound black people is a familiar story documented in a thousand books.

I have set forth the religious bind blacks are caught in from a historical perspective in *Black Religion: The Negro and Christianity in the United States.* The economic, sociological, and psychological aspects of black enslavement have been detailed in *The Politics of God* as well as in the first chapter of this work. We can assume here a common knowledge concerning the relentless degradation black masses have suffered from the beginning in America. There is no hard evidence of any basic change in the generations ahead. This reality is slowly forming a single black consciousness in America at a time in history when conditions are nearly right.

Given this total context, is Black Power as creative revolution for social justice, with freedom and equality for all, responsible? Insofar as Black Power's press is a mere threat, a denial of its intention, or a failure to carry out a buildup from the grass roots, it is irresponsible. Responsibility is as responsible men do. Responsibility is not a question of practicality, although for the end in view, Black Power is indeed pragmatic. At this juncture Black Power is a failure because it does not responsibly take on the yoke of wrenching the freedom believed to be necessary and therefore inevitable.

If Black Power emerges as responsible through the buildup of black masses into a revolutionary force, is this future goal justifiable? The answer lies in the fact that black people will not be delivered from evil unless they deliver themselves and with themselves the evildoers. To do this is heroic; not to do so is cowardice. Blacks have more cause for revolution than those who affirmed, "Give me liberty or give me death!" Authentic Black Power is the promise of a new soul for America. Its spirit can be tested by the extent to which it builds upon and goes beyond the beginning described by Abraham Lincoln in his Second Inaugural Address:

> Fondly do we hope, fervently do we pray, that this mighty scourge of war may speedily pass away. Yet, if God wills that it continue until all the wealth piled by the bondsman's two hundred fifty years of unrequited toil shall be sunk, and until every drop of blood drawn with the lash shall be paid

by another drawn with the sword; as was said three thousand years ago, so still it must be said, "The judgments of the Lord are true and righteous altogether."

Civil rights is a failure because it cooperates with a system that produces racism, poverty, and disrespect for black people in the name of overcoming that which the system feeds upon. Black Power's present failure is its acceptance of the system insofar as it permits black people to have a share in the decisions which are based upon the perpetuation of racism and poverty. The tactic of Black Power as interim strategy is to build up power blocs of blacks through politics, economics, culture, and pride. This is surely a no-win strategy, a stopgap measure. The mystique of the Black Power phenomenon is its illumination of the truth that through a liberating revolution, pride, self-love, initiative, consciousness, all emerge. The first task, then, is engagement in revolution; all else follows. A common cause, a common destiny, a common history become conscious in each black man as he participates with the black masses in the good fight. When the fight has ended, pride in self and culture will not die but will be built into the continuing work of remolding a nation. The war on poverty, disease, and ignorance can be given serious attention in the new society without racism. For racism has been and will be, until eliminated, the major stumbling block to overcoming the disasters plaguing Americans. Unlike Sweden, with a homogeneous population, America is a racist state, and this blind spot negates its power to wipe out catastrophes. Racism has to be wiped out first. This is the real expectation of Black Power and its justification.

The theme of self-determination, participatory democracy, and decision-making by persons whom the decisions affect is an important new stress in American society. It knocks into a cocked hat the basic American belief that only the elite intellectual experts can make responsible decisions because they alone can interpret the data. This new thrust says that this is the case only because the language is too complicated. Break the issues, problems, and possibilities down into basic English, and the people have a fund of experience and common sense with which to make the most responsible decisions. This sense is at work among those who engage with the black masses. The trouble is that a free people is not being asked to determine its destiny. Rather, an enslaved people is being asked to play games in the sense that the final outcome does not lie in the hands of the people. For example, the amount of money available for an antipoverty program depends upon the whims of the Congress, and Congressmen are not the representatives of the masses. In the revolution for liberation, the black masses will for the first time have a direct and undeniable share in the shaping of their destiny and that of the country. Following this venture, win, lose, or draw, there will be a new America. In this new America masses will not have to be coaxed into decision-making. As the revolution depends upon them, so will the new nation. There will be no question of condescension or gamesmanship. So, once again, the message of Black Power is tellingly basic. It needs to be about its prior business of calling blacks everywhere to fight to end racism in the only way they can be effective. They will answer, and if kept informed and consulted at all levels at all times, they will be both dependable and formidable.

Anglo-Saxon racism is so unyielding and uncompromising that even the minority of blacks who achieve within the system is forced back "to the level and limitations of the less advanced." This hard core of racism has led to some unintended consequences. Blacks who have a measure of success, or could have some real success if they chose this route, are acutely aware of their failure to become men and women with freedom and equality. They are in the same boat as the impoverished and illiterate masses. This reality becomes most conspicuous at exactly the time when advancement in the society appears rapid. As a result, racism slowly but surely demands the only possible response, the forging of "mass organization for group progress out of the discipline of solidarity." The conflict in the old-guard civil rights leadership groups is testimony to this dawning consciousness. The masses have been ready for a long time. They have been waiting the return of the advance guard. The masses are not surprised to find the advance guard returning with the message that they cannot make it alone; it will be all or none. The masses are not jealous of the material success which the "talented tenth" achieved; they welcome their return to reality without rancor. The confusion among the masses results from the inability of the leadership edge to resolve the tension between organizing the people to fight within the system and uniting them to fight for its overthrow. Black Power means the latter. Most black leaders believe the system of racism cannot be changed and has to be broken, but they cannot bring themselves to accept their deepest beliefs. A few black leaders are hung up between their rhetoric and the consequences. Only a handful are awaited who are committed to "the responsibility of the elite for the masses."

When that tiny minority of the black leadership class realizes the inevitable, it will become immediately clear that the readiness of the black masses all the while to give their lives is not enough to bring the results intended by Black Power. The enthusiasm and desire are there; commitment to the cause is there, but the black masses need guidance. Intelligence dictates the apprising of the black masses with respect to the essentials—the purpose of the revolution, its prospects, its methods, its objectives. Nothing short of grass-roots education, organization, discipline, indoctrination, and respect for informed and informing authority will suffice. Black leaders will realize that although the masses are so desperate they can be mobilized into a fearless fighting force, it is also the case that they are so desperate they can be easily led astray by establishment token gifts. It is this unenlightened desperation which has historically resulted in blacks' not being united, being easily divided and turned against themselves. To end racism, and in the process create a new black humanity, is not possible without the heightened quality of understanding, of black consciousness.

At this stage, the black masses have desperation enough but lack comprehension of what it means to engage in an intelligent and successful revolution. It is incumbent upon the black leaders to set forth a program, a strategy, an organizational chart, and a timetable for each local organization of blacks so that each local organization is coordinated with groups throughout the nation. The totality of this program requires architects, but constant communication with the masses, to the extent that they are thoroughly informed and participate in decisions, is imperative. It must become perfectly clear that the end result is not a return of the situation where there is an advance guard which becomes the exception proving the rule. The goal is the rise of a whole people into manhood, a condition which does not begin on the other side of the revolution but in and through it. Without the clear understanding of the fact that the masses are indispensable in every area, not just for their bodies, the revolution will fail because the masses will quickly become conscious of serving an interest other than their own.

Black Power makes sense only in this context of a dedicated, organized, intelligent, and disciplined development of a whole people through a struggle which brings them to manhood. The politics of revolution begins and ends with the increasing stature of black masses. It is to this end that brilliant leaders must give themselves. This is the test of the genuineness of Black Power, the advancement of the black masses. Black Power connotes violence as the only pathway which can end the vicious circle of racism. Violence is logical and justifiable to the extent that it unifies all the people through action with comprehension for social justice. Transformation of America is dependent upon the transformation of blacks. Their transformation is dependent upon direct participation in the struggle with knowledge gained through bringing the new society to birth. The terribly costly investment this means will not be a deterrent where the truth is communicated. The fantastic complexity of bringing a new order out of the chaos can be achieved by an informed people who are motivated by the will to never again allow their destiny to be in the hands of others.

Black Power is subreption or mere foaming at the mouth, destructive anger, a cruel joke played on the black masses, if it does not intend the revolution. If Black Power intends the revolution, its failure has been the lack of long and arduous dedication in the preparatory stage. If Black Power begins with the preparation for revolution, it is incumbent upon the leadership to ready the people for intelligent involvement in a new society. Black Power requires the precipitation of revolution and a vision of the new order. The seeds of revolution are strewn everywhere in the nation. "There are two Americas—black and white —and nothing has more clearly revealed the divisions between them than the debate currently raging around the slogan of 'black power.' "[8] The mystique of Black Power is its will to one America forged through the refining fires of violence. Whether Black Power is but a flash in the pan, a mere slogan to debate, or a violent revolution—that is the issue of its future or failure.

Black Power is the experience of black masses come full circle. It began in protest, it continues in protest, will it end in protest? The conciliatory side of the black masses finds expression in literature. There is, in addition, a very militant dimension upon which Black Power draws. It is found in spirituals, blues, work songs, secular writings, ballads, poetry, and prose. The history of the black man in America is the history of voices protesting for salvation and freedom. Usually, we are introduced to that literature which emphasizes only the sense of optimism and patience, although sometimes escapism is expressed in the literary creations of black souls. There is a less well-known but equally burning dimension which makes up the smoldering fire of Black Power. If the smoke of Black Power becomes the flame of revolution, its ember will be ignited by a very hot bed of coals, although a very old one.

Black Power first came to light when some black man in one of the slave fields reared his head and cried out:

Oh, Lawd, I'm tired, uuh
Oh, Lawd, I'm tired, uuh
Oh, Lawd, I'm tired, uuh
Oh, Lawd, I'm tired, a dis mess.

We have been led to believe that this is a line of humor, the unmatchable way blacks have of making it in this society. Consequently, our minds lead us to believe the final line refers to the following condition:

Way down yon'er 'un de Alerbamer way,
De Niggers goes to wo'k at de peep o' de day.
De bed's too short, and de high posts rear;
De Niggers needs a ladder fer to climb up dere.

De cord's worn out, and de bed tick's gone.
Niggers' legs hang down fer de chickens t' roost on.

Usually, though, we assume being tired "a dis mess" leads to a desire for escape to heaven which we do not admire but find non-threatening.

> O just let me get up in the house of God, Just let
> me get up in the house of God,
> Just let me get up in the house of God, and I'll
> never turn back any more.

Black Power is a cool statement of awareness as is "dis mess":

> We raise de wheat,
> Dey gib us de corn;
> We bake de bread,
> Dey gib us de crust;
> We sif de meal,
> Dey gib us de huss;
> We peel de meat,
> Dey gib us de skin;
> And dat's de way
> Dey take us in;
> We sim de pot,
> Dey gib us de liquor,
> And say dat's good enough for nigger.

Black Power has deep roots in the long memory of black Americans. It begins with respect for the beauty and glory of the original land as in these lines from Claude McKay's "Africa":

> The sun sought thy dim bed and brought forth light,
> The sciences were sucklings at thy breast;
> When all the world was young in pregnant night
> Thy slaves toiled at their monumental best.
> Thou ancient treasure land, thou modern prize,
> New peoples marvel at thy pyramids!
> The years roll on, thy sphinx of riddle-eyes
> Watches the mad world with immobile lids.

The upswing of pride is tapped from roots extended as in the black bard Countee Cullen's "Shroud of Color":

Lord, I will live persuaded by mine own,
I cannot play the recreant to these:
My spirit has come home, that sailed the
doubtful seas.

Of course, there is understandable despair which is set down in Fenton Johnson's "Tired":

I am tired of work; I am tired of building up
somebody else's civilization.

Thus, it is incumbent upon the black man to look elsewhere for guidance, although sometimes even this search seems futile, as Johnson concludes:

Pluck the stars out of the heavens. The stars mark
our destiny. The stars marked my destiny.
I am tired of civilization.

Despair has been but the hard reality shaking up the black spirit, sharpening the understanding of its condition. The despair lasts for a while; then the indomitable black spirit slowly rises and puts the despair to use by naming it as Countee Cullen has done in his "From the Dark Tower":

We shall not always plant while others reap
The golden increment of bursting fruit,
Nor always countenance, abject and mute,
That lesser men should hold their brothers cheap. . . .

Despair reveals the culprit as in James Whitfield's *America, and Other Poems*:

Thou boasted land of liberty
It is to Thee I raise the song
Thou land of blood, and crime, and wrong. . . .

From despair the black spirit rises to anger, the anger for which Claude McKay provides justification in these exceptional excerpts from "White Houses":

Your door is shut against my tightened face,
And I am sharp as steel with discontent.

But I possess the courage and the grace
To bear my anger proudly and unbent.

Black Power feeds upon anger in the face of economic exploitation, and this kind of anger is finely caught in Sterling Brown's "Old Lem":

I talked to Old Lem
And Old Lem said:
They weigh the cotton
They store the corn
We only good enough
To work the rows;
They run the commissary
They keep the books
We gotta be grateful
For being cheated;
Whippersnapper clerks
Call us out of our name
We got to say Mister
To spindling boys
They make our figgers
Turn sommersets
We buck in the middle,
Say 'Thankyuh, sah.'
They don't come by ones
They don't come by twoes
But they come by tens.

Black Power feeds on a long history of exclusion from the ballot box as Frank Davis underscores in his "The Cotton South":

There are some who say
Voteless blacks never get
A proportionate return of taxes paid
But since so many
Land in the hoosegow
On copyrighted charges
And the county pays their keep
In stockade, on chain gang,

They really use their share
Of public funds—
The arithmetic and logic
Are indisputable.

Black Power feeds on the endless night of racism as Robert Hayden pinpoints in his "Speech":

I have heard the words
They serve like barbed-wire fences
To divide yuh
I have heard the words—
Dirty niggers, poor white trash—
And the same voice spoke them;
Brothers listen well to me,
The same voice spoke them.

Black Power feeds as well on the unkept promises following wars "to make the world safe for democracy." In "Conversation on V" Owen Dodson is on target:

Now what is there here Victory?
It what we get when we fight for it.
Ought to be Freedom, God do know that.

Thus, Black Power is rooted in the dark night of experience known to all black people and caught by some in special times and places. Black Power begins in protest of "The Cotton South":

Well, you remakers of America
You apostles of social change
Here is pregnant soil
Here are grass roots of a nation
But the crop they grow is Hate and Poverty.
By themselves they will make no change
Black men lack the guts
Po' whites have not the brains
And the big land owners want Things as They Are.

This protest is also a challenge taken up by Black Power, the spirit which believes "Hate and Poverty" can no longer be tolerated, nor can it be any longer said that "black men lack the guts." Thus, Black Power moves from protest to a statement of conviction about the special task of black people. The past is largely defeat for the black masses, but no longer. Therefore, these lines from Langston Hughes's "Let America Be America Again" are interpreted as a promise of what America will be through aggressive black souls:

> O, yes
> I say it plain,
> America never was America to me,
> And yet I swear this oath—
> America will be!

Its evolution from protest to challenge to conviction leads Black Power to say "No" to the usual source of hope—expressed, for example, in Frank Davis' "The Cotton South":

> You disciples of Progress . . .
> . . . will you mold this section
> So its portrait will fit
> In the sunlit hall
> of Ideal America?

American disciples of progress have failed; Black Power affirms they will continue to do so. The inspiration must now be international in scope, and the last lines of Mark Tolson's "Dark Symphony" disclose a suggestion of this international scope:

> Out of abysses of Illiteracy,
> Through labyrinths of Lies
> Across wastelands of Disease . . .
> We advance!
>
> Out of dead-ends of Poverty,
> Through wilderness of Superstition,
> Across barricades of Jim Crowism . . .
> We advance!
>
> With the Peoples of the World . . .
> We advance!

The conviction Black Power holds beyond mere protest and

challenge is set forth in the final stanzas of "For My People" by Margaret Walker:

> For my people standing staring trying to fashion a better way
> from confusion, from hypocrisy and misunderstanding,
> trying to fashion a world that will hold all the people
> all the adams and eves and their countless generations:
>
> Let a new earth rise. Let another world be born. Let a
> bloody peace be written in the sky. Let a second
> generation full of courage issue forth, let a people
> loving freedom come to growth, let a beauty full of
> healing and a strength of final clenching be the
> pulsing in our spirits and our blood. Let the martial
> songs be written, let the dirges disappear. Let a
> race of men now rise and take control!

This, in a nutshell, is the conviction buoying up the black spirit and pervading Black Power. Protest and challenge are not threats to be hurled in confusion and anger. They are the spring-board for fashioning a new world, a new earth. Peace will come in the end, but not without blood "full of courage." There will be real healing, that is the strength of a black people "loving freedom come to growth"—it is in our "spirits and our blood." The final test of Black Power is its response to the yearnings of black bards through the centuries whose expressions of the masses Black Power has fed upon: "Let a race of men now rise and take control!" If Black Power is to be true to itself, beyond protest, challenge, and conviction, there must be action. "To fashion a better way" requires courage. "To fashion a world that will hold all the people" requires blood. To "let a new earth rise" requires death. "To let a second generation full of courage issue forth," this generation must let loose the "pulsing in our spirits and our blood." Thus, there is no getting around the reality that a generation must die if black men are to "let a race of men now rise and take control!" "If We Must Die," as Claude McKay puts it in his poem by this title, Black Power in his spirit determines that it be with "final clenching" to "let an-other world be born," "loving freedom," and with "a beauty full of healing":

If we must die—let it not be like hogs
Hunted and penned in an inglorious spot,
While round us bark the mad and hungry dogs,
Making their mock at our accursed lot.
If we must die—oh, let us nobly die,
So that our precious blood may not be shed
In vain; then even the monsters we defy
Shall be constrained to honor us though dead!
Oh, Kinsmen! We must meet the common foe;
Though far outnumbered, let us show us brave,
And for their thousand blows deal one deathblow!
What though before us lies the open grave?
Like men we'll face the murderous, cowardly pack,
Pressed to the wall, dying, but fighting back!

Violence is the means Black Power resorts to in the belief that all other means have been exhausted in the quest for freedom and equality with social justice. Hypocrisy is the real rub perceived by Black Power, for it once believed that freedom and equality with social justice were possessed within the system. This tendency toward violence is not irrationality in its mind. Rather, violence is the highest respect that can be paid to justice and reason, for direct action has been called for only after reason and justice are believed to be exhausted. This is the new dimension of Black Power, the "reason of unreason," the right to be unreasonable. We have just surveyed the ultimate conclusion of this "reason of unreason" for black masses. With respect to white people, it leads H. Rap Brown, former chairman of SNCC, to an appeal for support: "If you can't see yourself as being in the context of John Brown, then bring the guns to me." [9] In the same vein of countering the charge of being anti-white *per se,* of not seeking whites' cooperation, Malcolm X once threw out this lifeline: "If you are for me and my problem—when I say me, I mean *us,* our people—then you have to be willing to do as old John Brown did." [10]

It bears reiteration—this chapter is not an attempt to condone Black Power as violence. It is an attempt to make transparent its real base and appeal. A great deal of debate has ensued about what Black Power really means. In order to lay aside any doubts about the case here made, an appeal is made to the authority of the late and great Martin Luther King, Jr., of blessed memory. He wrote this of Black Power:

> It is, at bottom, the view that American society is so hopelessly corrupt and enmeshed in evil that there is no possibility of salvation from within.[11]

Dr. King came as close as any of the black leaders critical of Black Power to putting the finger on its pulse:

> Probably the most destructive feature of Black Power is its unconscious and often conscious call for retaliatory violence. Many well-meaning persons within the movement rationalize that Black Power does not really mean black violence, that those who shout the slogan don't really mean it that way, that the violent connotations are solely the distortions of a vicious press. That the press has fueled the fire is true. But as one who has worked and talked intimately with devotees of Black Power, I must admit that the slogan is mainly used by persons who have lost faith in the method and philosophy of nonviolence. I must make it clear that no guilt by association is intended. Both Floyd McKissick and Stokely Carmichael have declared themselves opponents of aggressive violence.[12]

Bayard Rustin once wrote about what he perceived as the no-win policy among black militants:

> Sharing with many moderates a recognition of the magnitude of the obstacles to freedom, spokesmen for this tendency survey the American scene and find no forces prepared to move toward racial solutions. From this they conclude that the only viable strategy is shock: above all, the hypocrisy of white liberals must be exposed. . . . They seek to change white hearts—by traumatizing them.[13]

With a sure grasp of the meaning of Black Power as violence, not for shock or traumatization, Dr. King picked up on Mr. Rustin's theme of the black militants' no-win policy. He misstated the issue of Black Power in declaring it to be rooted in the "conviction that the Negro can't win." [14] Dr. King held this to be the case because he saw rightly that Black Power is disenchantment with nonviolence. Black Power seeks the uplift of the masses. By any statistical measure available, black masses are worse off in 1968 than they were in 1960. On this score, nonviolence is a no-win policy. Whatever else may be said, Black Power is born of the conviction that violence is the only win policy. This is so, as John O. Killens tellingly puts it, because the objective of Black Power is freedom, and for nonviolence it is integration:

> Integration comes after liberation. A slave cannot integrate with his master. In the whole history of revolts and revolutions, integration has never been the main slogan of the revolution. The oppressed fights to free himself from his oppressor, not to integrate with him. Integration is the step after freedom when the freedman makes up his mind as to whether he wishes to integrate with his former master.[15]

Dr. King has no doubts—"any attempt of the American Negro to overthrow his oppressor with violence will not work." [16] The difficulty with Dr. King's thinking here is that he fails to make the important distinction between rebellion and revolution. The failures of Gabriel, Nat Turner, and Denmark Vesey lead Dr. King to hold that "violent rebellion is doomed from the start." [17] He overlooks the fact that these were rebellions of slaves who had not gained support from the masses of their brethren. These insurrections were without real planning, organization, firepower, and strategic location. Such is not the case in total today; where it is in part, it need not be so in the future. The point is that although blacks are outnumbered ten to one, the ratio is less important in the consideration of a revolution than in a rebellion. A rebellion is an uprising for limited objectives. The revolution Black Power intends as violence is to bring the nation as a whole to a halt and turn it around.

A development of this size is a real possibility. Of course, this is not the case today, and that is precisely the failure of Black Power. But the fundamental error in Dr. King's thinking was one of time. It may well be the case that Black Power is an idea whose time has not come. Nonviolence and integration can be documented as having failed in the past with respect to black masses. It cannot be assumed that Black Power as violence will fail or "is doomed from the start." In time, all the essential ingredients may be present. That is what Black Power is all about. Rigidity in the cities, an increasing birth rate among blacks, extended communication, intelligent leadership and planning, the heightening black consciousness—these are agents of time and energy. This realization may be in the future; it is not necessarily futuristic.

Strange things happen when a man's lifework is being attacked. Dr. King, of all people, found it necessary to lecture Black Power advocates on the price of violence: "In violent warfare one must be prepared to face the fact that there will be casualties by the thousands." He should know, for Dr. King taught this generation of young militants to be prepared for casualties. Nonviolence as direct action fed upon violence as a necessary response; there were "casualties by the thousands." Black Power advocates expect nothing less than the response through "exterminating thousands of black men, women and children." In fact, the objective of their revolution cannot be reached without thousands and perhaps millions being exterminated. Black Power is but nonviolence turned on its head. In the final analysis, Black Power may be able to grind this nation to a halt with good planning, intelligent sensitizing of black masses, and good luck. It cannot win, nor need it. Just as nonviolence was an appeal to white consciences on a minor scale, an appeal based upon fair play, so Black Power in the final analysis will be an appeal to white consciences. This time, however, white consciences will be reformed in the crippling of America's economic development, the destruction of her property, the death of thousands of whites, and, perhaps, the extermination of millions of blacks. Black Power really believes that only through "dis mess" will white consciences cry out, "Oh, Lawd, I'm tired, a dis mess." This may all be a deluded illusion. But wasn't it Dr. King who electrified us all when he said, "I have a dream"? The Bible puts it this way: "Your old men shall dream dreams, your young men shall see visions." "Where there is no vision, the people perish."

Will this occur in America? Dr. King believed "Anyone in his right mind knows that this will not happen in the United States."[18] Black Power believes that anyone in his right mind knows this has to happen in the United States. Dr. King held that internal revolution cannot succeed because it has never succeeded in a country where the government maintained effective control and the loyalty of the majority. This may be true. But it is no more difficult to believe that a successful revolution can occur than it is to believe that America will be turned around through nonviolence.

Black Power is ineffective because Dr. King did not conceive of powerless blacks challenging to any extent the white power structure and the militia at its command. Black Power is impractical since "a violent revolution on the part of American blacks would find no sympathy and support from the white population and very little from the majority of Negroes themselves." [19] The army, the national guard, the state troopers, and the local police are very formidable foes. So is the American military force in Vietnam. Not even the threat of nuclear bombs would be available in the United States. Guerrilla warfare in the United States executed by crack black revolutionists would be as effective as guerrilla warfare in Vietnam. It is just wishful thinking to conclude that the majority of blacks could not be indoctrinated and mobilized in their cause. As to whites, a growing minority is fully aware that the black revolution, if and when it comes, is not anti-white but pro-American. The telltale signs of this possible support are present in the New Left.* The "new politics" of Black Power may include an alliance of youth for a new society. A crystal ball is unavailable to predict the future. There is a will to shape it; strategies are being worked out for change that are indeed tactical. Black Power advocates agree with King: "This is no time for romantic illusions and empty philosophical debates about freedom. This is a time for action." [20] The disagreement is not over power, that is what Dr. King sought through nonviolence. Nonviolence was not simply power, but it was power rightly used and therefore good. He

* Huey P. Newton has hope in white radicals: "I've been inspired by the dedication of the white revolutionaries and the spirit they have shown. They're not just articulating euphemisms about what should be, but they are actually engaging in practice, they're integrating theory with practice and this is necessary to become a revolutionary." *New York Times,* September 8, 1968, p. 32.

took his cue from Alfred the Great: "Power is never good unless he who has it is good." If this is the condition, Black Power holds that since no man is good, it is a contradiction to talk in terms of power as good. Two thousand years have passed since the question of who is good was settled: "Why callest thou me good? none is good, save one, that is, God."

When Dr. King comes to his final criticism of Black Power, he is wrong. Here he claims that violence is unable to appeal to conscience. Nonviolence alone can do so. Violence demands hatred because it presupposes an enemy to be destroyed. In the first place, the lesson should have been learned long ago that an appeal to the conscience of whites in the majority is unadulterated nonsense. Even if their consciences are twinged through nonviolence, no fundamental change is produced for the black masses. If an appeal to conscience means this, it is as foolish as trying to get by in this world by looking to the next one. But there can be no doubt that violence appeals to the consciences of those who engage in it. It unites consciences around a single goal. It not only appeals to conscience as the history of all wars attests, but violence creates the consciousness so necessary for a meaningful conscience. The enemy may not love the violent aggressor who is right in his demand for justice, but one thing is sure—he respects him. The nonviolent man is not respected; he is tolerated because he is manipulatable. More than that, violence which is not rioting or revengeful can create community and brotherhood because it alone forces the oppressor to stop oppressing and join the once oppressed in building a mutually healthy new society. Of course, violence is chaotic, disruptive, contentious conflict. But conflict, as Dr. King has taught, is the condition for creativeness. The question is not one of violence or nonviolence as Dr. King suggests. Rather, it is one merely of quality.

It is no answer to declare that violence begets violence, that hate begets hate. Nonviolence begets nonviolence, and the movement is stopped dead in its tracks, an experience Dr. King knew in Chicago with Mayor Richard Daley. Black Power believes that it is not a question of there being too little violence with respect to racism but rather that there has not been enough violence. Racism runs deep in the American system. We have not rid ourselves of it. The first Civil War only repressed hatred for a while. It now is running rampant through the society. Instead of pretending hatred is not there, or merely manipulating it temporarily, Black Power wishes to assert precisely what Dr. King fears: "violence merely increases hate." Hate we will have with us always. But Black Power has a vision of a society where hate will not take the form of racism. It concludes that we must get the race hate out of our system once and for all; the cleanest and quickest way of doing so is through violence.

Perhaps Dr. King was such a keen critic of Black Power because he recognized in it the seeds of his own thought come to fruition. He used the term *militant* over and over again, but he did not take it seriously. Though opposed to Black Power, Dr. King claimed he would not "abandon our militant efforts." Black Power simply takes *militant* to mean what it implies. In his militancy, Dr. King desired to change the society, to rid it of "racial injustice." In their militancy, Black Power advocates intend no less. The objectives are the same, and that is why Dr. King worked so well with Black Power advocates and they with him. He understood Black Power as violence. He resisted it to the end, but it had an increasing effect upon him, even within the ranks of the Southern Christian Leadership Conference. Dr. King was a decidedly practical man. He knew that men cannot agree in our time on ideology, philosophy, or theology. They can agree on action in a common objective, although their reasons will differ widely. While this is true and characterized Dr. King's tactic, ideas do have consequences. Somewhere along the line, the disagreement about the why of what one does, which nevertheless permits agreement as to where one does it, will sooner or later emerge as disagreement as to how one does what one does, and when. This is the issue dividing nonviolence and Black Power. From the perspective of each, the other is a failure.

Black Power advocates believe the movement is condemned to freedom. Black Power critics believe it is condemned to failure. Whether it be freedom or failure in the end, in the present and foreseeable future Black Power possesses an inveterate faith to change this society in its own best interest—to stop it if need be and turn it around. Time alone will tell the depth of Black Power, the extent to which it keeps its faith:

O for a faith that will not shrink,
Tho' pressed by every foe,
That will not tremble on the brink
Of any earthly woe!

Change, fundamental change in this society, alone will determine whether or not the spirit of Black Power—"I ain't going to let nobody turn me around"—is a failure.

Black Power is the world and word of militant black youth who take their cue from the future. They have a vision not shared by their contemporaries dominated by the past. It is a vision of a time when white American power will be impotent in a world of color. Black Power militants have cut their eye teeth on such writings as those of W. E. B. Du Bois. Mr. Du Bois once wrote that the majority of

> American Negroes, even those of intelligence and courage, do not fully realize that they are being bribed to trade equal status in the United States for the slavery of the majority of men. When this is clear, especially to the black youth, the race must be aroused to thought and action and will see that the price asked for their cooperation is far higher than need be paid. . . .[21]

Black militants are not unaware of Barrington Moore, Jr., whose *Social Origins of Dictatorship and Democracy* deals with the interconnections between democracy and violence. This specialist on Soviet Russia at Harvard underscored the point of Black Power:

> As the one major segment of the American society with active discontents, the Negroes are at present almost the only potential recruiting ground for efforts to change the character of the world's most powerful capitalistic democracy. Whether this potential will amount to anything, whether it will splinter or coalesce with other discontents to achieve significant results, is quite another story.[22]

If, at the moment, Black Power as violence is a failure, we would do well not to underestimate it as the sound of things to come. Especially is this the case if, as Langston Hughes's poem suggests,

Negroes
Sweet and gentle,
Soft and kind
Pity the day
They change their mind.

The honorable and right intention of Black Power is to bring into being a society where the differences of black and white mutually enrich all and where to be white or black is equally good in the sight of all. This unswerving concern with justice confronts a racist society which could care less about justice denied. The present call to law and order shows not only that there is a priority of property rights over human rights, but that peace and business as usual cannot be disturbed no matter what the cause or its nobility. Little wonder Black Power does not expect this racist system to respond to a new order. In fact, the way whites respond to Vietnam, Cuba, and South Africa is fully expected here. Thus, Black Power prepares for the inevitable race war with the willingness to give up life:

> We are very close in this country to having to decide whether to commit *genocide*—and I'm not using that word symbolically—or to mobilize the resources of the nation to produce something approximating social justice.[23]

This succinctly expresses the growing messianism among blacks in every community across this nation, particularly among the youth. In reality, the very precariousness of Black Power lies at this crossroad.

Which way will Black Power go? Presently, Black Power is precocious; it will not always remain so. Black people, like all other people, may or may not have *a right* to revolution. But revolution may some time be *the duty* of black people, as it has been the duty of other people. Witness our Declaration of Independence:

> That whenever any Form of Government becomes destructive of these ends, it is the Right of the People to alter or to abolish it, and to institute new Government, laying its foundations on such principles and organizing its powers in

> such form, as to them shall seem most likely to effect their Safety and Happiness.

Will the dominant forces of this society do what is in their power—the right—or will Black Power force blacks to do their duty, that is, "the Right"?

A man cannot live without hope. I for one hope that the full humanity of blacks can come about without the clash of revolutionary war that must end in the loss of thousands, perhaps millions of blacks. Yet, I am not so tender-minded as to believe that the dignity and respect of all black people will automatically come by willing it. Nor will it come by some return to undiluted nonviolence in the Martin Luther King, Jr., tradition—only in a purer form. Neither will it come by the fantastic wish for some future leader who will bring about a new way which is a combination of the tried and the untrue with the true and the untried. My hope is that the holocaust will be prevented by the new respect black people have for themselves and by their aggressive internal power uplift through mutual regard, which will be responded to in kind by the dominant element of this society through a radical change in their political, social, economic systems and structures. Nevertheless, there is a tough-minded side of me which cannot see any real basis for a new society called for by Black Power apart from a racial war to this end.

To date, interpreters of Black Power have emphasized its tender-minded side, or pluralism, to the neglect of the tough-minded revolutionary side. Lest this militant call to creative violence be dismissed as neither important nor on the rise, it is well to recall in conclusion the fundamental beliefs of those who look to and prepare for the time when the idea of Black Power will come to fruition in the context of a world dominated by color.

James Forman, formerly of the SNCC staff:

> You must realize that we as the most exploited group in the United States, must assume leadership of our own struggle. And anyone who doesn't like it can go to hell.
>
> We're going to liberate you whether you like it or not.[24]

H. Rap Brown, former SNCC chairman:

The man tell you who your enemy is in Vietnam. I'll tell you who our enemy is. It's Lurleen Wallace. You're a fool not to shoot George, Lurleen, or little junior. The honkie is your enemy.[25]

Will Rogers, associated with SNCC:

I'm a *bad nigger.* The only language these white folks understand is an eye for an eye, a tooth for a tooth. Every time a black man gets killed, you ought to try to get two honkies. You spendin' all this money on expensive clothes and hair-dos. You better buy yourself some guns and ammunition. You gonna need them.[26]

James Baldwin:

You can't go back to Ireland or Poland or England, and I can't go back to Africa, and we will live here together, or we'll die here together, and it is not I who am telling you. Time is telling you. You will listen, or you will perish.[27]

Russ Meek of Chicago:

Now, you get this straight. You can kill all the black folks you want to, baby, but you will not kill the freedom of black folks. It's coming, we're going to get it. You think you're so great because you got all the weapons. I remember Mao Tse-tung once said—he wondered where he'd get his weapons from, and then we armed Chiang Kai-shek—and he said, "Thank you, Jesus," you see.

So don't misunderstand us, baby. We're dead serious. This country was founded on revolution. Those little settlers out there in the northeast section of this country had some muskets and some sticks and some stones, and they whipped the mighty professional British army, baby. And five thousand of them were black, and one black woman disguised herself as a man and fought with you all. And we don't have our freedom yet. We fought in every one of your damned lousy wars, and you give us nothing.

Now, the war is going to be here, because we're going to

be free. Now, you kill all you want to—but we kill too. And we don't frighten. We don't frighten at all . . .[28]

Ron Karenga, US, Los Angeles:

We must fight for the right of self-determination, race pride and pursuit of blackness. We must believe in our cause and be willing to die for it and we should stop reading other people's literature and write our own, and stop pretending revolution and make it.[29]

Stokely Carmichael:

I did not join the movement because of love, but because of hate. I hate racism and am out to smash it.[30]

Ron Karenga:

A revolt is an attempt to overthrow the system; while the revolution is the complete overthrow of that system.

A lot of brothers play revolutionary; they read a little Fanon, a little Mao and some Marx. Although this information is necessary it is not sufficient for we must develop a new plan of revolution for Black people here in America.

You can't fight a revolution on a local level. It has to be fought through a national struggle.

We must fight for the right of self-determination, race pride and the pursuit of Blackness.

The only thing that will make us invincible is for us to fight—to fight for our freedom and not our personal selves —to fight to get back the freedom we lost in 1565.

The white boy has been waging a race war ever since he has been here. Now that we plan to retaliate he calls us racists.

Blacks live right in the heart of America. That is why we are best able to cripple this man. And once we understand our role we won't talk revolution, we'll make it.

We are revolutionists. We believe in change. We believe in being realistic, but as for reality, we have come to change it.

We cannot have a revolution without direction, and that direction can only come through an ideology developed for our own situation.

To play revolution is to get put down.

We are the last revolutionaries in America. If we fail to leave a legacy of revolution for our children we have failed our mission and should be dismissed as unimportant.[31]

Black Power is the message and medium of the black masses; it is either subreption or soul power driven by single-mindedness and the will to this one truth: "that death precedes birth, that birth is the fruit of death, and that the soul is precisely the power of transforming an end into a beginning by obeying a new name." [32] It will come to this if need be. But it need not be. Which way will it be, dominant white America? The new humanity through the acceptance of a vigorous black manhood or the new humanity through black consciousness come to stature in a national war to liberate us all? Either way blacks are determined to be themselves; the only question is the way in which selfhood will be achieved. Is it necessary that truth trying to rise give birth to hatred which crushes it down? The final word of man to man should be the final word of God to man, peace—not war. War comes as the result of being caught in the gaps between the "too late" of our thoughts and the "too early" of our intuitions. "Life is an experiment in timing." The future is not determined; it is created. We must seek peace and pursue it because in peace alone do we come to our humanity, our manhood, black and white together. This is so because peace, unlike war, is never an accident. War may be necessary; it is never sufficient. Peace is both necessary and sufficient, for it is never a return to the past or a balancing on dead center. "Peace is the rhythm of a community which is still unfinished, still open to its true future." [33]

Postscript: June, 1969

The most recent illustration of Black Power subreption is James Forman's Black Manifesto. He demands $500 million or "$15 a nigger" from the "racist" religious establishment. This demand is a new form of the old request blacks made for "forty acres and a mule," though forty acres and a mule today would amount to considerably more than "$15 a nigger." "Reparations," historically understood to be an amount paid by the losers in war to the victors, is not what Forman seeks. He seeks restitution. The positive response from many white liberal leaders, after the initial shock, indicates their welcome of this opportunity to push white laymen further. Clearly, then, this acceptance of "reparations" or restitution reveals it as an essentially reformist Manifesto. If the choice is between "$15 a nigger" or eventually "$50 a nigger" and the necessary restructuring of this capitalist society to really meet the needs of poor blacks and subsequently of poor whites, white establishment churchmen find it in their best interest to go along with "reparations." White churchmen, in responding favorably to "reparations," while crying poor-mouth, may be acting out public penance for guilt. In this they are supported by the following statement of the National Committee of Black Churchmen:

> Reparation is a part of the gospel message. Zacheus knew well the necessity for repayment as an essential ingredient in repentance. "If I have taken anything from any man by false accusation, I restore him fourfold." The Church which calls itself the servant church must, like its Lord, be

> willing to strip itself of possessions in order to build and restore that which has been destroyed by the compromising bureaucrats and conscienceless rich. While reparation cannot remove the guilt created by the despicable deed of slavery, it is, nonetheless, a positive response to the need for power in the black community. This nation, and a people who have always related the value of the person to his possession of property, must recognize the necessity of restoring property in order to reconstitute personhood.

However, white and black churchmen are caught up in the Black Power subterfuge of this Manifesto. The Manifesto seeks less to serve as an outlet for guilt and more to call white oppressors to change their ways and provide the needed capital for blacks in a capitalistic society. But the churches do not have enough capital to meet the needs of blacks, though they can surely do more and even give up their riches to the poor. To do more is necessary; it is not sufficient. In the end the Manifesto may traumatize white churches, but it will not lead them to initiate radical changes in the society. In comforting the afflicted and in afflicting the comfortable, James Forman serves Black Power subterfuge as a secular if not a false prophet. We still await the true prophet of Black Power. He will be known because he will not "strain at a gnat and swallow a camel." The true prophet of Black Power will neither beg for pennies nor be a reformist. His demand of the churches and therefore of the nation will be as radical as that of Amos, the prophet of God:

> I hate, I despise your feasts, and I take no delight in your solemn assemblies. Even though you offer me your burnt offerings and cereal offerings, I will not accept them, and the peace offerings of your fatted beasts I will not look upon. Take away from me the noise of your songs; to the melody of your harps I will not listen. But let justice roll down like waters, and righteousness like an ever-flowing stream.

Notes

CHAPTER 2

1. Quoted in E. Franklin Frazier, *The Negro in the United States* (New York: Macmillan Press, 1949), p. 82.
2. *Ibid.*, p. 83.
3. *Ibid.*, p. 85.
4. *Ibid.*
5. *An Official Report of the Trials of Sundry Negroes Charged with an Attempt to Raise an Insurrection in the State of South Carolina,* prepared and published at the request of the Court by Lionel Kennedy and Thomas Parker (Charleston, 1822), p. 45.
6. *Ibid.*
7. Quoted in Gilbert Chinard, *Thomas Jefferson: The Apostle of Americanism* (Boston: Little, Brown and Company, 1948), p. 131.
8. *Douglass' Monthly, V* (August, 1862), p. 684.
9. *Douglass' Monthly, IV* (July, 1861), p. 484.
10. Quoted in James M. McPherson, *The Negro's Civil War* (New York: Pantheon, 1965), p. 163.
11. *Ibid.*
12. *Ibid.*, p. 169.
13. *Ibid.*, p. 192.
14. Quoted in Paul Lewinson, *Race, Class and Party* (New York: Oxford University Press, 1932), pp. 84–85.

CHAPTER 3

1. Quoted in W. E. B. Du Bois, *Black Reconstruction in America* (New York: Harcourt, Brace and Company, 1935), p. 177.
2. *Ibid.*, p. 136.
3. Kelly Miller, *Race Adjustment* (New York: The Neale Publishing Company, 1910), pp. 19–20.
4. Booker T. Washington and W. E. B. Du Bois, *The Negro Problem* (New York: James Potts and Company, 1903), p. 75.
5. Quoted in Robert L. Jack, *History of the National Association for*

the Advancement of Colored People (Boston: Meador Publishing Company, 1943), p. 2.
6. Charles E. Silberman, *Crisis in Black and White* (New York: Random House, 1964), p. 199.
7. Gunnar Myrdal, *An American Dilemma* (New York: Harper and Brothers, 1944), pp. 975–976.
8. Quoted in Amy Jacques Garvey, ed., *Philosophy and Opinions of Marcus Garvey,* Vol. 1 (New York: University Publishing House, 1923), pp. 1–9.
9. *Ibid.,* p. 77.
10. Marcus Garvey, *The New World,* February 14, 1925.
11. James Weldon Johnson, *Black Manhattan* (New York: Alfred A. Knopf, 1930), p. 256.
12. W. E. B. Du Bois, *Dusk of Dawn* (New York: Harcourt, Brace and Company, 1940), p. 277.

CHAPTER 4

1. This is a reference to Christianity in Eugen Rosenstock-Huessy, *The Christian Future* (New York: Harper Torchbook, 1966), p. 10.
2. *New York Times,* July 8, 1968, pp. 1, 18.
3. Stokely Carmichael, interview with Gene Roberts, *New York Times Magazine,* September 25, 1966, p. 128.
4. *Ibid.*
5. *Ibid.*
6. *New York Times,* July 21, 1968, p. 44.
7. *Ibid.*
8. Martin Luther King, Jr., *Where Do We Go from Here: Chaos or Community?* (New York: Harper and Row, 1967), p. 58.
9. John Benson, "Interview with Stokely Carmichael," *The Militant,* May 23, 1966.
10. Stokely Carmichael and Charles V. Hamilton, *Black Power: The Politics of Liberation* (New York: Vintage Books, 1967), p. 37.
11. *New York Times,* June 5, 1966, p. 75.
12. Bayard Rustin, "Black Power and Coalition Politics," *Commentary,* Vol. 41, No. 9 (September, 1966), p. 37.
13. Carmichael and Hamilton, *op. cit.*
14. Stokely Carmichael, "Speech at Mt. Holyoke College," November 17, 1966.
15. *Ibid.*
16. Carmichael and Hamilton, *op. cit.,* p. 53.
17. *Ibid.,* p. 54.
18. *Ibid.*
19. Benson, *op. cit.*
20. Carmichael and Hamilton, *op. cit.,* p. 55.
21. *Ibid.*
22. James Wechsler, "Killers of the Dream," *The Progressive,* Vol. 30, No. 12 (December, 1966), pp. 12–13.

23. Maulana Ron Karenga, "The Sevenfold Path of Blackness," in Floyd B. Barbour, ed., *Black Power Revolt* (Boston: Porter Sargent, 1968), p. 165.
24. *Ibid.,* pp. 165–168.
25. Carmichael, "Speech at Berkeley," November 19, 1966.
26. Carmichael, "What We Want," *The New York Review of Books,* September 22, 1966, p. 6.
27. Carmichael in *The Amsterdam News,* July 16, 1966.
28. Carmichael, "Speech at Mt. Holyoke."
29. Ernest Stephens, *Freedomways,* second quarter, 1967, pp. 131–138.
30. *Ibid.*
31. *Ibid.*
32. *Ibid.*
33. Quoted in Vincent Harding, "When Stokely Met the Presidents: Black Power and Negro Education," *motive,* January, 1967, p. 6.
34. *Ibid.,* p. 8.
35. *Ibid.,* p. 6.
36. *Ibid.,* p. 8.
37. Carmichael, "Speech at Berkeley."
38. King, *op. cit.,* p. 44.
39. Carmichael, "What We Want," *The New York Review of Books,* September 22, 1966, p. 6.
40. *Ibid.,* p. 5.
41. Charles Keil, *Urban Blues* (Chicago: University of Chicago Press, 1966), p. 185.
42. LeRoi Jones, *Blues People* (New York: William Morrow and Company, 1963), p. 236.
43. *New York Times,* June 22, 1966, p. 24.
44. Quoted in *Time,* June 28, 1968, p. 66.
45. *New York Times,* July 8, 1966, p. 16.
46. Carmichael and Hamilton, *op. cit.,* p. 47.
47. *Ibid.,* pp. 41–42.
48. *Ibid.,* p. 40.
49. *Ibid.,* p. 42.
50. Carmichael, "What We Want," *The New York Review of Books,* September 22, 1966, p. 5.
51. Carmichael and Hamilton, *op. cit.,* p. 47.
52. Quoted in Carl Rowan, "Crisis in Civil Rights Leadership," *Ebony,* Vol. 22, No. 1 (November, 1966), p. 28.
53. Carmichael, "Speech at Mt. Holyoke."
54. Carmichael and Hamilton, *op. cit.,* p. 46.
55. *Ibid.,* pp. 46–47.
56. A. Philip Randolph, "Keynote Address to Policy Conference, March on Washington Movement, 1962," in F. Broderick and August Meier, eds., *Negro Protest Thought in the Twentieth Century* (Indianapolis: The Bobbs-Merrill Company, Inc., 1965), pp. 203, 204.
57. *The Amsterdam News,* October 15, 1966.

58. Rustin, "From Protest to Politics," *Commentary,* Vol. 39, No. 2 (February, 1965), p. 29.
59. Rustin, "Black Power and Coalition Politics," *Commentary,* Vol. 41, No. 9 (September, 1966), p. 37.
60. *Ibid.,* p. 40.
61. Barry Sheppard, "Interview with CORE Leader," *The Militant,* August 8, 1966, p. 5.
62. Carmichael, *Jet,* June 2, 1966, p. 9.
63. Carmichael and Hamilton, *op. cit.,* p. 46.
64. Carmichael, "Speech at Mt. Holyoke."
65. "Interview with Stokely Carmichael, SNCC's *The Movement,* March, 1966, p. 1.
66. Carmichael and Hamilton, *op. cit.,* p. 62.
67. *Ibid.,* p. 66.
68. *Ibid.*
69. *Ibid.,* p. 20.
70. *Ibid.*
71. Carmichael, "What We Want," *The New York Review of Books,* September 22, 1966, p. 7.
72. Carmichael, "Speech at Mt. Holyoke."
73. Rowan, *op. cit.,* p. 34.
74. *Ibid.,* p. 32.
75. *Ibid.*
76. *Ibid.,* p. 24.
77. Carmichael, "What We Want," *The New York Review of Books,* September 22, 1966, p. 7.
78. *New York Times,* July 6, 1966, p. 5; July 9, 1966, p. 8.
79. *New York Times,* July 6, 1966, p. 14.
80. *New York Times,* July 8, 1966, p. 16.
81. Rustin, "Black Power and Coalition Politics," *Commentary,* Vol. 41, No. 9 (September, 1966), p. 39.
82. Samuel Du Bois Cook, *New South,* Vol. 21, No. 3 (Summer 1966).
83. *Ibid.*
84. Carmichael, "What We Want," *The New York Review of Books,* September 22, 1966, p. 7.
85. King, *op. cit.,* p. 48.
86. *New York Times,* July 7, 1968, p. 1.
87. Rowan, *op. cit.,* p. 28.
88. James Booker, *The Amsterdam News,* November 5, 1966.
89. *New York Times,* July 7, 1968, p. 38.
90. *Ibid.*
91. *Ibid.*
92. Robert Moses Parris, "Nonviolence in the Ghetto," in Paul Jacobs and Saul Landau, eds., *The New Radicals* (New York: Random House, 1966), p. 124.
93. *New York Times,* October 19, 1966, p. 35.

94. Rustin, "Black Power and Coalition Politics," *Commentary,* Vol. 41, No. 9 (September, 1966), p. 36.
95. *Meet the Press,* August 21, 1966, *Merkle Press* (Washington, D.C.), p. 22.
96. *Ibid.,* p. 26.
97. Benson, *op. cit.*
98. Roy Wilkins, *The Crisis,* Vol. 73, No. 7 (August–September, 1966), p. 354.
99. *New York Times,* July 8, 1968, p. 48.
100. *New York Times,* July 20, 1968, p. 10.
101. *Ibid.*
102. *Ibid.*
103. *New York Times,* July 29, 1968, p. 14.
104. *Ibid.*
105. *Ibid.*
106. *New York Times,* July 26, 1968, p. 39.
107. Quoted in *Time,* August 2, 1968, p. 11.
108. *Ibid.*
109. Benson, *op. cit.*
110. Carmichael, "Speech at Mt. Holyoke."
111. *New York Times,* July 10, 1968, p. 45.
112. *Ibid.*
113. Interview with Whitney M. Young, Jr., Public Broadcasting Laboratories, March 3, 1968.
114. *New York Times,* July 10, 1968, p. 45.
115. Quoted in *Time,* August 2, 1968, p. 11.
116. *Ibid.*

CHAPTER 5

1. Quoted in C. Eric Lincoln, "Theological and Ethical Implications of the Black Ghetto," *Christian Century,* March 1, 1967, p. 265.
2. *New York Times,* July 28, 1968.
3. "The Racial Crisis: An Exchange of Letters," Sarah Patton Boyle and John Howard Griffin, *Christian Century,* May 22, 1968, p. 679.
4. Nathan Wright, Jr., "Power and Reconciliation," *Concern,* October 1, 1967, p. 22.
5. Joseph R. Washington, Jr., *The Politics of God* (Boston: Beacon Press, 1967), p. 104.
6. *Ibid.,* p. 173.
7. Rosenstock-Huessy, *op. cit.*
8. W. E. B. Du Bois, ed., *Some Efforts of American Negroes for Their Own Betterment* (Atlanta: Atlanta University Press, 1898), p. 4.
9. W. E. B. Du Bois, ed., *The Negro Church* (Atlanta: Atlanta University Press, 1898), p. 5.
10. Interview in *Fortune,* January, 1968, p. 151.
11. "Interview: Al Cleage on Black Power," *United Church Herald,* Vol. II, No. 2 (February, 1968), pp. 27–30.

12. *Ibid.*
13. *Ibid.*
14. *Ibid.*
15. The Reverend Mr. Al Cleage, Jr., *Michigan Chronicle,* April 13, 1968.
16. The Reverend Mr. Archie L. Rich, Jr., "The Black Revolt," *Concern,* October 1, 1967, p. 18.
17. *Ibid.*
18. *Ibid.*
19. The Reverend Mr. Leon Watts, "A Modern Black Looks At His Outdated Church," *Renewal,* December, 1967, p. 3.
20. *Ibid.,* p. 6.
21. Tom Wicker, *New York Times,* February 15, 1968.
22. Henry H. Mitchell, "Toward the 'New' Integration," *Christian Century,* June 12, 1968, pp. 780–781.
23. Vincent Harding, "Black Power and the American Christ," *Christian Century,* January 4, 1967, p. 10.
24. *Ibid.*
25. *Ibid.,* pp. 10–11.
26. *Ibid.,* p. 13.
27. *Ibid.*
28. Vincent Harding, "The Religion of Black Power" in Donald R. Cutler, ed., *The Religious Situation: 1968* (Boston: Beacon Press, 1968), p. 36.
29. *Ibid.,* p. 37.
30. James H. Cone, "Christianity and Black Power" in C. Eric Lincoln, ed., *Is Anybody Listening to Black America?* (New York: Seabury Press, 1968), p. 3.
31. *Ibid.,* p. 4.
32. *Ibid.,* p. 5.
33. *Ibid.,* p. 8.
34. *Ibid.*
35. Nathan Wright, Jr., *Black Power and Urban Unrest: Creative Possibilites* (New York: Hawthorn Books, Inc., 1967), p. 135.
36. Quoted in *New York Times,* July 9, 1968, p. 3.
37. *Ibid.,* p. 23.
38. Quoted in *New York Times,* July 9, 1968, p. 3.
39. *Ibid.*
40. *Ibid.*
41. Quoted in *Esquire,* July, 1968, p. 52.
42. "Black Power," Statement by National Committee of Negro Churchmen (paid declaration), *New York Times,* July 31, 1966.
43. *Ibid.*
44. *New York Times,* November 6, 1966.
45. "Statement of the National Committee of Negro Churchmen on the Urban Mission in a Time of Crisis," April 5, 1968.
46. *Ibid.*

47. *Ibid.*
48. *Ibid.*
49. The Reverend Mr. Clayton E. Hammond, "Black Power and Methodism," *Christian Advocate,* August 24, 1967.
50. *Ibid.*
51. *Ibid.*
52. *Ibid.*
53. *Ibid.*
54. *Ibid.*
55. *Ibid.*
56. "Statement of the National Committee of Negro Churchmen at the Statue of Crispus Attucks, Boston," July 1967.
57. Claude Evans, "United Methodist Action," *Christian Century,* May 22, 1968, p. 673.
58. *NOW,* Newsletter No. 1, Black Methodists for Church Renewal, July 1, 1968, p. 1.
59. James Lawson, *Christian Advocate,* March 7, 1968.
60. Quoted in *New York Times,* July 28, 1968, p. 28.
61. *Ibid.*
62. *Christian Century,* July 3, 1968, p. 878.
63. Arnold Toynbee, *A Study of History*, Abridgment of Vols. I–VI by D. C. Somervell (New York: Oxford University Press, 1947), p. 129.

CHAPTER 6

1. Carmichael, "What We Want," *The New York Review of Books,* September 22, 1966, p. 22.
2. Carmichael Interview in *Christian Science Monitor,* July 23, 1966, p. 10.
3. Carmichael, "Speech at Mt. Holyoke."
4. *Meet the Press, op. cit.,* p. 22.
5. James Baldwin and Budd Schulberg, "Dialog in Black and White," *Playboy,* December, 1966, p. 282.
6. Carmichael and Hamilton, *op. cit.,* p. 53.
7. Column in *New York Times,* July 16, 1968, p. 14.
8. Rustin, "Black Power and Coalition Politics," *Commentary,* Vol. 41, No. 9 (September, 1966), p. 35.
9. Quoted in Truman Nelson, *The Right of Revolution* (Boston: Beacon Press, 1968), p. 3.
10. *Ibid.*
11. King, *op. cit.,* p. 44.
12. *Ibid.,* p. 54.
13. Jacobs and Landau, *op. cit.,* p. 303.
14. King, *op. cit.,* p. 44.
15. John O. Killens, *Negro Digest,* November, 1968.
16. King, *op. cit.,* p. 56.
17. *Ibid.*

18. *Ibid.*, p. 58.
19. *Ibid.*, p. 59.
20. *Ibid.*
21. W. E. B. Du Bois, *The World and Africa* (New York: International Publishers, 1965), pp. 267–268.
22. Barrington Moore, Jr., *Social Origins of Dictatorship and Democracy: Lord and Peasant in the Making of the Modern World* (Boston: Beacon Press, 1966), p. 154.
23. James Breeden statement to Workshop on Black Power of Metropolitan Associates of Philadelphia, Valley Forge, Pa., October 15, 1966.
24. Quoted in *The Progressive,* October, 1967.
25. Quoted in *Harvard Crimson,* October 20, 1967.
26. *Ibid.*
27. Interview with James Baldwin, Public Broadcasting Laboratories, March 3, 1968.
28. Conversation with Russ Meek, Public Broadcasting Laboratories, November 5, 1967.
29. Quoted in *Washington Post,* September 28, 1967.
30. Quoted in *Is Anybody Listening to Black America?* p. 97.
31. Barbour, *op. cit.*
32. Rosenstock-Huessy, *op. cit.*
33. *Ibid.*, p. 243.

Index